THE POETRY OF PROTEST
UNDER FRANCO

ELEANOR WRIGHT

THE POETRY OF PROTEST UNDER FRANCO

TAMESIS BOOKS LIMITED
LONDON

Colección Támesis
SERIE A - MONOGRAFIAS, LXXXIX

© Copyright by Tamesis Books Limited
London, 1986
ISBN 0 7293 0210 5

DISTRIBUTORS:

Spain:
 Editorial Castalia,
 Zurbano, 39,
 28010 Madrid

United States and Canada:
 Longwood Publishing Group, Inc.,
 51 Washington Street,
 Dover, New Hampshire 03820, U.S.A.

Great Britain and rest of the world:
 Grant and Cutler Ltd.,
 55-57 Great Marlborough Street,
 London W1V 2AY

Depósito legal: M. 11565-1986

Printed in Spain by Talleres Gráficos de SELECCIONES GRÁFICAS
Carretera de Irún, km. 11,500 - 28049 Madrid

for
TAMESIS BOOKS LIMITED
LONDON

CONTENTS

	Page
PREFACE	IX
INTRODUCTION	1
1. HISTORICAL BACKGROUND	6
Falangists and Neotraditionalists	7
Nonconformity and Social Conscience	14
Restoration of the Literary Past	19
2. NEW POETRY IN 1944	29
Dámaso Alonso and the Anguish of Existence	36
Victoriano Crémer's Nonconformist Poetry	42
3. POETRY OF RESISTANCE	53
Eugenio de Nora in the Vanguard	57
Modes of Protest	72
4. POETRY OF POLITICAL PROTEST	92
Blas de Otero's Epic for the Age of Man	98
I. Quest for Salvation	100
II. Social Logos	109
Gabriel Celaya and Agitprop Poetry	124
I. Praxis of SocRealism	127
II. The Red Thread	133

		Page
5.	POETRY OF SOCIAL PROTEST	145
	Poetry is Communication	149
	I. Angela Figuera Aymerich	154
	II. José Hierro	157
	III. A Christian Response	161
	IV. Fellow Travelers	170
CONCLUSION		179
LIST OF WORKS CITED		183
INDEX OF PROPER NAMES		191

PREFACE

During the course of this project many people, to whom I wish to offer public acknowledgement, aided me. First, I thank Paul Ilie for his thoughtful, prompt comments as my research took shape in a doctoral dissertation. I am also grateful to those helping me with this expanded version: John Crispin, Jan Lechner, Germán Bleiberg, and John Bingham. In collecting documentation, I received valuable advice and assistance from José Luis Cano, Agustín Millares Sall, Antonio Pereira, Asunción Fernández del Amo, José Castro Ovejero, Enrique Badosa, Manuel Molina, Victoriano Crémer, and from the staffs of the Biblioteca Nacional in Madrid, the Hemeroteca Municipal in Madrid, the Biblioteca de la Diputación in Barcelona, the Graduate Library of the University of Michigan, and the Jean and Alexander and Heard Library of Vanderbilt University. Finally, I would like to acknowledge support from the Fulbright-Hays Commission, which made possible a year's research in Spain, as well as assistance from the Mellon Foundation and the College of Arts and Science of Vanderbilt University, which allowed me to complete this version.

ELEANOR WRIGHT

Vanderbilt University.

INTRODUCTION

It is difficult to understand why the poetry of protest written during the Franco Dictatorship has been ignored to such an extent by critics and scholars that the tendency itself, as well as postwar poets of primary importance to the tendency, are still, decades later, in need of systematic study.[1] During the post-Civil War period writers of genres other than poetry, of course, brought pressing sociopolitical issues unredressed by the Regime to public attention. However, in contrast to the short story, novel, drama, or essay of protest, poetry of protest is particularly fruitful for study, having been least affected by institutional censorship.[2] This may have come about since poetry was read by a relatively small audience. While the actual size of this audience is uncertain, editions of poetic works, anthologies, and publications dedicated to poetry offer indications. To give a few examples, the Adonais collection published relatively large editions of 500-1,000 copies, but only 250 copies of the *Antología cercada* appeared and *Espadaña* usually printed issues of approximately the same size. These figures and published comments referring to the *mundillo literario* suggest that assiduous poetry readers in the Peninsula may have been more than 500 but probably fewer than twice that number. It does not seem unreasonable to me, therefore, that lighter censorship may have permitted more freedom of expression to poets than to novelists or dramatists. This possibility alone justifies a careful investigation.

Nonetheless, there are additional motives for such study. In the first place, we lack a chronological record of the poetry of protest, one incorporating available but little researched data from literary publications of the postwar period.[3] As sources of information —without regard for their

---

[1] A similar opinion, in reference to all postwar poetry, was stated recently by JAN LECHNER, «Preliminares para un estudio de las poéticas de posguerra», *Entre la cruz y la espada: en torno a la España de la posguerra. Homenaje a Eugenio G. de Nora* (Madrid: Gredos, 1984), pp. 205-09.

[2] Readers interested in the relationship between censorship and literature during the Franco Regime will find passing references in this study. The most authoritative book on the issue is by MANUEL L. ABELLÁN, *Censura y creación literaria en España (1939-1976)* (Barcelona: Ediciones Península, 1980); Abellán concludes that poetry was the least repressed genre in general, with exceptions made for poets who openly opposed or criticized the Regime and for publishers who tried to reprint works by exiled poets.

[3] The most complete guide to postwar literary publications is by FANNY RUBIO, *Las revistas poéticas españolas (1939-1975)* (Madrid: Turner, 1976). Of the hundreds of postwar literary publications in Spanish libraries, perhaps fifty contain significant information concerning the poetry of protest. The most important titles

irregular esthetic quality— these publications illuminate the way in which this tendency dialectically challenged ruling conventions, imposed its own norms, and eventually was overtaken by different conventions arising during the 1950s. Secondly, critical commentary about the poetry of protest has most often been unexamined opinions concerning landmarks such as *Hijos de la ira,* the *Antología consultada,* and *Veinte años de poesía española,* even when information about their reception indicates that the role of these works was more complex than generally believed. A disinterested study of such works and their relation to the poetry of protest is consequently overdue.[4] Thirdly, existing studies perpetuate confusion by failing to examine how irreconcilable ideological differences among poets and critics determined essential qualities of the tendency.[5] In the ranks of those opposed to the Regime, some sincerely favored the goals of anarchism, socialism, or communism, others defended those of traditional bourgeois liberalism. All believed themselves humanists seeking democratic government with human rights and political tolerance, but they differed on how such a state ought to be achieved. Seldom made explicit, this point of contention provoked heated exchanges. Later, in response to a change in the world's diplomatic climate, increasing numbers of Spanish intellectuals claimed liberal, if not socialist, beliefs as their own. Nevertheless, many laid the authenticity of their commitment open to doubt by reaping benefits through obedience to the Regime. Thus, I believe that if postwar poets are not clearly distinguished according to ideology, the process generating the poetry of protest remains concealed and central polemics seem trivial or incomprehensible. Accordingly, it seems to me that ideological outlook ought to be taken into account in textual interpretation as a complement to customary analytic methods. Fourthly, the

---

are: *Acento Cultural, Cisneros, Correo Literario, Entregas de Poesía, Escorial, Espadaña, La Estafeta Literaria, La Hora, Insula, Laye, Rocamador,* and *Verbo.* The information I sought concerns the first appearance of individual poems, the content of declarations, definitions, objections, and challenges, as well as book reviews for the initial reception of individual works. Other valuable sources of information were prologues, epigraphs, dedications, anthologies, published letters, etc.

[4] HANS ROBERT JAUSS, «Literary History as a Challenge to Literary Theory», *New Directions in Literary History,* Ralph Cohen, ed. (Baltimore: Johns Hopkins, 1974), p. 11, whose theory helped me develop the method I follow, claims that reception studies bridge the gap between historical and esthetic approaches by taking into account the audience as it actually was constituted instead of assuming, with formalists, that it is a perceiving subject or, with Marxists, that it is well-versed in historical materialism.

[5] The three most extensive studies, which deal abstractly with the relation of poetry and politics, are an anthology by LEOPOLDO DE LUIS, *Poesía española contemporánea. Antología (1939-1964). Poesía social* (Madrid: Alfaguara, 1965); a well researched investigative study by JAN LECHNER, *El compromiso en la poesía española del siglo XX. Parte segunda de 1939 a 1974* (Leiden: Universitaire pers Leiden, 1975); and an introductory survey by SANTIAGO DAYDÍ-TOLSON, *The Post-Civil War Social Poets* (Boston: Twayne, 1983).

theory of Socialist Realism is an undervalued but significant key to the poetry of protest. The literary and ethical force of this theory was often masked by the euphemistic title *social*. This may have been for esthetic reasons, since political efficacy is an uncommon goal in poetry, or for political reasons, because Spaniards were reluctant openly to espouse Marxism or its literary manifestation, Socialist Realism, during the first two postwar decades. However, in the interest of scholarly fairness, the norms of postwar Spanish Socialist Realist poetry must be identified and Socialist Realist works examined in their light and not only in that of inappropriate, misleading norms. And, finally, we must recognize as leaders of the tendency Eugenio de Nora, Blas de Otero, and Gabriel Celaya.

With these motives for study, I suggest that the poetry of protest be viewed as a tendency developing during the Regime of General Franco, where poetry and politics overlapped, led by those committed to a literary doctrine, Socialist Realism. This view, for which I provide documentation, is supported by a method whereby I interpret texts within a diachronic reconstruction of events to distinguish between what commonly is held to be true and what is substantiated by evidence.

Textual interpretation is, naturally, a complex creative activity. The same poem of protest, for instance, has different meanings according to the reader's ideological and methodological persuasion; moreover, these meanings change as time passes. A poem that, in 1946, embodied authentic sentiment lost its evocative capacity a decade or two later.[6] Also, textual interpretation is affected by factors seldom acknowledged because their analysis is considered, by critics, beyond the bounds of literary history and criticism. The circumstances of a poem's origin, the contemporary sociopolitical situation, not to mention a poet's ethics and poetic theory, inevitably enrich textual interpretation. Consequently, I dispense with any boundary between text and context, seeking instead explicit links between them. Furthermore, I examine poems for more than intrinsic structure and style, seeking also their communicative potential. That is, I look not only for the possibility of «deautomatization», defamiliarization, but also for that of «automatization», in other words, unobstructed reference to a topic.[7] In fact, we ought to recognize that poems are both autonomous and communicative: autonomous, because they are an assembly of signs;

---

[6] EUGENIO DE NORA's *España, pasión de vida* shows how a work's significance changes through time. Most of the poems appeared in *Espadaña* and other literary publications between 1945 and 1950, when they had great impact on readers. Finally published as a book in 1954, the work —seen against the openly political poetry of Blas de Otero and Gabriel Celaya, not to mention that of the legion of poets then writing poems of protest— received only modest acclaim. De Nora, who wrote little poetry after 1950, became an almost forgotten figure of postwar poetry.

[7] For a review of these terms and their usage, see: F. W. GALAN, «Literary Change and Systemic Change: The Prague School Theory of Literary History, 1928-49», *PMLA*, 94, No. 2 (March 1979), pp. 275-85.

communicative, because they refer to intellectual, religious, ethical, or social principles.

This accounts for the interpretative divergence between poets and critics favoring Marxist ideals and those advocating traditional liberal values. From the Marxist perspective, of course, there exists a relation of identity between ideological beliefs and literary practice. Messages in poems of protest are held to be homologous to messages in oral discourse. Both sorts of messages are instruments with which to further a cause. According to the practices of Socialist Realism, writers are obliged to promote Marxist social goals and to convince the skeptical that these offer the correct solution to sociopolitical problems. Gabriel Celaya, for example, challenges poets to choose sides; for, as he argues, a neutral position favors the opposition:[8]

> Poetas entregados a esa ambigua delicia
> ... ...
> levantaos, sed hombres que aceptan sus deberes,
> escuchad lo que el pueblo con alarma os exige,
> pensad que ser neutrales es pronunciarse en contra.

In the Marxist view, this poetic challenge legitimately uses available means to protest injustice. The traditional liberal perspective, on the other hand, holds that poetry and ideology are independent realms, which, when dealt with jointly, usually prejudice the former by limiting interpretive range to a totally historical context. Celaya's challenge, therefore, is not seen as the natural utterance of a real person as a result of actual circumstances; rather, framed by the poem's esthetic boundaries, the challenge is viewed as fictive, a representation of what it pretends to be.[9] The testimonies, harangues, and pleas of the poetry of protest are viewed similarly — not as real utterances but as their representations. The incompatibility between these views of a poem's status led to the polemics that energized the tendency's development. Customarily, Marxists claim that ideological values form the axis of signification in their works, that they and their poetry are political. What is not so obvious is that the same is true of traditional liberals. While holding different values, traditional liberals also emit messages susceptible to political interpretation. Thus, the divergence between Marxist and traditional liberal beliefs concerning poetry mirrors

---

[8] GABRIEL CELAYA, «Vivir para ver», *Cantos iberos* (Madrid: Turner, 1976), p. 64.

[9] Discussing this view, BARBARA HERNNSTEIN SMITH, «Poetry as Fiction», *New Directions in Literary History*, Ralph Cohen, ed. (Baltimore: Johns Hopkins, 1974), pp. 165-87, separates natural utterances from fictive ones depending upon whether the poet and reader share a set of conventions by which poems represent various kinds of spoken discourse. According to such conventions, readers interpret poems by creating plausible contexts, but the readers can neither discover nor verify the truth of such utterances, which are «historically indeterminate».

a similar divergence in world-views.[10] This profound discrepancy is also responsible for a division between critics and scholars today, some taking the side of Marxists, others, that of traditional liberals.

The lack of commonly accepted terms with which to discuss what I call the poetry of protest presents only apparent methodological problems. Certainly many different names have been used: realism, social realism, objectivism, practical poetry, social poetry, nonconformist poetry, and so on. Yet this abundance of terms, rather than evidence of critical carelessness or confusion, may be viewed as a sign of the tendency's vitality. From a theoretical perspective, these numerous terms referring to the same historical phenomenon reveal why I use historical categories rather than analytic ones. Useful analytic categories, of course, are exclusive, defined in such a way that poems or works clearly belong to one category or another. Analytic categories, which prescribe the characteristics of hypothetical class members, are inflexible when defining works already in existence. Since I discuss the poetry of protest historically, I prefer categories encompassing the contemporary understanding of distinct sorts of poetry, and, where pertinent, how that understanding changed through time. Unlike clear-cut analytic categories, historical ones lack unambiguous boundaries; differentiation among categories can vary according to circumstances. For example, what I call poetry of resistance in Chapter 3 thematically overlaps what I call poetry of political protest in Chapter 4 and poetry of social protest in Chapter 5. Poetry of resistance, however, is chronologically prior to the other two types.

The selection of poets discussed in each category may seem, at first, arbitrary. While we generally agree upon the poets in the tendency's forefront, less consensus exists concerning those of secondary importance. Thus, Blas de Otero, Gabriel Celaya, José Hierro, and Angel González must be included, but we may differ on whom else to include, particularly, as the adherents increased during the late 1950s. Therefore, among figures of secondary importance with respect to the poetry of protest —never to their stature as poets— my selection is representative rather than exhaustive: I discuss the poetry of José Agustín Goytisolo and Jaime Gil de Biedma, but not that of José María Caballero Bonald or Carlos Alvarez; that of Angela Figuera Aymerich and Gloria Fuertes, but not that of Angel Crespo or José Angel Valente. A maximum number of participants in the interest of completeness seems to me less valuable to progress in a significantly understudied field than a concise commentary including representative poets and their relationship to the tendency's development.

---

[10] ARNOLD HAUSER, *Teorías del arte. Tendencias y métodos de la crítica moderna* (Madrid: Guadarrama, 1975), pp. 231, 260, 271, emphasizes the need to leave the realm of art in order finally to identify reasons for changes in taste, since artistic forms are not only sensorial expressions, they are also expressions of a socially determined world view.

I

HISTORICAL BACKGROUND

A strong censorship law, promulgated for all of Spain on 22 April 1938 and scarcely changed for almost thirty years, is often thought to have stilled artistic development and exchange of ideas in post-Civil War Spain. Frequently repeated metaphors intended to capture in a phrase the complex postwar atmosphere, such as «the years of silence» or «a culture in hibernation», strengthen this view by supposing unrelieved harshness where selective enforcement existed. The effectiveness of Francoist censorship is seldom examined and this serves to reinforce claims that anyone who published in Spain, especially during the 1940s, was subservient to the Franco dictatorship. Yet this view is an oversimplification. It fails to take into account how competing factions within the Regime, in pursuit of power and influence, allowed exchange of heterodox ideas and tolerated the development of poetry of protest. Although political parties other than the Movimiento did not exist officially in Spain, many writers held a range of ideological views ranging from anarchist, socialist, and communist to traditional liberal and Christian democrat. All were humanists sympathetic to the causes of freedom and justice, their common concern uniting them. Rather than be silenced, they wrote against and in spite of authoritarian power. Some deflated dogma and bombast with satire, others advocated a Marxist revolution. Whether moderate or extremist, Spanish intellectuals were less hindered than pessimists implied, but doubtless more inhibited than their counterparts abroad, either through self-censorship or imposed deletions by official readers.

Since the early postwar period is not generally well-known, questions arise immediately: Did the Franco government silence all expression of dissent? Was dissent possible, perhaps in disguised form? Some answers to these questions are provided by documentation in this chapter. In later chapters facts concerning the polemical phases of the poetry of protest, the role played by specific writers in its development, as well as the rationale, themes, and rhetorical practices specific to each phase provide additional answers. What becomes clear is that Spanish culture did not begin *ex nihilo* in the postwar period. The recuperation of existentialism and Marxism, of such important writers as Antonio Machado and Miguel Hernández, and discussion of the problem of Spain were achievements of the 1940s. The process of recuperation was influenced by events and loyalties beyond the realm of literature; thus a review of the relationship between the Regime and publishing practices is germane to the question of censorship.

FALANGISTS AND NEOTRADITIONALISTS

The historical twists and turns that affected literary publishing in the 1940s were first mapped by Falangist ideologues, such as Dionisio Ridruejo, Pedro Laín Entralgo, and Antonio Tovar.[1] Members of the Delegación de Prensa y Propaganda, they were responsible to Serrano Súñer, the Interior Minister, then an outspoken admirer of National Socialism. These intellectuals chose to ignore the pre-Civil War political activity of such writers as Unamuno, Antonio Machado, Valle-Inclán, and Ortega y Gasset. By regarding them as literary figures, they hoped to stress the important place of Spanish literature in twentieth-century European culture.

When the tide of World War II changed, Franco distanced himself from the Axis through dismissal of the Germanophile minister, Serrano Súñer. In repercussions, Ridruejo and Tovar were dismissed as well and the Delegación de Prensa y Propaganda transferred to the authority of the Ministry of Education. Franco held that Spain's interests would be served best by a neutral position concerning the outcome of World War II. By 1942 he created the internal structure that would define the character of the Regime for many years to come. Franco became a power broker among sometimes conflicting groups vying for his favor. By his arrangement, Church traditionalists were awarded control of the educational system, the Falange authorized to organize industries with vertical syndicates supervising workers, and the army charged with enforcing civil peace.

At the same time Franco found it advantageous to attribute Spain's troubles to the influence of foreign ideas. He condemned alike rationalism, liberalism, and Marxism and praised Spain as one great family over which he presided, hoping to erase social divisions. Furthermore, he exploited as propaganda a spiritual return to the Golden Age when Spanish power was at its zenith, a crusade that depended upon the calculated use of

---

[1] For background, see: FANNY RUBIO, *Las revistas poéticas españolas (1939-1975)* (Madrid: Turner, 1976), pp. 31-32; JOSÉ-CARLOS MAINER, *Literatura y pequeña burguesía* (Madrid: EDICUSA, 1972), pp. 39-44.

nostalgia.² Declaring he had the best interests of Spaniards at heart, Franco portrayed himself as a bridge spanning the separation between government and people. *Escorial,* a Regime-sponsored literary publication, assured its readers that there was no need for the *Caudillo* to offer lengthy explanations, it was sufficient to see new buildings being raised and fields once more tilled.³ The change of government, seats of power, and political outlook required new slogans or at least new interpretations of familiar ones. A psychiatrist prominent within the Regime claimed that the notion of «mass man» was incompatible with Spanish character, based upon eternal values.⁴ Later he added that «mass rebellion» was only an attempt to escape responsibility, an alternative fortunately unavailable since the conclusion of the Civil War.⁵ Franco himself claimed that social justice was the foremost concern of the Regime: «Sobre todas nuestras inquietudes de gobierno... predomina como la principal la de servir al pueblo: ésta es nuestra tiranía.» ⁶ And Franco's love for the people seemed reciprocated when, for instance, he visited Granada in May 1943. One observer wrote that the presence of the *Caudillo* turned hatred to friendship, the cordial crowds seemed to offer Franco a political prayer: «Te respetamos como un Caudillo. Te queremos como un padre.»⁷

The neotraditional tone of cultural life under José Ibáñez Martín, Education Minister until 1951, gained strength with the founding of the Consejo Superior de Investigaciones Científicas. Ibáñez Martín, distrustful of prewar liberal intellectual institutions, intended the C.S.I.C. to be a conservative agency circumscribing theoretical speculation in the humanities and the social sciences. Upon appointing José María Albareda as Secretary-General of the C.S.I.C., Ibáñez Martín opened the door to infiltration by the reactionary and semi-secret Opus Dei.⁸ Opus members,

---

² A definition of the neotraditionalist attitude has been offered by José Luis L. Aranguren, «La condición de la vida intelectual en la España de hoy», *La Torre,* 1, No. 4 (October-December 1953), p. 86: «Lo esencial es mantener incontaminados a los españoles de los 'errores modernos'. Aislarles, si es posible —desde esta perspectiva es como cobra pleno sentido la censura— del exterior, sofocar en el silencio los problemas espirituales del hombre contemporáneo, tener callados a los 'disconformes' de dentro, negar la obra y casi la existencia de los 'inquietos' emigrados, conjurar los 'peligros' de toda índole y lograr, en fin, una estable, una permanente *seguridad.*»
³ «Hechos de la Falange. El Caudillo y su pueblo», *Escorial,* 6, No. 16 (1942), pp. 279-80.
⁴ Juan J. López Ibor, «Pathos ético del hombre español», *Escorial,* 4, No. 9 (1941), p. 82.
⁵ Juan López Ibor, «Se aleja el hombre masa...», *El Español,* 27 February 1943, pp. 1, 10.
⁶ Elías Gómez Picazo, «El imperativo de lo social», *Fénix,* No. 2 (1944), pp. 63-65.
⁷ *Vientos del Sur,* No. 2 (10 May 1943), pp. 5-6.
⁸ See: Elías Díaz, *Notas para una historia del pensamiento español actual (1939-1973)* (Madrid: EDICUSA, 1974), pp. 39-44; Vicente R. Pilapil, «Opus Dei in Spain», *The World Today,* May 1971, pp. 211-21.

whether ordained priests or not, served in lay clothing and were indistinguishable from non-members. They followed the maxims of the society's spiritual guide, *Camino,* whose ideology systematically attacked the liberal tradition while stressing religiosity and obedience. Ibáñez Martín was aware that the Opus members would take over the investigation centers, the University, and even the Ateneo de Madrid as they were named to key positions. Opus members gave preference to each other when awarding generous fellowships, grants, and scholarships. Ediciones Rialp, and publications such as *Nuestro Tiempo, Arbor, Atlántida, Gaceta Universitaria, La Actualidad,* and *Telva* were their channels of ideological influence. The Opus founded the University of Navarre in the early 1950s in order to groom promising young Spaniards in the tenets of the society. Through this institution the society exerted an influence far beyond the relative numbers of its members. Enjoined to secrecy concerning their activities, members acknowledged few links with the society despite its importance to postwar cultural affairs and the postwar economic recovery.

Ibáñez Martín gained control over the publishing industry in the move that put the Delegación de Prensa y Propaganda under his authority. This enabled the Education Minister to disseminate neotraditionalist views and curb the publication of whatever he considered improper with punitive measures: regulation of paper allotments, holding publishers answerable for whatever they printed, prior censorship in Madrid and Barcelona, and threats of fines, dismissals, and seizures of entire issues judged to contain infractions. Freedom of the press was forgotten, publications were ideological instruments of those in power.[9]

The founding of independent publications, such as *Espadaña* or *Verbo,* was subject to a law of 4 March 1942 designed to provide readers with «indispensible political and spiritual guarantees».[10] This law required in requests a description of the proposed format, a declaration of purpose,

---

[9] See XAVIER DE ECHARRI, «Libertad de la prensa», *Fénix,* 1, No. 5 (November 1943), p. 23: «El periodismo —refirámoslo ya directamente a nuestro periodismo, al periodismo español— ha pasado de ser una profesión al servicio de grupos de partidos o de personas, a ser una misión al servicio directo y exclusivo de la Patria.» And also, PEDRO GARCÍA SUÁREZ, «Nuestra Prensa. En todos los periódicos de España», *Fénix,* 2, No. 9 (March 1944) p. 22: «El periódico sirve de antena y de enlace entre el mando y el pueblo español; transmite al pueblo la consigna del mando, y a éste, la emoción y la inquietud del pueblo... Es entonces la Prensa el altavoz español que lleva a todas las cardinales ibéricas la emoción de nuestra doctrina, el amor a la hermandad de nuestra Falange, la resurrección y el brío del ímpetu de nuestro pueblo.» Compare Article 2 of the Press Law, reprinted by MANUEL PRADOS Y LÓPEZ, *Etica y estética del periodismo español* (Madrid: Espasa-Calpe, 1943), p. 146: «En el ejercicio de la función expresada, corresponde al Estado: 1.º La regulación del número y extensión de las publicaciones periódicas. 2.º La intervención en la designación del personal directivo. 3.º La reglamentación de la profesión de periodista. 4.º La vigilancia de la actividad de la Prensa. 5.º La censura, mientras no se disponga su supresión.»

[10] *Boletín Oficial del Estado,* No. 63 (March 1942), pp. 1591-94.

and a funding plan, as well as socio-political reports on all editors, managers, and administrators. Furthermore, the editor-in-chief had to belong to the Registro Oficial de Periodistas de la Delegación Nacional de Prensa y Propaganda. In the case of *Espadaña,* the permit application was submitted under the name of Eugenio de Nora, a student in Madrid at the time, while practical matters of editing and printing fell to Victoriano Crémer, whose political record might have jeopardized the application. Permit approval entitled the editor to rationed allotments of paper, these to be used only for the purposes stated in the application. This control was consistent with the Regime's mandate that the Spanish press eliminate past and potential ideological discrepancies within public opinion and ensure that what was published coincided with Franco's socio-political doctrine.[11]

Apparently the industry was under tight control. In practice, this policy was strictly enforced only for the daily press. Periodicals with small circulations were not brought under the close supervision which existed for newspapers though they were just a step away from such control since, from the Regime's point of view, there was no reason why periodicals should be subject to different norms, especially when they could become vehicles of subversive ideology and of socio-political agitation.[12] Outside of Madrid and Barcelona infractions were less rigorously hunted by publishers. This provided a loophole through which passed literary journals and magazines, most with fewer than two hundred copies per issue, works in luxury editions, and books of special interest numbering one hundred to three hundred copies.

Juan Aparicio, who replaced Ridruejo as director of the Delegación de Prensa y Propaganda in 1941, furthered Franco's goal of a unified Spain, gathering literary figures to replace those dispersed by the Civil War. Among the selected were Camilo José Cela, Agustín de Foxá, Lorenzo Villalonga, Adriano del Valle, José María Pemán, and Luis Felipe Vivanco.[13] He also founded periodicals as showcases for art at the service of the Regime: *El Español, La Estafeta Literaria,* and *Fantasía.*

---

[11] ANTONIO ESPINA (GARCÍA), *El cuarto poder: cien años de periodismo español* (Madrid: Aguilar, 1960), p. 295. Compare these words by JUAN APARICIO in the prologue to *Etica y estética del periodismo español,* p. 9: «La prueba más palpable de que la presente Revolución española es una auténtica Revolución nacional nos la ponen delante de los ojos los periódicos de las cincuenta provincias de España. Aquí existe un hombre nuevo —el periodista español del minuto actual—, que ha construido una unánime Prensa española a la altura de las circunstancias del mundo. Se alejan las jornadas de 1934, en las que podían publicarse —por ejemplo— en Soria cuatro y en Tortosa tres periódicos diarios, que eran los portavoces de los sorianos y tortosinos, partidos y repartidos en ligas y banderías. Ya no rige el mito de la libertad de Prensa, sino la verdad dogmática de la comunidad de la Prensa española para fines espirituales, trascendentales y educativos.»

[12] «Advertencia», *Anuario de la Prensa Española,* 4:2 (Revistas), 1957, p. v.

[13] «Proteccionismo literario», *El Español,* 3 July 1943, p. 15.

Aparicio took advantage of the fact that Madrid was the literary capital of Spain. Though writers from elsewhere formed groups, they were acutely conscious of their peripheral relation to the center of literary activity. Cultural centralism was a challenge to which they could not remain indifferent. The outcome of the Civil War did not change this situation, but it empowered an entirely different group of writers from those featured in prewar publications such as *La Gaceta Literaria* or *El Mono Azul*.

Though unwilling to depart from neotraditionalist ideological orthodoxy, Aparicio encouraged polemics. One of the longest running was over the alleged decadence of Spanish literature, reasons for which avoided the question of literary quality. An important factor was said to be competition of books imported from Argentina, Chile, and Cuba.[14] Additional competition to works by Spaniards came from translations published within Spain for the domestic market.[15] In 1943 it was pointed out that about forty percent of all literary works published in Spain, from serious poetry to popular novels, were written by non-Spaniards. Spanish writers blamed publishers for refusing to risk money on unproven works, preferring to reissue classics and proven commercial successes. Publishers blamed writers for expecting cash advances. Everyone agreed that the high cost of publishing was another serious problem.[16] Worsening the situation was the fact that the Regime set paper prices high in order to protect the Spanish paper industry. In 1944 the price of paper in Spain was more than three times that on the international market. Consequently a book produced in Argentina, for example, sold there for the equivalent of less than four *pesetas* and for very little more in Spain. On the other hand, a comparable book printed and sold in Spain would cost eight or even nine *pesetas*. The reading public, seldom mentioned in this polemic, would not read only Spanish authors, even in the name of patriotism, when books by foreign writers were available at a more reasonable price.

The Propaganda Director created a «literary life» thoroughly reported in his publications. He filled pages with little more than gossip about the members of various *tertulias* meeting in Madrid's cafés. According to the historian Fernando Díaz-Plaja, the ruling principle of this clubby atmosphere was that personality counted higher than accomplishment and friendship higher than disinterested respect:[17]

---

[14] «De Argentina llegó un barco cargado de libros», *La Estafeta Literaria*, No. 25 (1945), p. 25.
[15] «La autarquía de la inteligencia y la anarquía de las traducciones», *El Español*, 4 December 1943, p. 12.
[16] «El libro español y sus problemas de hecho», *El Español*, 29 April 1944, p. 29.
[17] FERNANDO DÍAZ-PLAJA, «Gente que escribe en Madrid y Barcelona», *El Español*, 11 September 1943, p. 7.

> En Madrid se valora más al *Hombre* que a su obra... abundan los seres de quienes *se espera mucho,* hayan publicado o no... El hombre —el autor— tiene importancia en Madrid porque aparece de una forma física, se le ve por las calles, en los cafés, tiene una solidez material. Se da *un valor* a su amistad, y los libros dedicados son considerados superiores a los que van a manos del vulgo, desconocedor de personalidades.

In this kind of setting, Aparicio found a group of poets willing to assume roles left vacant by the scattered Generation of 1927. He introduced his protégés in *El Español* and authorized funding so they could begin their own publication: *Garcilaso*.[18] The most favored of the group, José García Nieto, began a successful poetic career; he would receive many awards — the Adonais, the Garcilaso de la Vega created just for him, the Fastenrath from the Academia Española, and the Nacional from the Ministerio de Educación Nacional. García Nieto's name became synonymous with the literary tendency called *garcilasismo*.

Because publicity swelled the importance of this minor neoclassic current, conscientious critics were obliged to evaluate the group. Valbuena Prat acknowledged the importance of neoclassicism, but minimized the role of García Nieto when he identified the most important poets of 1944 to be Luis Rosales, Luis Felipe Vivanco, and Dionisio Ridruejo.[19] Vicente Gaos named major neoclassic poets from 1935 to 1945 as Luis Rosales and Germán Bleiberg, followed by Dionisio Ridruejo, with García Nieto appearing in the postwar «epilogue» of the movement.[20] Antonio Vilanova remarked that the only active poets left in Spain were those who, in their eagerness to display formal virtuosity, seemed to forget advances made in poetic expression during the 1920s and 1930s.[21]

Despite bias in government-sponsored publications, occasional articles suggested political ambiguity or tolerance that modify accusations of intransigency. In an early issue of *Escorial* Torrente Ballester criticized the extravagant trivialization of historic commonplaces: «Nunca se ha dicho tanta tontería del Imperio y de Trento, de la Contrarreforma, de la

---

[18] For studies of *Garcilaso,* see: RUBIO, *Las revistas poéticas,* pp. 108-21; JAN LECHNER, *El compromiso en la poesía española del siglo XX. Parte segunda de 1939 a 1974* (Leiden: Universitaire pers Leiden, 1975), Chapter 2; VÍCTOR G. DE LA CONCHA, *La poesía española de posguerra. Teoría e historia de sus movimientos* (Madrid: Prensa Española, 1973), Chapter 5.

[19] ANGEL VALBUENA PRAT, «El momento actual de la poesía española», *La Estafeta Literaria,* No. 15 (1944), p. 15.

[20] VICENTE GAOS, «De Luis Rosales a José García Nieto. Diez años de poesía: 1935-1945», *La Estafeta Literaria,* No. 25 (1945), p. 5.

[21] ANTONIO VILANOVA, «Poesía española y poesía europea», *Entregas de Poesia,* No. 1 (January 1944): «... no queda ya más que una pléyade de garcilasistas, que remansan los caminos de nuestra poesía en un delicado marasmo de inquietud y que basan su retorno a lo clásico en un recuerdo de Garcilaso y en la añoranza perenne de su voz. Una incomprensión profunda de los más logrados avances de nuestra lírica ha llevado a estos poetas a un culto denodado de la belleza formal y a una valoración excesiva de su virtuosismo lírico.»

Ilustración o del Carlismo como se dice hoy.»[22] Another contained an article that dealt with, among others, Pierre Emmanuel, a poet of the French Resistance.[23] And *Escorial* even printed some early poems by Blas de Otero.[24]

Garcilaso's magnanimous editorial policy seemed to invite contributions from all quarters, regardless of political antecedents:[25]

> Nuestras puertas están francas. Somos contrarios a toda barrera, a todo grupo cerrado, a toda torre de marfil. Haced, si queréis, aquí un elemental juego de símbolos con la muerte de nuestro caballero. Os podemos llamar abiertamente porque tenéis el paso libre y esperamos gozosos vuestra obra. Así os damos también la nuestra emplazada y destinada a la más justa atención, a la más serena acogida.

Two poets of the Generation of 1927 associated with the Republican side who remained in Spain after the Civil War contributed to *Garcilaso*. Dámaso Alonso's elegy to García Lorca appeared prior to its inclusion in *Oscura noticia*.[26] And a poem from Vicente Aleixandre's forthcoming *Sombra del paraíso* was published, arousing interest in a book whose favorable reception by the literary world carried political significance.[27]

Some writers aligned with the Republican side also won roles in a postwar literary scene dominated by the Regime's partisans. Germán Bleiberg is one representative. The poems of *Sonetos amorosos* from 1936, two of which Bleiberg published from prison in *Redención*, «Organo del Patronato Cultural para la redención de penas por el trabajo», were acknowledged models for much neoclassical poetry of the 1940s.[28] José Luis Cano, another Loyalist, was a critic who promoted poetic trends and shaped literary taste in the direction of his own traditional ideology.[29] With

---

[22] GONZALO TORRENTE BALLESTER, «Epístola a Antonio Tovar sobre su libro *El Imperio de España*», *Escorial*, No. 9 (1941), p. 126. One excessive example: PABLO ANTONIO CUADRA, «Carta de relación de un conquistador del Siglo XX a la Majestad primera del Imperio Doña Isabel, la Católica: Reina perenne en el recuerdo», *Escorial*, No. 8 (June 1941), pp. 425-36.

[23] RICARDO JUAN [BLASCO], «Sobre algunos poetas de la actualidad en Francia», *Escorial*, No. 30 (1943).

[24] BLAS DE OTERO, «Poesías en Burgos», *Escorial*, No. 34 (1942) [Cited by RUBIO, *Las revistas poéticas*, p. 34].

[25] *Garcilaso*, No. 2 (June 1943).

[26] DÁMASO ALONSO, «A un poeta muerto (fragmento)», *Garcilaso*, No. 8 (December 1943).

[27] VICENTE ALEIXANDRE, «Plenitud de amor», *Garcilaso*, No. 12 (April 1944); CHARLES DAVID LEY, *Spanish Poetry Since 1939* (Washington, D.C.: Catholic University of America, 1962), p. 40.

[28] RUBIO, *Las revistas poéticas*, p. 52; CHARLES DAVID LEY, *Spanish Poetry Since 1939*, p. 40.

[29] BIRUTÉ CIPLIJAUSKAITÉ, *El poeta y la poesía: del romanticismo a la poesía social* (Madrid: Insula, 1966), p. 397, attributes a traditional ideology to Cano, who reported at least three different dates for the purchase of Adonais by Rialp, which was represented by FLORENCIO PÉREZ EMBID: «a comienzos de 1947» in «Historia de una colección de poesía», *Cuadernos Hispanoamericanos*, No. 8 (1949),

Enrique Canito he founded *Insula,* the most respected independent literary publication of the postwar period. His twenty-year association with the prestigious collection Adonais, which he co-founded, continued long after the collection was purchased by Rialp, a change that affected the integrity of the collection; for in 1949, to cite one example, Blas de Otero's *Angel fieramente humano* was denied deserved recognition and had to be published elsewhere.[40]

Other writers remained in Spain to begin anew even after, in some cases, having been imprisoned on war-related charges. To Bleiberg's name may be added others, such as Blas de Otero, José Hierro, and Victoriano Crémer. A large number of writers and intellectuals, many of whom held ideas that were far from extremist, risked accusations of nonconformity in order to follow the dictates of conscience, performing a necessary service that bore fruit when the neotraditionalist dominance yielded to traditional liberal ascendence.

Nonconformity and Social Conscience

The neotraditionalists directing Spanish culture placed a high value on protecting a supposedly innocent public from pernicious notions and expected strict observance of their warnings. Anyone who raised questions ran the risk of over-stepping limits, falling into the stigmatized category of *inconformistas*. What made this situation even more difficult was that socially and morally defined boundaries were more strict than those defined by law.[31] The clergy in particular discouraged flocks from reading authors associated with «progressive» thinking, even when approved by state censorship. Academic figures, such as Joaquín de Entrambasaguas, University professor and a C.S.I.C. director, believed that the integrity of Spanish culture should be protected by restricting the flow of foreign books into the country.[32] Since Entrambasaguas thought the gravest ideological threats were posed by foreign ideas, he called for the founding of a translation institute in which persons of recognized wisdom and literary prestige, such as himself, would set necessary standards, screening works to be translated into Spanish.

p. 350; «en 1946» in «Recuerdo y homenaje a Juan Guerrero», *Insula,* No. 113 (15 May 1955), pp. 4-5; and «al finalizar el año 1949» in «Historia y sentido de una colección de poesía: Adonais», *El libro español,* Revista del Instituto Nacional del Libro Español, 2, No. 17 (1959), p. 275. Cano was, perhaps, less concerned by historical accuracy than by the threat to the continuing existence of the collection.

[30] See Chapter 4, pp. 20-21.

[31] «Lo que no se puede leer en España», *Demócrito,* 2, No. 34 (December 1946), p. 2.

[32] JOAQUÍN DE ENTRAMBASAGUAS, «¿Qué libros no debieron traducirse nunca?», *La Estafeta Literaria,* No. 2 (20 March 1944), p. 5.

After the first postwar years, direct references to Franco were absent from the pages of cultural publications. Nevertheless, the mass media, in which he appeared as the personification of neotraditional values, formed an authoritarian background against which existentialist and Marxist notions stood out. This is why the labels *existencialista* and *inconformista* were not neutral epithets. During World War II, *El Español* took advantage of its readers' presumable interest in forbidden texts with series of articles whose titles are provocatively self-explanatory: «Razones y sinrazones de la filosofía... San Agustín, Heidegger y Nicolai Hartman» (24 July 1943), p. 13; «El Komintern dentro de nuestra Patria» (14 November 1942), page 1; «Actuación en España del Comunismo internacional» and «Rusia al desnudo... Sustitución del culto a Dios por el culto al hombre» (30 January 1943), pp. 1, 10; «Contrabando marxista» (27 March 1943), p. 1.

Although an elaborate clandestine press such as the *samizdat* never developed in Spain, the student press of the 1940s, clandestine and official, mentioned Marxism. Whether the result of inquisitive interest or favorable sentiment, mentions were indirect. This may be observed in an article in *Cisneros,* where during a discussion of nationalism and internationalism the author dealt with the attraction Marxism had for new adherents by succintly describing Marxist doctrine and its propaganda method.[33]

Some clandestine publications, such as *Demócrito,* written and distributed by the Unión de Intelectuales Libres between 1945 and 1947, dispensed with precautions. This publication depended upon militant slogans dividing society between Fascists and revolutionaries, demagogic innuendos, urgings to victory, and yearnings for a new Vanguard, in which an *intelligentsia* composed of students would unite with peasants, workers, and guerrillas in the struggle: [34]

> La idea de unir a la mayoría de los intelectuales españoles en un movimiento común de resistencia contra la tiranía hermanados en una misma línea de combate con los obreros y los campesinos, con los guerrilleros y los exiliados, es una empresa noble y generosa.

Some measure of underground activity was as inevitable as it was dangerous. Even in 1947, eight years after the end of the Civil War, hundreds of Spaniards were arrested every month, their trials continued endlessly at Alcalá de Henares, and prisoners released on conditional liberty could seldom obtain a work permit, forcing them to live in the streets, shining shoes, peddling lottery tickets, and begging.[35]

---

[33] THIERRY MAULNIER, «Más allá del nacionalismo», trans. José Perdomo García, *Cisneros,* No. 5 (1943), pp. 73-85.
[34] «Política del intelectual», *Demócrito,* No. 18 (March 1946), p. 2.
[53] SAUL BELLOW, «Spanish Letter», *Partisan Review,* 15, No. 2 (February 1948), pp. 217-30.

A less direct form of resistance took literary form. Picking up the thread of revolutionary poetry written by Miguel Hernández, Pablo Neruda, and Rafael Alberti, postwar poets elaborated conventions for poetry of protest. Two collections illustrating the new conventions are *Pueblo cautivo,* long considered anonymous, and the *Antología cercada,* gathering the work of five poets.[36]

Though not forced underground by authorities, existentialism, censured by the Pope in the 1950 encyclical «Humani generis», was notorious. A series of articles about existentialism in the government-funded *Correo Literario* expressed disapproval in keeping with the Pope's judgment.[37] And yet, between 1945 and 1950 it was such a widely discussed topic and practised literary attitude that by 1947 writers were accused of being «too existentialist» and of adopting «*existencialismo a ultranza*».[38] Certainly, the claim that a writer was responsible to his fellow man and to his historical circumstance was neither new nor exclusively French. Commitment was discussed freely before and during the Civil War. Moreover, Spanish roots of existentialism already existed in the vitalist speculations of Unamuno; and Heidegger, Jaspers, and Marcel were read in Spain. But the popularization of *engagement* was primarily due to Jean-Paul Sartre. Before Sartre gained adherents, especially among Spanish novelists, with the publication of *¿Qué es la literatura?,* he was introduced to Spaniards in writings reported in publications such as *Insula.*[39]

Perhaps the richest source of existentialist ideas was *Espadaña,* published between 1944 and 1950 in León.[40] Often driven by polemical zeal, it began as the literary voice for a countermovement to *garcilasismo.* The writers of *Espadaña* rejected labels, including that of *existencialista.*[41] They noted, however, that the name was given to them because they were

[36] See Chapter 3, pp. 62-67; 73-76, *passim.*
[37] MIGUEL OROMI, O.F.M., «Existencialismo por penúltima vez», 1, No. 1 (June 1950), p. 5; «Escolasticismo ante existencialismo», 1, No. 7 (1 September 1950); pp. 1, 4; P. MIGUEL OLTRA, O.F.M., «La Encíclica 'Humani generis' y el Existencialismo», 1, No. 9 (1 October 1950), p. 5.
[38] JOSÉ CASTRO OVEJERO, «Filosofemas», *Espadaña,* No. 26 (n.d.).
[39] L. DUMONT WILDEN, «El existencialismo de Jean-Paul Sartre», No. 3 (15 March 1946), p. 5; GABRIEL MARCEL, «El existencialismo cristiano», No. 4 (15 April 1946), p. 7; PAULINE GARAGORRI, «Una novela existencialista de Jean-Paul Sartre», rev. of *La Nausée,* No. 14 (15 February 1947), p. 2; «Entrevistas. Jean-Paul Sartre», No. 32 (15 August 1948), p. 3.
[40] *Espadaña. Revista de poesía y crítica* (rpt., León: Espadaña, 1978); JOSÉ MANUEL LÓPEZ-BERNASOCCI, «La reedición de *Espadaña,* la revista española más representativa de su época», *Insula,* No. 392-93 (July-August 1979), p. 4. For studies of *Espadaña,* see: DE LA CONCHA, *La poesía española de posguerra,* pp. 304-63 and «*Espadaña* (1944-1951) (Biografía de una revista de poesía y crítica)», *Cuadernos Hispanoamericanos,* No. 236 (August 1969), pp. 380-97; RUBIO, *Las revistas poéticas,* pp. 256-72; LECHNER, *El compromiso en la poesía española del siglo XX. Parte segunda,* Chapter 3; and an issue of homage to *Espadaña: Peña Labra,* No. 14 (Winter 1974-1975).
[41] «Polémica. Poetas existencialistas y de los otros», *Espadaña,* No. 43 (1949).

not indifferent to the surrounding tragedy.⁴² Articles about sincerity, authenticity, and the ethical concerns of a writer in the 1940s added to the perception of an existentialist tenor in *Espadaña*.⁴³

One of the earliest postwar statements about the responsibility of the writer appeared in this publication.⁴⁴ An anticipation of Sartre's *engagement*, it confirmed that Spanish writers were willing to take an ideological view of writing. Answering a question about the value of poetry in times of great social distress, one *espadañista* admitted that the workman, the businessman, and the soldier might be skeptical of the value of poetry, but that did not make poetry useless:

> Para nosotros, habituados a mirar cara a cara lo que hay; a no eludir ni poner disfraz a nada, la Poesía es, entre otras cosas, con todas sus consecuencias, un modo de atestiguar la existencia y persistencia de un pueblo silencioso... Nuestra voz es, quiere ser, el mensaje de la vida que llega.

Toward the end of the 1940s, *Espadaña* became an arena testing two historically important positions: ethical commitment to social justice and political commitment to revolutionary change.⁴⁵ The profound seriousness toward existentialism shown by *Espadaña* was taken by many as an expression of dissent that seemed to polarize opinion.

The significance of a conjunction of politics and literature varied according to the vantage point of the observer. To a left-wing writer it meant the opportunity to publish Marxist propaganda defining human endeavor in ideological terms; to a right-wing writer it meant the limitation of literary creativity, the renunciation of control over the creative act in order to fulfill a predetermined political function.⁴⁶

---

⁴² «Filosofemas», *Espadaña*, No. 26 (n.d.).
⁴³ Compare this statement from «Poesía y vida», *Espadaña*, No. 16: «Resulta sobremanera fácil escribir sobre sinceridad poética, sobre lealtad consigo mismo, sobre la autenticidad, en suma, que el menester de escribir exige de más imperiosa manera que ningún otro... [Pero] lo auténtico, lo leal, lo sincero, se da en el escritor sin pensar en ello, y creemos que en la mayor parte de las ocasiones; aun en aquellas en que la obra se nos muestra desprovista de estos atributos... Todas estas variaciones nos llevarían a una exigencia de la que el arte no puede prescindir: la exigencia de la libertad más absoluta. Porque sin ella todo cuanto se diga o se escriba sobre sinceridad, sobre lealtad y sobre autenticidad, es ganas de turbar la creación intelectual y de falsear la verdadera verdad.» And from *Espadaña*, No. 8 (1945): «No; no es la guerra quien nos ha hecho tristes. Lo somos por temperamento, por formación, por ambiente. Y ésta es nuestra terrible virtud nacional; de la que ni el poeta puede desligarse, si no quiere verse reducido a la condición de inefable flautista. ¿Cuál será en nuestra hora la intensidad de esta fiereza y hasta qué dramáticas honduras no llegará la tristeza de España? Asomarse un poco a esta realidad perturba; pero, aun con el horror que un buceo tal pueda producir, debiera intentarse para poder fijar con exactitud al hombre que a nuestro alrededor se mueve, profundamente serio e intensamente recomido de continua agresividad.»
⁴⁴ «Poesía y vida», *Espadaña*, No. 19 (1945).
⁴⁵ See Chapter 3, pp. 85-87.
⁴⁶ «Necesidad y propósito», *Correo Literario*, 1, No. 1 (1 June 1950), p. 1;

Those intellectuals who out of prudence or skepticism remained uncommitted or those who were undecided between points of view found it progressively more difficult to remain aloof from political issues. Confronted by opposing views over freedom of expression, each writer felt forced to choose sides in order to remain in touch with reality, to sway the readership. General dissatisfaction with reigning social conditions in the late 1940s as well as the memory of the revolutionary 1930s —by right-wing Falangists and left-wing Marxists— led to suggestions of a Marxist revolution in the clandestine press and calls for a revolt against capitalism in the name of spiritual values in *La Hora,* published by SEU, the official student union.[47]

However, through a melding of Marxist and Falangist slogans lacking concrete reference, ideological discourse became exceedingly vague. Thus, articles in *La Hora* maintained the bias of the Regime, but adopted a progressive tone by repeating quasi-Marxist notions such as social revolution and dialectical materialism.[48] Representative articles illustrate this process in detail.

«Razones frente al socialismo» commenced with an unequivocal statement in favor of Spanish National Syndicalism; however, the author wanted to examine the concepts underlying a socialist economy because many fellow students believed that it offered a solution to Spain's dormant economy.[49] The substance of the article was a point-by-point refutation of the premises of a socialist economy with appeals to various authorities. Thus, socialism, morally defective, was repudiated by the Church; its practice of state-run collectives opposed doctrines of the Falange, which called for social organization based on the «natural unities» of family, municipality, and syndicate; moreover, socialism was an unnecessary detour on the way to National Syndicalism; and finally, it was incompatible with Spanish character. The author explained the popularity of socialism in Spain during the 1930s as due to the doctrine of class struggle, not to that of a state-owned economy.

An article examining «twentieth-century myths» expressed concern for the way man under the power of numerous mystifications renounced in-

J. RUIZ, «Intelectuales enrolados», *Laye,* No. 1 (March 1950), p. 7; JUAN EUGENIO BLANCO, «Más sobre los intelectuales», *Laye,* No. 4 (June 1950), p. 11.

[47] BLAS SÁENZ, «Juventud revolucionaria», *La Hora,* No. 70 (14 February 1948), p. 5.

[48] «Sobre la revolución social», *La Hora,* No. 43 (31 March 1947), p. 8; «¡Proletarios de todo el mundo: uníos!», *La Hora,* No. 70 (13 February 1948), p. 6; «La verdad del materialismo marxista», *La Hora,* 2, No. 7 (17 December 1948), p. 2; «Mundo burgués y marxismo», *La Hora,* 2, No. 9 (31 December 1948), p. 2.

[49] JOSÉ LUIS RUBIO, «Razones frente al socialismo», *La Hora,* 2, No. 21 (25 March 1949), p. 5.

dividual judgment for blind allegiance to mass movements.[50] Identifying *lo social* as perhaps the most important myth of the twentieth century, the author claimed that, with this cliché, demagogues tried to destroy the natural hierarchy of society. Other myths, those of technology and speed, changed the nature of daily life, placing an inflated value on rushing from one appointment to another, from one city to another. The political myths were the most noxious because they lacked precision. In the name of democracy and of communism entire peoples were enslaved. Even philosophy created a myth that stressed existential anguish. Both the theater and the novel were invaded by the man-in-the-street and the anguished individual, figures about to become myths too. The criticism in this article hinted at nostalgia for simpler times. Its distrust of foreign ideologies was consistent with the Regime's bias in the early postwar period.

In another student publication the tendency toward extremism was analyzed.[51] The author argued that the success of the Movimiento, single political party during the Franco Dictatorship, was measured by the extent to which it modified the inclination of Spaniards to consider cultural life representative of an underlying political reality. That is, Spaniards postulated leftism or rightism without recognizing the existence of plural values. In this respect, concluded the author, the Movimiento failed in its mission. Following José Antonio Primo de Rivera, he favored separating the various spheres of life, treating politics as politics and other problems —cultural, administrative, economic— independently of political formulations.

Small publications during the 1940s were a medium for ideological discussion widely prohibited elsewhere. Articles such as those in *Espadaña* and *La Hora* imply that discussion of ideological principles did not cease during the early postwar period, but even achieved a differentiation beyond crudely outlined postures of the left and right. This recuperation of the previous decade's ideological debate was paired with a deliberate effort to recognize the importance of unjustly forgotten writers of the same era.

Restoration of the Literary Past

Under normal conditions, free of coercive measures with ideological motives, literary publications inform their readers of important writers whose work is contemporary in idea or expression. They introduce foreign writers and revive interest in forgotten national writers as part of an

---

[50] Carmen Alonso Blanco, «Los mitos del siglo», *La Hora,* No. Extraordinario (24 June 1950), n. pag.
[51] Rodrigo Fernández Carvajal, «Contramovimiento», *Alcalá,* No. 1 (25 June 1953).

informative function taken for granted. During unusual conditions, such as those prevalent in the postwar period, fulfilling a normally routine function becomes a valuable mission. In this sense, little magazines such as *Corcel,* published without state subsidy, contributed to the vitality of postwar Spanish poetry by including poems of exiled writers whose works were inaccessible in Spain. In one issue of *Corcel,* No. 10-12 (December 1945), appeared three selections by Luis Cernuda, two by Juan Ramón Jiménez, and one by Pablo Picasso. All the major figures from the prewar and from abroad who were commemorated in such publications of the 1940s and 1950s are too numerous to be listed here. However, several poets who played important roles in postwar poetry must be mentioned. Two were Juan Ramón Jiménez, who enjoyed a select following, and Antonio Machado, admired and respected by all regardless of social class.[52] Juan Ramón Jiménez was a model for many poets of the Generation of 1927; in 1956 he received the Nobel Prize for Literature in recognition of his literary contribution. But the poets of the next generation, sometimes called *los nietos del 98* for their admiration of Miguel de Unamuno and Antonio Machado, were more drawn to the Machadian concept of poetry. Machado's notion of *intrahistoria,* holding that man's inner reality was the source of his humanity and the most authentic measure of his existence, guided the central branches of postwar Spanish poetry.[53] Following the Civil War, during which an existentialist tendency unfolded, Spanish lyric separated in two directions, one toward a personal, intimate poetry and the other, toward a social poetry in search of communion. Both tendencies, nevertheless, looked to Machado as a true predecessor.

Machado's renown as a poet was established long before the Civil War, earned by his major poetry and selections from *Juan de Mairena.* After the war his poems appeared in numerous publications, but the motive for inclusion was either to introduce one of Spain's foremost modern poets to new readers or to present previously unpublished or uncollected poems. Re-editions of his *Poesías completas* were enjoyed by increasing numbers of readers during the 1940s.[54] Not even an essay, in which Dionisio Ridruejo confirmed that Machado was a truly Spanish poet though politically «in error», dampened enthusiasm of the interested.[55]

---

[52] ARTURO SERRANO PLAJA, *Antonio Machado* (Buenos Aires: Schapire, 1944), pp. 33-36.
[53] LUIS FELIPE VIVANCO, *Introducción a la poesía española contemporánea* (Madrid: Guadarrama, 1974), 1, pp. 32, 39.
[54] Early postwar editions of *Poesías completas* (Madrid: Espasa-Calpe) are: 1st, 17 September 1940; 2nd, 5 November 1940; 3rd, 30 June 1943; 4th, 30 April 1946; 5th, 9 December 1949; 6th, 22 February 1953.
[55] See: DIONISIO RIDRUEJO, «El poeta rescatado», *Escorial,* 1, No. 1 (November 1940), pp. 93-100.

From the early postwar period until the middle of the 1960s, Machado's existential vitalism permeated postwar poetry.[56] It is well-known that Machado was a decisive influence on such poets as Rosales and Panero. But he was also a model thinker for the poets of *Espadaña*. Like Machado, they denounced excessive formalism for its intemporality, and excessive romanticism for emphasizing idiosyncracies, rather than common characteristics among men.[57] Despite sectarian claims and narrow political labels, Machado earned universal esteem for his profoundly inspiring humanist sentiments.[58] Widespread admiration for him resulted in articles and special publications dedicated to his memory.[59] On the tenth anniversary of his death, an elaborate homage was offered by *Cuadernos Hispanoamericanos*. It published, for the first time in Spain, a selection of posthumous papers and excerpts from *Los complementarios,* then added formerly uncollected poems from diverse pre-Civil War sources, several critical studies, numerous plates, and an «*Homenaje poético*». On the twentieth anniversary of his death *Indice* and *Insula* prepared homage issues, but the most significant tribute was the anthology José María Castellet dedicated to Machado's memory.[60]. Castellet's argument in the prologue of the anthology was based upon his analysis of *Los complementarios,* which had only recently become available.[61] In Machado's preference for colloquial language and his belief in brotherhood, Castellet saw a prophecy of the course of postwar poetry.

---

[56] For a study of this influence on major poets, see: JOSÉ OLIVIO JIMÉNEZ, *Cinco poetas del tiempo* (Madrid: Insula, 1964).
[57] VÍCTOR G. DE LA CONCHA, *La poesía española de la posguerra,* Chapter 4; LUIS GONZÁLEZ NIETO, «Eco de Antonio Machado en la poesía de la posguerra», *Peña Labra,* No. 16 (Summer 1975), pp. 48-50.
[58] LEOPOLDO DE LUIS, *Antonio Machado* (Madrid: SGEL, 1975), p. 121, summarizes this view: «Machado no es un poeta político. No pone su obra al servicio de nada que no sean sus propias emociones, sus propios sentimientos; pero entre esos sentimientos está la comunión con los demás... Machado es, pues, un poeta humanista, no un poeta político.»
[59] ANGEL LACALLE, «Notas a la obra de Antonio Machado», *Mediterráneo,* No. 1-4 (1943), pp. 91-107; *Albores del espíritu,* No. 28 (February 1949) [Cited by MANUEL TUÑÓN DE LARA, *Antonio Machado, poeta del pueblo* (Barcelona: Laia, 1975), p. 371]; ELADIO SOS, «Antonio Machado y la nueva poesía», *Raíz,* No. 6 (November 1949) [Cited by RUBIO, *Las revistas poéticas,* p. 93]; «A la memoria de Antonio Machado», *Cuadernos Hispanoamericanos,* No. 11-12 (September-December 1949); *Alfoz,* No. 4 (September-October 1952) [Cited by RUBIO, *Las revistas poéticas,* p. 365]; *Indice,* No. 123 (March 1959), p. 7; *Insula,* No. 158 (January 1960). Also, cited by BERNARD SESÉ, *Antonio Machado (1875-1939)* (Madrid: Gredos, 1980), p. 928: *Estudios segovianos,* No. 4 (1952); *Caracola,* No. 84-87 (October-December 1959, January 1960); *Cuaderno* de la Cátedra *Antonio Machado,* Soria, No. 1 (1960); *Machado, siempre (1939-1959). Aula del momento,* No. 18 (1960).
[60] JOSÉ MARÍA CASTELLET, *Veinte años de poesía española, 1939-1959* (Barcelona: Seix-Barral, 1960). See Chapter 5, pp. 171-73.
[61] ANTONIO MACHADO, Guillermo de Torre, ed., *Los complementarios y otras prosas póstumas* (Buenos Aires: Losada, 1957).

Poems by Miguel Hernández, who in 1939 was sentenced to death, pardoned, then returned to prison where he died in 1942, began appearing in *Espadaña, Verbo, Proel, Raíz,* and *Alcándara* around 1946.[62] Yet, in view of obvious echoes of his poetry in that of others writing in the early 1940s, it is not unreasonable to believe that Hernández's unpublished poems circulated before the first Spanish edition in 1952.[63] One of Hernández's most valuable contributions to postwar poetry was his exploration of autobiographical technique, elaborating his own inner life.[64] Hernández, in effect, wrote a personal version of the *intrahistoria* of 1936-1942, beginning with his passionate surrender to the cause of social justice recorded in *Viento del pueblo,* continuing with his reflections upon the tragedies of war in *El hombre acecha,* and concluding with testimony of his longings for family and freedom in *Cancionero* and *Romancero de ausencias.*[65] The tragic existentialist tone of his poetry anticipated the postwar poetry of Dámaso Alonso, Blas de Otero, and Gabriel Celaya.[66] Since Hernández was a controversial political figure, few poetic tributes to him were published until 1945.[67] The first elegy written to Hernández may have been «Al poeta Miguel Hernández» by Ildefonso Manuel Gil, which appeared in *Poemas del dolor antiguo* (1945).[68] But one of the first published was the final sonnet of *El canto cotidiano,* «En la muerte de Miguel», by Enrique Azcoaga.[69] One of the first publications to honor Hernández

[62] «Poema del hijo» [Four parts. In a fascicle of the *Antología parcial.*] *Espadaña,* No. 24 (1946); «Madre», *Verbo,* January-February 1947; «Sepultura de la imaginación», *Espadaña,* No. 42 (1949); «Silencio divino», «Huerto mío», «Pozo mío», and «Poemas del cancionero y romancero de ausencias: 12, 38, 51, 56», *Verbo,* No. 30 (April 1954). Also, cited by Rubio, *Las revistas poéticas,* p. 242 [5 unpublished poems], *Proel,* No. 2 (Summer 1946); p. 92. «Antes del odio», *Raíz,* No. 5 (June 1949); p. 395 [2 poems], *Alcántara,* No. 1 (1951). And, cited by Lechner, *El compromiso en la poesía española del siglo XX. Parte segunda,* p. 55: «El pez más viejo del río», «Casida del sediente», *Espadaña,* No. 44 (1950). Finally, Darío Puccini, *Romancero de la resistencia española* (Mexico: Biblioteca ERA, 1967), p. 40, noted the publication of late Hernández poems in *Halcón,* No. 6 (May 1946).
[63] Miguel Hernández, *Obras escogidas: poesía teatro* (Madrid: Aguilar, 1952).
[64] Juan Cano Ballesta, *La poesía de Miguel Hernández* (Madrid: Gredos, 1962), p. 262.
[65] Luis Felipe Vivanco, *Introducción a la poesía española contemporánea,* 2, p. 200.
[66] Manuel Durán, «Miguel Hernández: Poet of Clay and of Light», *Spanish Writers of 1936. Crisis and Commitment in the Poetry of the Thirties and Forties* (London: Tamesis, 1973), p. 75.
[67] A few early examples are: Juan Eduardo Cirlot, «Elegía a Miguel Hernández», *Espadaña,* No. 16 (1945); José Luis Cano, «Elegía», *Verbo,* May-June 1947, p. 3; Ramón de Garciasol, «Miguel Hernández», *Poesía de España,* No. 1 (1960), p. 3.
[68] Lechner, *El compromiso en la poesía española del siglo XX. Parte segunda,* p. 17, says Gil wrote the poem in 1942.
[69] Enrique Azcoaga, «En la muerte de Miguel», *El canto cotidiano* (Madrid: Editorial Hispánica, 1943), p. 66:

> La tierra al recibirte habrá sentido
> todo el calor del trigo más granado;

was *Indice* in 1951.⁷⁰ Finally, on the fiftieth anniversary of his birthdate, Hernández was commemorated in several tributes.⁷¹ Gradually, the great debt owed to this poet by admirers who learned from his poetry became acknowledged. His contemporaries, Victoriano Crémer, Eugenio de Nora, Rafael Morales, and José Hierro, continued the social poetry that he initiated, while younger poets such as José Angel Valente, José Agustín Goytisolo, and Claudio Rodríguez sometimes wrote in a similar vein.⁷²

The delayed recognition of Hernández as a major poet was not due to lack of interest in his stirring poetry, but rather to his political significance. As late as 1952, an equanimous literary essay exploring the theme of death in Hernández's poetry, mentioning neither circumstance nor reason for the poet's death, provoked a sharp exchange of editorial comment with the national press.⁷³

Rafael Alberti, an avowed Communist since the 1930s, who sought exile in Argentina, then in Rome, seldom appeared in Spanish literary publications of the 1940s and 1950s, but traces of his poems were recognizable to initiates. An example was a poem by the Andalusian Salvador Pérez Valiente, «Deliberado homenaje a R. A.», from 1948.⁷⁴ Not until his sixtieth birthday in 1963 was Alberti honored in his native land and publicly recognized for his importance to Spanish poetry.⁷⁵

> todo el amor de un hombre inacabado;
> la gloria de un poeta conseguido.
>
> El surco que tu sangre ha redimido
> sembrando injustamente tu truncado
> destino pedirá justicia airado
> a Dios desde unos olmos sin olvido.
>
> Tu estirpe campesina quiso un día
> salvar al hombre fértil del secano
> monstruoso en que brotó tu voz lograda.
>
> Y Dios perpetuará tu lozanía,
> tu corazón sin muerte, fiel hermano,
> en troncos como tu alma destrozada.

---

⁷⁰ RUBIO, *Las revistas poéticas*, p. 84.

⁷¹ «En memoria de Miguel Hernández en el 50.º aniversario de su nacimiento», *Poesía de España*, No. 4 (1960); *Agora*, No. 49-50 (November-December 1960); *Insula*, No. 168 (November 1960); *Caracola*, No. 96 (1960) [Cited by RUBIO, *Las revistas poéticas*, p. 390].

⁷² JUAN CANO BALLESTA, *La poesía de Miguel Hernández*, p. 262.

⁷³ ENRIQUE BADOSA, «La conciencia de la muerte en la poesía de Miguel Hernández», *Laye*, No. 18 (March-April 1952), pp. 7-12. Cf. *Laye*, No. 19 (May-June 1952), p. 3: «De las responsabilidades de Miguel Hernández juzgaron en su sazón los tribunales a quienes incumbía y dictaron una sentencia que aquél estaba cumpliendo al fallecer. Pero *Madrid*, acaso por creer que la sentencia fue liviana, parece desear que a la pena temporal de cárcel se añada una condena eterna de silencio para su obra, que conocemos a través de ediciones legalmente autorizadas.»

⁷⁴ *Verbo*, No. 13 (1948), pp. 3-4.

⁷⁵ *Agora*, No. 59-60 (1961); *Insula*, No. 198 (May 1963); *Papeles de Son Armadans*, No. 88 (July 1963).

Latin American poets also helped shape postwar Spanish poetry in essential ways. Pablo Neruda's lyric experiments and revolutionary ideas, which polarized those around him in Madrid during the 1930s, created a second wave of influence a decade later. In *Españada,* his own poems and prose as well as poems dedicated to him appeared between 1947 and 1950.[76] Apart from his presence in *Espadaña,* largely a result of Eugenio de Nora's sponsorship, Neruda appeared at least twice in *Verbo:* in a poem of tribute written by Concha Zardoya, Chilean by birth, and in a book review of *Tercera residencia* that eluded mention of «España en el corazón», inspired by the Spanish Civil War.[77] Though Neruda's importance to poetry of protest was obvious, the extent to which his influence reached beyond a few poets is unclear. According to a statement in *Insula,* Neruda's importance may have been limited and superseded very early in the postwar period.[78] However, his poetry seems to have parallels, not only with that of Celaya, but even with that of Angela Figuera.[79] His *Canto General* affected Leopoldo Panero in a negative manner by eliciting from him a complex response in *Canto Personal.* Beyond these few poets, evidence of consuming interest in Neruda's poetry is lacking. Because copies of his works were difficult to find in Spain, *Espadaña* acquired a limited supply of complete works through arrangement with a Chilean publisher and then advertised them from 1947 to 1949. Despite a reasonable price, Crémer finally gave the copies away.[80]

Another Latin American poet important to the development of the poetry of protest was César Vallejo. He seldom appeared in publications before 1949, but was honored twice that year, perhaps in enthusiastic response to the recently available edition of his poetry.[81] A precipitously formed group, «Poesía total», signed a vehement declaration in Vallejo's

---

[76] «Invocación», «Cómo era España» [from *España en el corazón*], No. 25 (n.d.); «Alturas de Machu-Picchu» [selections], No. 30 (1947); «Poesía y vida. Textos no clásicos» [«Conducta y poesía», *Caballo verde para la poesía,* No. 3 (1935)]. No. 30 (1947). Louis Aragon, «La caja de mariposas», «España en el corazón» [Dedicated to Neruda], No. 36 (1948). Gabriel Celaya, «A Pablo Neruda», No. 46 (1950).

[77] «Las manos del espejo», No. 11 (April-May 1948), p. 3; review of *Tercera residencia,* February 1948, p. 28, which commences: «Siempre dentro de su peculiar modo de expresión, Pablo Neruda reúne en 'Tercera residencia' algunos de sus popularizados últimos poemas. La nota social, vinculada a la segunda gran guerra, acaso sea la nueva en esta colección de versos.»

[78] «Neorrealismo poético», *Insula,* No. 126 (15 May 1957), p. 2.

[79] Charles David Ley, «Influencia de Pablo Neruda y de otros poetas hispanoamericanos en la moderna poesía de España», *Actas del Tercer Congreso Internacional de Hispanistas,* Carlos H. Magis, ed. (México: El Colegio de México, 1970), pp. 543-52.

[80] Lechner, *El compromiso en la poesía española del siglo XX. Parte segunda,* p. 55.

[81] César Abraham Vallejo, *Poesías completas (1918-1938)* (Buenos Aires: Losada, 1949).

honor in *Espadaña*.[82] *La Hora* featured a brief introduction to the life and works of the Peruvian that mentioned both *Poemas humanos* and *España, aparta de mí este cáliz*.[83] The selection of poems offered to readers, however, was drawn exclusively from *Los heraldos negros*. A review article in *Verbo* acknowledged Vallejo as one of the most powerful lyric poets of the twentieth century, well-known in Spain despite a veil of silence raised for diverse reasons.[84] Félix Grande, admirer of Vallejo, remembered that the Peruvian poet became known in Spain during 1940s, but was not widely read until the 1950s.[85] New interest in Vallejo no doubt was stimulated by articles such as a thematic study of his poetry by José María Valverde, published in 1949.[86]

With firm dedication, literary publications honored officially censured poets during the early years of the postwar period. They were sources for information about writers barred from periodicals with wider readerships. Special issues of homage, poetic tributes, republication of important poems maintained continuity between the committed poetry of the pre-Civil War period and the poetry of protest in the postwar period.[87]

At mid-century, a nucleus of critics, securely placed in well-paid positions, utilized officially sponsored publications to propagate neotraditionalist opinion concerning postwar literature. That contrasted significantly with a new wave of opinion coming to light in *Indice, Alcalá,* and *Cuadernos Hispanoamericanos* under a revised editorial policy beginning in 1951 and made possible by Joaquín Ruiz-Giménez, Education Minister. The neotraditionalist *excluyentes* and the more liberal *comprensivos,* to use Ridruejo's terminology, were poles apart on most cultural issues.[88]

---

[82] *Espadaña*, No. 39 (1949): «*César Vallejo* nació el día 6 de junio del año 1893 en Santiago de Chuco (Perú) y murió en París el día 15 de abril de 1938. José Luis Aranguren, Antonio G. de Lama, Victoriano Crémer, Eugenio de Nora, Leopoldo Panero, Luis Rosales, José María Valverde y Luis Felipe Vivanco LE RECUERDAN.»
Two other appearances in *Espadaña:* «Los desgraciados», No. 22 (1946); «Masa», No. 45 (1950).
[83] *La Hora,* 2, No. 16 (18 February 1949), p. 13.
[84] *Verbo,* No. 22 (June 1951), pp. 51-53.
[85] Félix Grande, *Apuntes sobre poesía española de posguerra* (Madrid: Taurus, 1970), pp. 39, 46-47.
[86] José María Valverde, «Notas de entrada a la poesía de César Vallejo», *Cuadernos Hispanoamericanos,* No. 7 (January-February 1949), pp. 57-84.
[87] Juan Cano Ballesta, *La poesía española entre pureza y revolución (1930-1936)* (Madrid: Gredos, 1972), pp. 260-61: «En la primavera de 1936, tras el triunfo del Frente Popular, sube de grado la fiebre revolucionaria en círculos de escritores. Se multiplican las publicaciones de este tono y se intensifica su ardor... Se vive en un ambiente de intensa fermentación espiritual que somete a severa crítica todos los hechos culturales, artísticos y sociopolíticos, y prepara el cambio más profundo en las concepciones poéticas de nuestro siglo, llevándolo en parte a feliz término. Toda la llamada poesía social de décadas posteriores tuvo allá su planteamiento y su germen.»
[88] Elías Díaz, *Pensamiento español 1939-1973* (Madrid: EDICUSA, 1974), p. 56.

However, knowledge of this schism within prominent circles —the University, the periodical press, informal groups of intellectuals— remained confined to the Peninsula until the Third International Congress of the Catholic Press in Rome, held in 1950.[89] There, the question of Spanish censorship came to world-wide attention when American correspondents interpreted a comment by the Pope as an accusation that the Franco Dictatorship censored religious publications. The Regime was forced to admit publicly that, though surveillance existed, it was limited to «political» matters. One result of international attention to Spanish cultural affairs was foreign scholarly concern about censorship's regressive effects upon postwar Spanish literature. Robert G. Mead claimed that a comparison of exiled Spanish intellectuals with those who remained in Spain following the Civil War demonstrated the negative effect of political censorship; he argued that, since politics and literature were interrelated, what occurred in one realm affected the other.[90] Even when Julián Marías provided a list of outstanding Spaniards and their accomplishments, Mead denied that his position had been refuted. In the debate, which continued for several years, other writers, such as José Luis Aranguren and Guillermo de Torre, participated.[91]

This scrutiny of the Regime's workings revealed the authoritarian nature of the Franco Dictatorship precisely when Spain, wishing to join the post-World War II recovery, needed to adopt a moderate image in order to be accepted by other Western nations. Therefore, in 1951 Franco reorganized the ministerial departments and redistributed responsibility. This move effectively closed the period of autarky existing since the Civil War. An important result of the reorganization, in which Joaquín Ruiz-Giménez became Education Minister, was a more liberal publication policy.

One of Ruiz-Giménez's decrees directed provincial deputations, municipalities, and other public corporations to hold book competitions for new works, republish out-of-print books, and foster interest in cultural affairs by means of programs, courses, and expositions.[92] This policy also encouraged subsidies to literary publications, a step both necessary and overdue in the opinion of representative editors.[93] Survival of publications

---

[89] Manuel Fernández Areal, *La libertad de prensa en España* (Madrid: EDICUSA, 1971), pp. 62-63.
[90] Elías Díaz, *Notas para una historia del pensamiento español actual*, pp. 95-98.
[91] Guillermo de Torre, «Hacia una reconquista de la libertad», *La Torre*, No. 3 (July-September 1953), pp. 107-26; José Luis Aranguren, «La evolución espiritual de los intelectuales españoles en la emigración», *Cuadernos Hispanoamericanos*, No. 38 (1953), pp. 123-57; «La condición de la vida intelectual en la España de hoy», *La Torre*, 1, No. 4 (October-December 1953), pp. 83-97.
[92] *Boletín Oficial del Estado*, No. 224 (11 August 1952), pp. 1746-48.
[93] «Preguntas a los 'hombres que hacen revistas'», *Correo Literario*, 3, No. 42 (15 February 1952), p. 6. José Luis Cano stated: «Lo ideal sería que el Estado no

depended upon a steady source of funding, whether from the State, subscriptions, patronage, or the editors' pockets. The sometimes by-monthly, other times weekly *Estafeta Literaria,* financed by the Dirección General de Prensa y Propaganda, circulated as many as 10,000 copies per issue. The monthly *Poesía Española,* also assisted by the State, distributed between 1,500 and 2,000 copies. Some publications were sponsored by organizations within the Regime, such as *Cuadernos Hispanoamericanos,* issued by the Instituto de Cultura Hispánica. *Luz de Tomelloso* was supported by Acción Católica; other publications accepted aid from official sources, the Delegación de Educación y Cultura, in the case of *Al-Motamid* in Tetuán, and the Círculo Cultural del Movimiento, in that of *Rocamador* in Palencia.[94] These literary reviews seldom had a sharply defined ideological purpose. Rather, they provided a forum for would-be writers and poets.[95] As long as publications confined their comments to literary life, they ran little risk of censorship, particularly under Ruiz-Giménez in the early 1950s. On the other hand, censorship did not cease. The «Servicio de Lectorado», as it was called in 1952, became part of the newly formed Dirección General de Información under Gabriel Arias Salgado.[96]

This first concerted effort toward intellectual liberalization had unexpected results. For instance, against all attacks, Ruiz-Giménez supported the homages to Ortega y Gasset on the philosopher's seventieth birthday.[97] He took an active role in literary and artistic affairs, but his policy was moderate; in these areas he intended to neither disregard beauty nor scorn truth.[98] Ruiz-Giménez believed that art, as an expression of the individual, was autonomous and not to be used by the State to promote its own interests. Yet he also believed that the State ought to stimulate and compensate the arts since society no longer provided adequate support.

---

tuviese que ayudar a las revistas literarias... Desgraciadamente, faltando en España un público cultivado capaz de mantener unas revistas literarias, creo necesario que el Estado llene esa lamentable ausencia. Ahora bien, a mi juicio, el sistema más honesto de ayuda a una revista literaria por parte del Estado sería, más que patrocinarla directamente, convirtiéndola en órgano de su propaganda cultural, adquirir una parte de la edición de cada número para difundirla gratuitamente en el extranjero.»

[94] «Vida y aventura de las revistas de poesía», *La Estafeta Literaria,* No. 94 (4 May 1957), pp. 1, 4.

[95] «Desde San Sebastián», *La Estafeta Literaria,* No. 51 (7 July 1956), p. 5: «En el Círculo Cultural existen pequeños grupos con inquietudes literarias... no sería extraño que surgiera una revista... esta entidad es la única que económicamente podrá hacerlo. En otras ciudades las Delegaciones Provinciales de Educación, merced al carácter activo y emprendedor de sus miembros, suelen impulsar la vida de las letras.»

[96] *Boletín Oficial del Estado,* 21 March 1952. The pay established in *pesetas* per 200 pages read was: Spanish, 100; Catalan, Galician, French, Italian, 150; English, 200; German, Slavic, and Oriental languages, 300.

[97] ELÍAS DÍAZ, *Pensamiento español 1939-1973,* p. 108.

[98] «Exposición Bienal Hispanoamericana de Arte. Inauguración», *Diez discursos* (Madrid: Educación Nacional, 1954), pp. 21-24.

The University was of particular interest to Ruiz-Giménez. He wished to develop dialogue between students and professors to encourage a corporative style of life, self-government, and communication with the surrounding society, so that the University might reflect the concerns of the entire nation. Ideologically, Ruiz-Giménez intended to achieve these goals within the spirit of Christianity. In an outline of his plan to democratize culture, he emphasized the need for political representation for all, policies that benefited the majority, and also «un ascenso simultáneo y armónico en el orden de la vivencia de los valores espirituales que constituyen el alma misma de la cultura».[99] He planned for this to occur without loss of respect for the dignity of man, without discrimination, but with justice and service to the community. This idealistic policy was to guide Spaniards from mutual distrust to brotherhood in which each lived fully; rather than *coexistencia,* he encouraged *convivencia.*[100] Ruiz-Giménez, after dismissal as Minister following the student strikes in 1956, joined other intellectuals to found *Cuadernos para el diálogo.* This publication, begun in 1963, was deliberately political and remained in the forefront of cultural liberation. The policy of *convivencia,* supported by Ruiz-Giménez, seemed confirmed by Pope John XXIII's encyclical of freedom, «Pacem in terris».[101] Directed to all men of good will, the encyclical eased tension in Spain over increased freedom coming about in the liberalization of Spanish culture, begun around 1950, halted in 1956, and rapidly expanded after 1963, the years when poetry of protest rose to prominence.[102]

---

[99] JOAQUÍN RUIZ-GIMÉNEZ, «Entre el dolor y la esperanza», *Alcalá,* No. 23-24 (10 January 1953), n. pag.
[100] «La democratización de la cultura», *Cuadernos para el Diálogo,* No. 20 (May 1965), pp. 5-7.
[101] ELÍAS DÍAZ, *Pensamiento español 1939-1973,* pp. 173-85.
[102] Attributing the variety of terms used to designate this poetry to the large number of ethical and esthetic approaches of critics and poets, observed FANNY RUBIO, «Teoría y polémica en la poesía española de posguerra», *Cuadernos Hispanoamericanos,* No. 361-362 (July-August 1980), p. 205: «En cuanto al concepto en sí, aparte de poesía 'social', indistintamente se usan los calificativos de 'realismo crítico', 'poesía práctica' (J. Hierro), 'militante' o 'comprometida' (E. de Nora), y 'socialrealismo' (A. González, A. Sastre).»

2

NEW POETRY IN 1944

The abrupt change of direction in postwar poetry, dubbed «La revolución de 1944» by Víctor G. de la Concha, seems obvious now. That *Sombra del paraíso* by Vicente Aleixandre, *Hijos de la ira* by Dámaso Alonso, and *Espadaña*, edited by Victoriano Crémer and Eugenio de Nora, contributed significantly to a change of taste is a claim often made in book reviews and in declarations. Contemporary critics differed, however, on how these four poets changed taste; and they used a range of terms to identify the new poetry. During the 1940s, it was called neoromanticism or *tremendismo,* though neither term gained universal acceptance. The former called attention to familiar qualities found in earlier poetry, the latter, to the qualities constituting the antithesis of *garcilasismo;* both designated poetry written within an esthetic conception distinct from, and in opposition to, that of pure poetry. *Sombra del paraíso,* significant for other reasons, was not seen as noticeably affecting development of the poetry of protest. On the other hand, the relation of *Hijos de la ira* was mentioned frequently. The case of *Espadaña* is more complex. This publication was largely the creation of Victoriano Crémer, a figure almost forgotten today, whose poetry appearing in *Espadaña* conformed to the new esthetic practice during the crucial years when poetic norms were redefined.

One of the first announcements concerning a new poetry was made by Antono G. De Lama in his critique of *Garcilaso*.[1] After claiming that a high regard for polished lines and nostalgic tone was depriving poetry of substance, De Lama praised literary romanticism and encouraged poetry with fewer metaphors and less stylistic perfection, but more spontaneity and prophetic sensibility. He offered a lengthy description while discussing the two major tendencies of 1944: «*la poesía formalista*» and «*la otra poesía*».[2] According to De Lama, metaphysical poetry, unlike «formalistic»

---

[1] ANTONIO G. DE LAMA, «Si Garcilaso volviera», *Cisneros*, No. 6 (1943), pp. 122-24.

[2] ANTONIO G. DE LAMA, «Poesía y verdad. La poesía actual». *Espadaña*, No. 9 (1944).

poetry, could not be learned nor cultivated, its excellence depended upon a gift, the humanity of the poet. De Lama revived the idea of the *poeta vate,* whose calling to poetry was destined. Such a poet uttered truths about the noumenal realm, which could not be intellectually known. To evoke a passionate reader response, the *poeta vate* shunned neoclassic precepts, adopting instead a fervid manner. Rather than concentrate on the composition of perfect songs, sonnets, madrigals, and odes, he tried to express a level of reality requiring freer verse forms. De Lama ascribed the major reason for this esthetic change to the historical moment: «La época que nos ha tocado vivir es demasiado trágica para que nos dediquemos a jugar con las palabras y con la música fácil de los versos.»

De Lama's definition of major tendencies contrasted with one by Eugenio Frutos that avoided moral discussion.[3] Frutos indicated no preference between neoclassicism and neoromanticism and omitted mention of any dialectical relation between historical events and poetry, thus achieving detachment for esthetic analysis. Frutos elsewhere discussed the historical development of the new poetry, suggesting that the major romantic themes of postwar poetry —love, family, country— were used extensively by Aleixandre, Lorca, Cernuda, and Hernández before 1936.[4] Furthermore, he believed romanticism accentuated in both the poetry of the Civil War and, except for the brief popularity of *garcilasismo,* that of the postwar period.

More complex definitions usually took for granted a relationship between poetic tendencies and the situation in which they developed to propose connections and speculate on the future trajectory of poetry. In a study of three tendencies, *garcilasismo, el virtuosismo de la sencillez,* and *neoromantismo,* Rodrigo Fernández Carvajal isolated the defining features of each tendency, remarking on the dangers each incurred through exageration.[5] Although he believed all three sorts had authentic roots in the contemporary world, he dismissed the importance of the first two: one, as a Petrarchan revival that already served its purpose by correcting earlier styles, the other, as a pale imitation of German and English poems that sought profundity in verbal simplicity, but failed. He affirmed that the newest poetry drew inspiration from prewar neoromanticism while criticizing *garcilasismo.* In support he cited the attitude of a voice crying out in the wilderness and that of existential alienation, patent symbols of homage to Unamuno. He also found Aleixandre's *La destrucción o el*

---

[3] EUGENIO FRUTOS, «Los poetas dicen», *Verbo,* May-June 1947: «Apuntemos dos [direcciones] que no son de ahora, sino eternas: un neoclasicismo y un neorromanticismo. Los dos 'neos' suponen una cierta retórica, un amaneramiento...»

[4] EUGENIO FRUTOS, «La poesía actual y el romanticismo», *Correo Literario,* 1, No. 6 (15 August 1950), pp. 1, 4.

[5] RODRIGO FERNÁNDEZ CARVAJAL, «Notas a la poesía joven», *Cisneros,* No. 11 (1946), pp. 96-103.

amor, with its unique universe and long lines, a pervasive presence in recent poetry. On the other hand, though he believed the influence of Machado extensive, he found it difficult to isolate.

In the reconstruction of a poetic tendency, studies that pinpoint authors and works help recreate the contemporary understanding of an era. For this reason, one of the most useful documents in which to discover the perception of poetry in the 1940s is the *Antología parcial*.[6] This pioneering analysis of a complicated period of Spanish poetry was issued by fascicules in regular numbers of *Espadaña* from No. 22 (1946) through No. 38 (1949). It conformed to De Lama's criteria for anthologies by listing principle groups, affinities, and tendencies, noting each author's place and importance in the literary panorama, and providing a brief sketch of each author.[7] The *Antología parcial* analyzed the poetry of 1936-1946; thus it spanned the Civil War, tracing prewar tendencies in relation to their postwar variations.[8] The anthology divided recent poetry among cross-generational groupings. Under «Neoromanticism» were Alberti, Cernuda, Alonso, and Aleixandre, as well as younger poets Cano, Gaos, and Morales. «Pure poetry» included Diego, Guillén, Salinas, Prados, Altolaguirre, and Carmen Conde. In a group labeled «Transition» were Hernández, León Felipe, Bleiberg, Panero, Rosales, Vivanco, with Bousoño and Valverde included as religious poets. The remaining category, with Crémer and De Nora, carried as title, «Federico García Lorca». Links between the Leonese poets and their Andalusian mentor were perhaps a neopopulist style from the *Romancero gitano* and a *tremendista* manner. Crémer and De Nora easily might have used the term *tremendismo,* coined by another poet but associated earliest with them, to describe their poetry.[9]

---

[6] Studied by LECHNER, *El compromiso en la poesía española del siglo XX. Parte segunda,* pp. 62-63.
[7] ANTONIO G. DE LAMA, «Poesía y verdad. Antologías», *Espadaña,* No. 27 (1947).
[8] Compare this description of the new poetry given in *Antología parcial,* p. 6: «Quizá esté en el repudio de la poesía pura y en esa tendencia metafísica que intenta dar a los versos una trascendencia, cargando el acento sobre el dolor, sobre la angustia del hombre. Hay mucho falso y hueco en esto que alguien ha llamado 'tremendismo'; pero es evidente que en esa órbita se ha movido los mejores intentos de la poesía de estos últimos años.
Como se ve, esto que denunciamos como nuevo es ya viejo; estaba ya en el superrealismo e islas adyacentes. Pero aquí está su más claro síntoma de autenticidad. Solamente lo que es desarrollo tiene auténtica novedad.»
[9] ENRIQUE CASAMAYOR, «Tremendismo poético», *Cuadernos Hispanoamericanos,* No. 9 (May-June 1949), pp. 746-47: «Este fenómeno de la poesía desbordaba de gestos y dolor, de gritos y silencios desolados, 'el impresionante afán hacia lo trascendente y grande, hacia lo fuerte y violento', fue bautizado por un poeta, A. de Zubiaurre, con el nombre de *tremendismo...* Hay una muchedumbre de adjetivos como *sideral, cósmico, horrible, horrendo, abismal, espantoso, infinito, desierto...,* y muy especial el *tremendo* etimológico, que subraya, junto a la idea de magnitud potenciadora, la acepción de conmoción, de sacudida, de acromegálico proceder; es como un *tremo* anímico que subvierte valores usados, para cantar la soledad amorosa fatalista y doliente, buscándole límites al infinito.»

The *Antología parcial* was edited over several years, though the introduction presented the original plan and ranking in the first fascicule. Evidently the initial roster of poets proved incomplete because other poets were added later. Some, such as Gabriel Celaya and José Hierro, became known around 1947 and properly were included. Others, such as Entrambasaguas, however, may have been included for non-literary reasons.[10] The most conspicuous omission was that of Blas de Otero, whose poetry was important by 1948. Though he had not yet published *Angel fieramente humano,* his poems circulated in various publications and in manuscript. Despite the boast of partiality, this anthology actually omitted few prominent poets and in a rare instance of oversight, perhaps intentional, *Espadaña* apologized to the offended individual.[11] The *Antología parcial* was the first collection to pay special attention to the youngest generation of poets, treating the *Garcilaso* group with more fairness than they received in *Espadaña* articles.[12] This anthology, with easily criticized classifications when judged by academic standards, was one of the first independent assessments of postwar directions.[13]

The rapidity of stylistic change during the 1940s was evident in Gabriel Celaya's declaration that a new humanized poetry was in formation and was different from *tremendismo,* only the most recent of numerous romantic postures coming to the fore from 1928 to 1948.[14] In Celaya's view, a poet under the aegis of Unamuno and Machado was a prophet who refused to treat poetry as a plaything, speaking instead of mankind's anxieties in the convulsive atmosphere of postwar Europe. Celaya's definition resembles De Lama's in some respects, but differs by valuing highly the surrealist technique of image, the irregular verse, and the frequent long

---

[10] Also added later were Leopoldo de Luis, Enrique Azcoaga, Concha Zardoya, José María Pemán, José Luis Hidalgo, Alfonso Moreno, Fernando González, Joaquín Romero Murubi, Rodríguez Spiteri, and Adriano del Valle.

[11] «Cuando ya no hay remedio», *Espadaña,* No. 37 (1949): «No entonamos un 'yo pecador' colectivo, porque esto no remediaría el cósmico trastorno originado por nuestra parcialidad, pero queremos seguir su consejo de mínima generosidad, de excesiva generosidad y enmendar nuestro profundo error reproduciendo un fragmento poético original de S. P. Valiente...»

[12] CHARLES DAVID LEY, *Spanish Poetry Since 1939* (Washington, D.C.: Catholic University Press, 1962), p. 246.

[13] By contrast, Alfonso Moreno's anthology —«antología de aquí y ahora»— followed criteria establecidos by the Regime's Editora Nacional. Moreno expanded the imposed limits to include Unamuno, Machado, Jiménez, Lorca, Salinas, Guillén, Alberti, Cernuda, Altolaguirre, and Hernández, as he stated in the introduction to *Poesía española actual* (Madrid: Editora Nacional, 1946): «Los límites impuestos por la Editora Nacional han sufrido cierta ampliación al incluir algunos fallecidos o actualmente residentes fuera de España. En ambos casos, la salvedad se ha hecho en favor de aquellos nombres sin los cuales no podría entenderse, en su verdadero arranque y significación, el panorama actual de nuestra poesía.»

[14] GABRIEL CELAYA, «Veinte años de poesía», *Egan,* No. 2 (April-June 1948), pp. 27-31.

lines. Within prewar Spanish neoromantic poetry, which he judged comparable in quality to European poetry of the same period, Celaya included all the «isms», neopopular poetry of Lorca and Alberti, «poesía mágica» influenced by Bécquer, and «poesía iluminada» of Aleixandre, Cernuda, and Pablo Neruda, who affected Peninsular poetry through *Residencia en la tierra*. Celaya believed prewar neoclassicism a successful check on the torrential verse of many neoromantic poems, but found postwar neoclassicism «*rabiosamente hispánica*» for non-literary reasons, seldom rising above pastiche and preciosity. By 1945-1946, he thought the reaction to *garcilasismo* widespread in the form of *tremendismo*, which in turn was losing ground to humanized poetry. José Albí and Joan Fuster, less optimistic than Celaya about the state of postwar poetry, agreed there was a «retorno a lo humano» led by *Espadaña* and *Hijos de la ira*.[15] They saw humanized poetry, exacerbated by the Civil War, as the normal reaction to an academic style, but one in danger of artistic stagnation through excessive repetition. Albí and Fuster concluded that it was time for renovation, perhaps toward a new surrealism.

Several critics assigned a relation between the Civil War and the postwar return to humanized, vitalized poetry. The concurrence of ethics and esthetics in what became known as *tremendismo* seemed correct for the times. But fewer than six years passed between De Lama's announcement of new poetry, and the first notices that it was an exhausted style. *Tremendismo* was not a new tendency, judged by its typical vocabulary and most frequently used techniques. Quevedo, Valle-Inclán, and Lorca drew upon similar semantic categories and used techniques of substitution such as animate for inanimate and vice-versa in order to personify animals and objects and dehumanize persons. But the popularity of *tremendista* poetry most likely depended upon reading protest as an authentic reaction to historical conditions, as suggested by assertions in *Espadaña*. When imitators divorced exaggerated gestures and emotion, shouts and desolate silences from the ethical context in which they were legitimate, *tremendismo* was diminished to a mere style based on a few rhetorical figures and overworked adjectives. According to José Luis Cano, the decline of *tremendismo* occurred after a few years of inordinate popularity, in which epigoni counterfeited the tone solely for effect.[16] Cano believed that a newer anti-romantic tendency, based on personal references, nostalgia, sincerity, and hope, was exposing the melodramatic falseness of *tremendismo*. He stressed that no one sort of poetry was dominant in 1950. To those tendencies just named, he added romanticism, as cultivated by

---

[15] «Orientaciones de nuestra poesía», *Verbo*, No. 14 (January-February 1949); «Balance poético, suma y sigue», *Verbo*, No. 15 (March-April 1949).

[16] José Luis Cano, «Romanticismo y antirromanticismo en nuestra poesía actual», *Correo Literario*, 1, No. 11 (1 November 1950), p. 9.

Bousoño, Montesinos, and himself, Catalan surrealism, and the Baroque poetry of the *Cántico* group in Córdoba.

Despite the early conviction of the founders of *Espadaña* and others that they were creating a new poetry, little evidence suggests 1944 was then widely accepted as a turning point or that Alonso, Aleixandre, Crémer, and De Nora were protagonists. Juan Guerrero, often called the «Cónsul de la Poesía Española», named as poets most read that year: Machado, Juan Ramón Jiménez, Adriano del Valle, García Lorca, Lugones, Acosta, Rosales, Concha Espina, and Gabriel y Galán.[17] Similarly, outside a few circles, *Espadaña* was almost unknown. At the national level it was merely a promising publication, not yet distinguished from others such as *Proel, Entregas de Poesía,* and *Lazarillo.*[18]

From this discussion, it is apparent that critical terminology used in the 1940s lacked homogeneity. How many tendencies existed and the relative importance of each depended upon the critic cited. Writers for *Espadaña,* actively renovating Spanish poetry, published declarations against pure poetry with its ivory towers, horror of sentimentality, and distaste for epic narration.[19] Other critics, such as Pedro Caba, did not concur with the *Espadaña* view. Caba claimed lyric poetry to be in decadence beginning with certain poets of the Generation of 1927 — Salinas, Alonso, and Diego. He excepted Aleixandre as the only great living poet in addition to Juan Ramón Jiménez.[20] Jesús Juan Garcés refused to accept Caba's rejection of all poets but Jiménez and Aleixandre, claiming that Spanish poetry was in the midst of a Renaissance: *Garcilaso* had just published fourteen issues, and «Adonais», its first ten collections of poems.[21]

Given a perspective of fifteen years, José María Castellet proclaimed 1944 significant to the history of postwar poetry, making *Hijos de la ira* primary evidence in his argument for realism in Spanish poetry, a tendency

[17] Interview with Juan Guerrero, *La Estafeta Literaria,* No. 3 (15 April 1944), p. 9.
[18] RAFAEL S. TORROELLA, «La literatura de mañana», *La Estafeta Literaria,* No. 12 (1944), p. 29.
[19] L. LÓPEZ SANTOS, «Fichas provisionales. Como la Poesía del último siglo», *Espadaña,* No. 2 (1944): «... el campo poético se ha restringido de un modo exagerado. (A la vez se ha restringido al público poético y el influjo social de la poesía.) ... Se trata de ampliar el radio del instrumento poético y de ventilar las torres de 'marfil'. Para nuestros grandes autores, la poesía abarcaba toda la gama del sentir y del pensar. Lope, Góngora o Quevedo poéticamente lloraban o reían, rezaban o insultaban, volaban o reptaban; eran hombres o niños, populares o cultos, escribían Epopeyas o Letrillas... Si a todas estas divagaciones se opusieron la poesía pura —sin realidades, sin ideas, sin sentimientos— peor para la poesía pura.»
[20] PEDRO CABA, «La decadencia de la poesía lírica», *La Estafeta Literaria,* No. 7 (1944), p. 5.
[21] JESÚS JUAN GARCÉS, «Algunas notas urgentes sobre la poesía contemporánea», *La Estafeta Literaria,* No. 8 (1944), p. 5.

he characterized as hastily begun during the Civil War and reborn in the postwar period.[22] He distinguished the impact of *Hijos de la ira* from that of *Sombra del paraíso;* the former's was limited at first, but set the tone for much later poetry, while the latter's was immediately pervasive. Castellet emphasized that *Sombra del paraíso* gained influence in part because Aleixandre shared his new poems prior to publication with young poets seeking his advice who then adapted or imitated his distinctive style.[23]

Manuel Lamana called 1944 crucial without mentioning either Alonso or Aleixandre. He cited instead the founding of *Espadaña* as a rallying point for opposition to *Escorial* and *Garcilaso* by poets from all corners of the Peninsula.[24] Though Castellet and Lamana found evidence of change in different sources, they agreed that poetry became more realistic in the 1940s. Félix Grande repeated that 1944 was important because of *Hijos de la ira* and *Espadaña,* but argued against the supposed influence of *Sombra del paraíso.*[25] To Grande, Aleixandre's irrational, pantheistic world seemed incompatible with the existentialist view of reality then in formation. J. P. González Martín concurred that 1944 was a key date for new poetry, adding only that Alonso's importance was also enhanced by *Oscura noticia,* published the same year.[26] Perhaps the most extensive study in support of 1944 as turning point is that by Víctor G. de la Concha.[27] De la Concha identified *Hijos de la ira* and *Sombra del paraíso* —different in tone and theme, but sharing a tragic vision of man's life on earth— as having initiated the new sensibility. De la Concha also included in the «Revolution of 1944» the founding of *Espadaña* by De Nora, Crémer, and De Lama.

The formative effect of *Hijos de la ira* and *Espadaña* upon the poetry of protest is taken for granted today. Whether *Sombra del paraíso* was equally important to this sort of poetry in the 1940s is more doubtful. Why this is so was implied in the first reviews of the work. José Luis Cano conceded that *Sombra del paraíso* adhered to romantic metaphysics, yet insisted that its language, expression, and tone were serenely classic,

---

[22] JOSÉ MARÍA CASTELLET, *Veinte años de poesía española (1939-1959)* (Barcelona: Seix Barral, 1960), pp. 65-71.

[23] JOSÉ LUIS CANO, Review of *Sombra del paraíso, Mediterráneo,* No. 9-11 (1945), pp. 171-74: «Este libro, que aún nonnato ya influía en los jóvenes poetas amigos del autor que iban conociendo sus poemas, viene a aportar al panorama presente de nuestra poesía lo que apenas era posible encontrar en él...»

[24] MANUEL LAMANA, *Literatura de posguerra* (Buenos Aires: Nova, 1961), p. 77.

[25] FÉLIX GRANDE, *Apuntes sobre poesía española de posguerra* (Madrid: Taurus, 1970), pp. 35-36.

[26] J. P. GONZÁLEZ MARTÍN, *Poesía hispánica 1939-1969 (Estudio y antología)* (Barcelona: El Bardo, 1970), p. 51.

[27] DE LA CONCHA, *La poesía española de posguerra,* Chapter 7. See also: GUSTAV SIEBENMANN, «Los cambios estéticos en los últimos 40 años de poesía en España», *Boletín de la Asociación Europea de Profesores de Español,* 4, No. 7 (October 1972), pp. 83-92.

beautiful and nostalgic at the same time.[28] Carlos Bousoño emphasized the Platonism of Aleixandre, who eliminated disturbing present-day elements from the ideal world of *Sombra del paraíso* where the only imperfection was human mortality.[29] He later noted that Aleixandre adopted solidarity with mankind as a premise of his work after 1940, but that it was not fully integrated until 1947.[30] Gonzalo Sobejano, addressing the question of whether *Sombra del paraíso* contained allusions to the postwar, concluded that there was no direct reflection, although he observed the indirect reflection in the preference for union over separation.[31] Both Aleixandre and Alonso were important figures for the younger generation of poets, but Alonso, in *Hijos de la ira,* was closer in tone and theme to the poetry of protest.

Dámaso Alonso and the Anguish of Existence

One of the first landmarks of postwar poetry, *Hijos de la ira* has been analyzed both as a single work and as part of Alonso's complete poetry from many perspectives in the last four decades. Without questioning the unmistakable importance of the work, critics arrived at rather different conclusions, some of which radically changed the significance of the work for later readers. Perhaps the most widely circulated view interpreted the work as the beginning of postwar social poetry. Yet neither a reading of *Hijos de la ira* keeping this interpretation in mind, nor an examination of the reception of the work since its publication in 1944, seems to uphold the validity of this view. Instead, these procedures suggest that *Hijos de la ira* properly belongs to a religious tendency and can be taken as a work of social protest only by ignoring several important poems.

Alonso attracted much critical attention in 1944 when *Hijos de la ira* appeared. During the Civil War he was an editor of the Republican monthly *Hora de España* and in 1939, one of the few well-known intellectuals remaining in Spain. Highly respected as a literary scholar and philologist, he would eventually be elected to the Real Academia de la Lengua. Alonso's prestige alone could justify the first critical interest in *Hijos de la ira,* but he prepared the way for its reception by reading se-

---

[28] José Luis Cano, Review of *Sombra del paraíso*, p. 171.
[29] Carlos Bousoño, Review of *Sombra del paraíso*, Cisneros, No. 9 (1944), pp. 97-98.
[30] Vicente Aleixandre, *Obras completas*, v. 1, prólogo de Carlos Bousoño (Madrid: Aguilar, 1977), pp. 14-19.
[31] Gonzalo Sobejano, «*Sombra del paraíso*, ayer y hoy», *Vicente Aleixandre. A Critical Appraisal,* ed. Santiago Daydí-Tolson (Ypsilanti, Michigan: Bilingual Press, 1981), pp. 172-86.

lected poems to friends prior to publication.[32] When it became available, critics eagerly reviewed Alonso's first work of poetry in over two decades.

Those who compared *Hijos de la ira* to works written in the dominant neoclassic style were astonished by Alonso's use of varied line lengths, irregular strophic patterns, and a vocabulary that mixed colloquial and scientific terms with traditional diction. They perceived *Hijos de la ira* as highly original both for Spain and abroad.[33] The strident tone Alonso used in numerous poems led critics to sketch the poet as a «monstruoso niño prodigio (a pesar de sus 45 años), desamparado, aterrorizado en medio de la tiniebla virginal del mundo» or as a child who «llora y patalea (su ira es más bien eso: una rabieta infantil)».[34] Leopoldo Panero, personal friend of Alonso and the work's censor, was impressed by the dramatic qualities, the juxtaposition of diverse thematic material, and the symbolic use of character and conflict.[35] Finally, Panero likened Alonso's achievement to Unamuno's and Antonio Machado's because he presented a developed conception of reality. The publication *Cisneros* hailed Alonso for avoiding superficial sensuality in order to reveal the spiritual sensibility of the moment with poetry that came from submerged layers of man's nature.[36] De Lama asserted that Alonso humanized Spanish poetry: His new rhetoric, based on themes from the Bible, Unamuno, and the surrealists, was profoundly rooted in a world haunted by death and obsessed by God.[37] Alonso received well-earned admiration from most critics, but one offered inexplicable derision.[38]

---

[32] EMILIO ALARCOS LLORACH, «Hijos de la ira en 1944», *Insula*, No. 138-39 (May-June 1958), p. 7.
[33] CHARLES DAVID LEY, «Some Spanish Poets of Today», *Bulletin of Hispanic Studies*, 22, No. 86 (April 1945), pp. 69-76.
[34] LEOPOLDO PANERO, «El último libro de Dámaso Alonso. *Hijos de la ira*», *La Estafeta Literaria*, No. 8 (30 June 1944), p. 12; C. R. DAMPIERRE, «Dámaso Alonso: Hijos de la ira. Diario íntimo», *Escorial*, No. 15 (June 1944), pp. 136-46.
[35] PANERO, «El último libro de Dámaso Alonso», p. 12.
[36] J. R. C., Review of *Hijos de la ira*, *Cisneros*, No. 10 (1945), pp. 111-12.
[37] ANTONIO G. DE LAMA, «La poesía de Dámaso Alonso», *Espadaña*, No. 2 (June 1944).
[38] GABRIEL GARCÍA GILL, «Entrambasaguas contra novelistas y poetas», *La Estafeta Literaria*, No. 19 (1944), p. 9: «Cuando Ricardo Molina... preguntó a don Joaquín su opinión acerca de la obra de Dámaso Alonso, *Hijos de la ira*, una gran carcajada, tan ancha y tan elemental como pudiese haberla dado el menos complicado de los hombres, subrayó el comentario inicial del crítico. Según éste, el poeta de referencia vive demasiado felizmente para sentir determinadas preocupaciones de orden teológico, para estremecerse frente a los agudos problemas que chispean entre los versos del citado libro de poemas. No queremos exponer los minuciosos detalles de índole privado que utilizó como esencia de esta tesis original. Después de un recorrido completo a través de *Hijos de la ira* con salpicaduras de humor y jocosos paréntesis ilustrativos, el señor de Entrambasaguas condensó su opinión sobre la obra defecto fundamental de la misma de Dámaso Alonso, diciendo que él se polarizaba en esa idea doméstica de Dios, ridícula y estrecha, con que el poeta había querido «epatar» [sic] el pensamiento contemporáneo. (Hubo alguien en la reunión que sonrió detrás de los cristales de sus gafas

Many works of protest poetry owe their epic character to poems arranged in narrative order. Rather than incidental to meaning, this device promotes an underlying ideology through the structure of a work. The deliberate exposition of an ideology is typical of didactic works; in this sense, *Hijos de la ira* seems a model for later works by, say, Blas de Otero. Although the parallel with protest poetry would not be made until the 1950s, in the first reviews a recognizable progression along a unified theme received comment.[39]

The argument of *Hijos de la ira* is organized as a quest that alternates between the apocalyptic and the pastoral as the protagonist-speaker meditates upon the themes of existence and essence, life and death.[40] Surrounded by hatred, ugliness, turmoil, and evil, the speaker suffers hellish torments in a chaotic world peopled by writhing creatures and mutating beings. He yearns for changelessness and peace, a paradise of love and beauty. To this end, he calls repeatedly for a sign from God that death is not as terrible as he imagines. Though receiving no answer, the speaker elects salvation through religious commitment, an act of faith resolving his anguish and terror of death.

Alonso carefully prepares readers for the speaker's confession of faith. The subtitle, «Diario íntimo», reduces terrifying visions and multiple addresses to the subjective limits of interior monologue and uses this illusion to control readers' reactions to the speaker.[41] The speaker's epistemological search is framed between the moment when he receives a mandate from God to sing —«porque la mano de mi Dios me tocó, / porque me ha dicho que cantara: / por eso canto» (46)— and another where the speaker asserts that singing was the correct diagnosis: «Tenía que cantar para sanarme» (143). Once the speaker renounces his quest for the meaning of death, he likens his former doubt to an illness, whose cure is religious faith. This cancels the horror of earlier visions for the speaker, and for readers as well.

In the first sequence of poems, the speaker engages in philosophical discourse to rationalize death. The answer he awaits, as «Insomnio» (37-38) indicates, must be valid for all mortals — himself, other *madrileños*, the dead, and those who have yet to die. He rephrases his question to

---

imaginando, acaso, que no era un argumento demasiado contundente para desautorizar las inquietudes de Dámaso Alonso el que su vida discurriese de forma próspera y feliz.).»

[39] AUDREY LUMSDEN, Review of *Hijos de la ira*, *Bulletin of Hispanic Studies*, 23, No. 89 (January 1946), pp. 65-67.

[40] DÁMASO ALONSO, *Hijos de la ira. Diario íntimo,* edition by Elias L. Rivers (Barcelona: Labor, 1970). Page references to this edition appear in the text. Poems added to later editions —«La Injusticia», «El último Caín», «En la sombra», «La obsesión», «A la Virgen María»— are omitted from the commentary.

[41] ANDREW P. DEBICKI, «Satire and Dramatic Monologue in Several Poems of Dámaso Alonso», *Books Abroad*, 48, No. 2 (Spring 1974), pp. 276-85.

ask the meaning of existence and essence in «En el día de los difuntos» (43-50). Since existence leads inevitably to death, the speaker wonders if its permanence could be the perfect state he seeks. Perhaps, he reasons, the succession of selves we leave behind are only alienated images of our essential self. Uncertain still, the speaker looks to the natural world for a definite answer. Yet a rock, silent and sorrowful, and a tree, its branches caressing his face, are as mute as God himself in «Voz del árbol» (51-53). Even those in the throes of death, eyes wide open, are silent when the speaker asks what they see beyond the veil in «Preparativos de viaje» (55-58). To arrive at an intelligible definition of essence, he describes the properties of an object in «Cosa» (59-60), then tries to capture its essence by holding the object in his hands; but neither naming nor physical possession yields essence. He follows a similar procedure in «Yo» (69-70) to define his own unchanging essence; but again he is defeated, this time by a bewildering array of alienated former selves, evidence of his transitoriness.

The central poems of *Hijos de la ira* present existence as a blind force tormenting an irrational universe. Some poems —«Mujer con alcuza» (71-77), «Elegía a un moscardón azul» (79-83), «A Pizca» (93-94), «Los insectos» (115-17)— are among Alonso's best known. To display horror in these poems, Alonso invents grotesque agents of torture for unwitting victims, prisoners of a hostile, incomprehensible environment. For instance, in a prayer for deliverance, «Monstruos» (85-86), the speaker requests an explanation of the monsters who transform him into another creature as uncommunicative and unloving as themselves. The certainty that this is his fate brings about an attack of self-loathing:

> No, ninguna tan horrible
> como este Dámaso frenético,
> como este amarillo ciempiés...
> como esta bestia inmediata
> transfundida en una angustia fluyente...

In the ironic comparison of mankind to a dog without a master, found in «Hombre» (119-20), the speaker alludes to the death of God. Forgotten in this catastrophe are mortals, engaged in an absurd attempt at dialogue with the Deity. Alonso exempts neither mankind nor the speaker from cosmic loneliness and anguished torment:

> ¿... dices algo, tienes algo
> que decir a los hombres o a los cielos?
> ¿Y no es esa amargura
> de tu grito, la densa pesadilla
> del monólogo eterno y sin respuesta?

Other poems of dread strip everyday sights and experiences of comfortable familiarity by placing them in an exploding cosmic dimension. This device reduces the speaker to insignificant proportions or to endlessly replicated images, driving him to the edge of madness. The single respite in a crescendo of suffering is «La Madre» (87-91). Here, the speaker retreats in time to the source of his essence, escaping the decline of physical existence. In this fantasy, the speaker and his mother would remain children forever in a perfect land if possible.

The work reaches a crisis in «Raíces del odio» (121-25). The speaker, who always sought perfection —«flor celeste, rosa total»—, finds the roots of hatred everywhere. He seeks a world of perfect beauty, but the Furies and daughters of wrath, crueler than man himself, offer the human race unending agony. This is the point where the work clearly turns to religious repentance. In the final poems, dramatic development is resolved as the speaker cries out in remorse to an omnipotent God in «La isla» (127-32), makes an abject plea for mercy in «De profundis» (133-34), and dreams of divine forgiveness in «Dedicatoria final (Las alas)» (139-45). To discover the meaning of death in redemption and eternal life, the speaker abandons his epistemological quest based on systematic doubt. Affirming new-found faith, his «wrath» is cured and he finds spiritual peace. These final poems, rather than merely introducing the religious theme, send readers back to earlier poems to reconsider their meaning in light of divine purpose.

Hijos de la ira, in the appraisal of Charles David Ley, is one of the finest works of modern religious poetry, a story of victory over uncertainties.[42] José Luis Cano, after citing lines from «De profundis», called the work truly religious poetry in an agonizing and dramatic sense, similar to that of Unamuno.[43] He found Alonso's view of life as a bitter, dramatic journey emblematized in «Mujer con alcuza». The acceptance of *Hijos de la ira* as religious poetry gained more weight with a study revealing that God, whom the speaker frequently addressed, was represented by distinct identities: a pantheistic God of creation, a dualistic God of love and hate.[44] Individual poems of *Hijos de la ira* reveal Alonso's religious attitude; the arrangement of poems as a narrative ending in redemption underlines the religious character of the work.[45]

At first reading, Alonso's «impure» poems may seem to follow the

---

[42] LEY, *Spanish Poetry Since 1939,* p. 49.
[43] JOSÉ LUIS CANO, «Ira y poesía de Dámaso Alonso», [*El Español,* 10 June 1944] *La poesía de la generación del 27* (Madrid: Guadarrama, 1973), pp. 102-07.
[44] LUIS DÍAZ MÁRQUEZ, «La temática de la poesía de Dámaso Alonso», *Cuadernos Hispanoamericanos,* No. 209 (May 1967), pp. 231-65.
[45] ANGEL ZORITA, *Dámaso Alonso* (Madrid: EPESA, 1976), pp. 65-67, argues that *Hijos de la ira,* rather than a sudden change in direction for Alonso was an intensification of interest in metaphysical topics observable in his essay on San Juan and in the poems of *Oscura noticia,* written during the same period as those of *Hijos de la ira,* that is, from before 1936 through 1943.

esthetic declared by Neruda in *Caballo Verde para la Poesía*.[46] Indeed, Neruda's manifesto describes certain features of *Hijos de la ira:* «Una poesía impura como un traje, como un cuerpo, con manchas de nutrición y actitudes vergonzosas, con arrugas, observaciones, sueños, vigilia, profecías, declaraciones de amor y odio, bestias, sacudidas, idilios, creencias políticas, negaciones, dudas, afirmaciones, impuestos.» Neruda summarized the nature and purposes of rehumanized poetry, already important in pre-Civil War Spain. However, he and other sympathetic poets —Alberti and Hernández— deliberately interpreted this esthetic ideologically. That is, believing mankind perfectible and social justice possible, they wrote poetry openly promoting a Marxist social order. Alonso of course would reject such ideological claims because he believed that politics should be restricted to the voting booth or to conversations with close friends.[47] He would disagree too with the Marxist belief that alienation lies within the individual, not in life on earth. For Alonso, religious, not social, commitment was the path from alienation to redemption. This is the crucial difference between Alonso's poetry and that from which develops the poetry of protest.

The first reviewers drew a parallel between *Hijos de la ira* and contemporary facts only in the broadest sense. They spoke of a world torn by war, but not of Spain under the dictatorship of Franco. If there is a reason for believing that *Hijos de la ira* represents Spain in the 1940s, textual evidence is slight. Obvious references are the mention of Madrid (37), a line using the English phrase «blackout» (49), and a possible hint of bombed cities (65). Yet these few allusions initiated an interpretation of *Hijos de la ira* as a protest of the Civil War and of World War II, which gained support from a footnote Alonso added to the essay «Una generación poética (1920-1936)».[48] Writing in 1948, he said he needed the terrible jolt of the «Spanish War» to express himself as he did in *Hijos de la ira*. Later, he included himself among poets writing what he called «up-rooted» poetry after a phrase from Otero's poem «Lo eterno» in the essay «Poesía arraigada y poesía desarraigada».[49]. These are the cues that José Luis Cano, in an article, and José María Castellet, in his anthology, followed when they said that the two wars and the bombings of Japan were echoed

---

[46] «Sobre una poesía sin pureza», *Caballo Verde para la Poesía*, No. 1 (October 1935; rpt. Nendeln-Liechtenstein: Verlag Detlev Auvermann KG, 1974).

[47] José Luis Castillo Puche, «Dámaso Alonso: 'Yo siempre mantuve la amistad con los poetas exiliados'». *El País*, Arte y Pensamiento, 18 December 1977, pp. vi-vii: «... yo no soy ni fui nunca un político, tengo mis ideas políticas como cualquier hijo de vecino, pero no soy hombre político, y reservo, por eso, mis ideas políticas para hablar con mis amigos más íntimos, o para usar de esas ideas cuando se tiene la ocasión de votar en una urna como por fin la hemos tenido.»

[48] Dámaso Alonso, *Poetas españoles contemporáneos* (Madrid: Gredos, 1952), p. 169.

[49] *Ibid.*, pp. 333-80.

in Alonso's work.[50]. Before growing opinion that *Hijos de la ira* expressed social protest, Guillermo de Torre observed that it was possible to believe Alonso's vision spoke of real surroundings, but the essential intent of the work was neither open protest nor bitter dissent.[51] The tide of opinion turned abruptly with publication of Elias L. Rivers' edition of *Hijos de la ira* in 1970. In the prologue, Alonso cautioned against reading any specific protest in the work. He emphasized that his protest was, first, universal and cosmic and, second, a literary response to *garcilasismo,* pure poetry, and surrealism.[52] The same year, Philip Silver called the belief that Alonso was the «father of social poetry» a grave mistake for Alonso was, above all, a religious poet and highly dependent upon literary tradition for the originality of *Hijos de la ira.*[53] Silver added that, given the deplorable socio-economic conditions of the 1940s, readers said *Hijos de la ira* was a work of protest because they thought it should be, when it was really hermetic and aloof from contemporary events.[54] Since then, other critics denied that the work was social poetry: De la Concha in 1973 and Lechner in 1975.[55]

Despite the profound humanity of *Hijos de la ira,* its existentialist rhetoric, and even its epic quest structure, the reading of *Hijos de la ira* as poetry of social protest seems to owe more to incidental aspects —Alonso's circumstantial association with the Loyalists during the Civil War, the rising tide of social poetry after 1950— than Alonso's underlying purpose, that is, to protest man's mortality —«una protesta universal, cósmica, que incluye, claro está, todas esas otras iras parciales» (30)—, to examine and experience the irreconcilable aspects of human existence.

Victoriano Crémer's Nonconformist Poetry

Victoriano Crémer's reputation as a poet was overshadowed by the fame of *Espadaña,* a publication envisioned by De Lama as a channel for Crémer and Eugenio de Nora, aspiring but almost unpublished poets in 1943.[56] De Nora, the titular director, was seldom in León and therefore

---

[50] José Luis Cano, «Fervor de Dámaso Alonso», *Insula*, No. 138-39 (May-June 1958), pp. 12-13; José María Castellet, *Veinte años de poesía española*, pp. 66-67.
[51] Guillermo de Torre, «Contemporary Spanish Poetry», *The Texas Quarterly*, 4, No. 1 (1961), p. 70.
[52] Dámaso Alonso, *Hijos de la ira*, pp. 29-30.
[53] Philip Silver, «Tradition as Originality in *Hijos de la ira*», *Bulletin of Hispanic Studies*, 67 (April 1970), pp. 124-30.
[54] Philip Silver, «On Entering Creation: A Second Look at *Hijos de la ira*», *Books Abroad*, 48, No. 2 (Spring 1974), pp. 286-96.
[55] De la Concha, *La poesía española de posguerra*, p. 299; Lechner, *El compromiso en la poesía española del siglo XX. Parte segunda*, p. 21.
[56] De la Concha, *La poesía española de posguerra*, p. 311.

Crémer became the effective director, editor, and, since he was a typographer by trade, publisher from 1944 until *Espadaña*'s demise in 1950.[57] In multiple roles —critic, theorist, editor— Crémer accomplished more than perhaps any other single writer of the 1940s toward the *rehumanización* of Spanish literature.[58] *Espadaña* was the primary vehicle not only for his poems, most republished as books, but also for his reviews of new poetry and general articles of opinion. Together these varied contributions were largely responsible for the vitality of the publication over its seven-year life. Crémer was well-cast in his role as a poet of protest. Like Miguel Hernández, he was born in obscure circumstances, mainly self-taught, cognizant of his responsibility to others; and he wrote to a wide audience in a colloquial, direct manner. He cultivated a style echoing the strongest voices of the 1930s —Lorca, Alberti, Hernández— in his first cycle of works that included *Tacto sonoro, Caminos de mi sangre, Las horas perdidas,* and *La espada y la pared.*[59]

Tacto sonoro, published at the same time as *Hijos de la ira* as the first offering of Ediciones Espadaña, obtained neither the wide circulation nor literary reputation of Alonso's work. Yet more than *Hijos de la ira, Tacto sonoro* was a protest against *garcilasismo* in the vanguard of opposition initiated by De Lama's manifesto.[60] More importantly, *Tacto sonoro* differed from *Hijos de la ira* by proposing commitment to humanism rather than to Christianity as an ethical alternative to the despair of nihilism.

Prior to the appearance of *Tacto sonoro,* several of the poems were published by *Cisneros.*[61] Crémer also read the poems at various cultural gatherings in Northwestern Spain. At the conclusion of a recital in 1943, José María Pemán, author of *Poema de la bestia y el ángel,* donated his honorarium to Crémer to publish *Tacto sonoro,* which he admired for continuing the «poetic revolution» of the previous fifteen years.[62] It is ironic that *Tacto sonoro,* written by a former anarchist, was published with the assistance of a poet always in good standing with the Regime during his long career.

In order to satirize the dominant literary styles, Crémer evokes genres in vogue among followers of neoclassicism. His poem titles name

---

[57] *Ibid.,* p. 358: «... fue Crémer el verdadero *factotum*. El era quien recibía el material, lo valoraba, lo *modificaba no pocas veces,* lo disponía, lo confeccionaba y hasta ayudaba a editarlo.»

[58] SERGIO MORATIEL, *La poesía en acción de Victoriano Crémer* (León: Imprenta Diocesana, 1973), p. 41.

[59] Poems are cited in text according to the following abreviations: PT: *Poesía total (1944-1966)* (Barcelona: Plaza y Janés, 1970); TS: *Tacto sonoro* (León: Espadaña, 1944); CS: *Caminos de mi sangre* (Madrid: Adonais, 1947).

[60] See above, pp. 29-30.

[61] «Canción para submarinos», *Espadaña,* No. 5 (1943), pp. 112-13; «Oda malherida del avión en picado», «Fábula de la persecución y muerte de Dillinger», «Poema sin sosiego (Homenaje a Espronceda)», *Espadaña,* No. 6 (1943), pp. 104-14.

[62] MORATIEL, *La poesía en acción,* pp. 27-28, 33.

traditional forms —odes, songs, elegies, fables, ballads— to remind readers of the literary conventions he mocks. The titles of several sections within the work invert neoclassic *topoi*. «Puertos de tierra adentro» reverses the topic of Spain as Empire by focusing on the wretched life of isolated, impoverished Spaniards. «Romancero de hierro» takes a sidelong view of the heroics of warfare. «Poemas sin sosiego» oppose the virtues of moderation and tranquillity. Crémer alludes to his iconoclastic intention in the paradoxical title of the work with its synesthetically crossed meanings.

Crémer degrades the literary *status quo* through systematic distortion. He is also critical of hackneyed themes, but not everything he criticizes is related to *garcilasismo*. In one exception, «Torero yo» (PT, 57-59), the speaker mocks the fashion for bullfighting motifs by comparing himself, a man in a crowded street, to a bullfighter and concludes that he himself shows more courage in the fight for survival. In other poems, Crémer views death unconventionally. His «Canción serena» (PT, 53-54) is not the wish for a tranquil life one might expect in a poem whose epigraph is a line from «Vida retirada» but a plea for deliverance from the perplexing torment of a certain but absurd death. And, in «¿Y es eso sólo la muerte?» (PT, 43-44), the dramatic dialogue between a recently deceased person, a mourner, and a passerby rob death of transcendant significance. A similarly skewed perspective undercuts religious nostalgia in «Melchor» (PT, 47). The speaker, one of the Wise Men, is impatient to see Christ, hidden from his view by Joseph, a palm tree, a cloud, and the moon, like so many adornments of a crib.

The most characteristic poems of the collection, however, satirize the conventions of *garcilasismo*. Crémer does not exalt the figure of the warrior. Sometimes his satire is playful, as when he composes an elegy to a «Napoleon» in a nightshirt astride a wooden horse in «Jineterías» (PT, 49-50). Or, he portrays a soldier's natural fear of night vigils through the speaker of «Centinela» (TS, 77-78). Crémer mocks Petrarchan love motifs when he sketches a distant setting, reminiscent of Lorca's *Romancero gitano,* for a patiently waiting lover in «Novia del recuerdo ya» (TS, 61-62) and when he recounts a midday encounter between indifferent lovers unable to emulate a courtly manner in «Frente a frente, los dos» (TS, 55-56).

The world Crémer portrays is permeated with violence and fear; it is as irrational as the realm discovered by surrealists, nihilism its dominant ethic. Crémer sees mankind almost incapable of heroism and subject to fear or cowardice regardless of social position. Personified machines are predators threatening mankind in «Canción para submarinos» (PT, 48-49). Crémer portrays as «buccaneers of the deep» some (quite real) submarines massing for war off coastal Spain. Similarly, he depicts a nose-diving plane as a fierce Lucifer about to destroy the speaker of «Oda malherida del avión en picado» (PT, 51-53). Descriptively more complex, this poem is an incantation to power by a terrified victim paralyzed by fear. Crémer elaborates the same relationship of man and fear in «Fábula de la persecución y muerte de Dillinger» (PT, 60-65). Formal division into scenes suggests a cinematic perception of reality. Using the technique of montage, Crémer vividly combines different verse forms, enhancing the text with cruel and bizarre images. Set in New York, the poem contrasts Dillinger's boldness to the witnesses' cowardly silence at his murder:

> Volvía todo el mundo apresurado,
> para esconder su miedo bajo llave,
> ... ...
> Y en lo hondo, los hombres como orugas,
> recomían la vida.

Crémer cultivates moral nihilism in «Poema. Homenaje a Espronceda» (TS, 131-36). The speaker, indebted to romantic oratorical tradition, invites his listener to accompany him on a search for the unfathomable secret of life. In a descent through the spheres of the universe that reaches beyond the beginning, the speaker finally comes to man, trembling with fear between Chaos and Nothingness, insensible to reason. Perhaps Crémer's best known poem in the nihilist vein is the «Fábula de B.D.» (PT, 80-87), written long before its first publication in 1946.[63] The initials refer to Buenaventura Durruti, popular Anarcho-Syndicalist militant from León, assassinated on 22 November 1936. In this poem the magnetic hero is portrayed as fearless in contrast to his assassins who shoot him from behind. Crémer uses the legendary death of Durruti, commemorated in many popular ballads, as a pretext for exploring his own vision of mankind. He alternates static urban sketches with active lyric passages to intensify a mood of pursuit and fear. In climactic stanzas, using anaphora to lend gravity, he implies that a corrupt society is responsible for Durruti's death.

Crémer's irony concerning the perfidy of human —and divine— nature is more pronounced in «Fábula de Judas el Iscariote» (PT, 88-96). Narrative passages recount a gathering of the disciples where the Lord admonishes them to love one another. When Christ meets Judas, contrary to Biblical accounts, He kisses Judas. Then Crémer's Judas realizes that, false disciple or not, he is doomed. This inversion of Christian doctrine is the most extreme position Crémer adopts. Such cynicism is at

---

[63] According to a letter from Crémer to Lechner, *El compromiso de la poesía española del siglo XX. Parte segunda*, p. 39.

odds with the mystic transcendence inspiring several poems important in the trajectory of his poetry.

The question of Crémer's commitment has been discussed by De la Concha and Lechner. Both refer to «Recuerdo de la nada» (PT, 73-76), arriving at somewhat different conclusions. De la Concha believes this poem clearly states the existentialist commitment integral to much of Crémer's poetry and therefore relegates to marginal status elements of transcendental commitment.[64] Lechner reads the same poem as referring to a particular, rather than representative, man and suggests that Crémer may be affirming his commitment to the men of his own calamitous times.[65] However, Crémer's commitment is more complex than this when «Recuerdo de la nada» is read in conjunction with thematically related poems. Despite stylistic differences between the poem in homage to Espronceda, mentioned earlier, and this one, which honors Cernuda, there exists an underlying metaphysical and narrative unity. In the earlier poem, the speaker discovers man on the threshold of Nothingness, frightened, ignorant of who and what he is. In this poem, the speaker describes man's return from Apocalypse, aware of his fate, in terms from Heidegger: «Silencioso, recóndito; sosteniéndose el alma / con las manos. ¡Sabiéndose arrojado a la Vida!» Read in sequence, the two poems cohere into a metaphysical journey from dread to existentialist commitment.

Transcendental aspects of Crémer's commitment appear too when taking into account a confessional poem, in which the speaker is God's agonist. The center of discussion is «Hombre habitado» (PT, 55-57). De Lama, in his review of *Tacto sonoro,* alluded to the concluding stanza of the poem:[66]

> Te siento, sí. Me siento por tu peso.
> Y soy en Ti porque tu voz me suena.
> Porque tu fresco tacto derramado
> desbordó las acequias de mi alma.

Then he remarked that Crémer's book was an anguished itinerary from the world to God, even though the presence of God illuminated only brief instants in the work. De la Concha disagreed with De Lama's emphasis on transcendental themes in Crémer's poetry. Seeking a more comprehensive view, Sergio Moratiel argued that for Crémer God could be engaged in dialogue, but man had to rise to speak with God as an

---

[64] DE LA CONCHA, *La poesía española de posguerra,* pp. 411-12.
[65] LECHNER, *El compromiso en la poesía española del siglo XX. Parte segunda,* pp. 43-44.
[66] ANTONIO G. DE LAMA, «La poesía de Victoriano Crémer», *Espadaña,* No. 4 (July 1944).

equal.[67] He also cited a statement published by Crémer in 1945 that substantiated this interpretation.[68]

Developing this view, Crémer's ethics seems to derive from man's essential dignity, which enables him to meet the Creator face-to-face. Crémer's commitment to *El Hombre,* protagonist of several poems, does not seem to exclude commitment to God, but rather views commitment to God from a human vantage point, as in «Hombre habitado». The speaker of this poem compares himself to an empty dwelling, silent, lonely, and useless until entered by angels of peace bearing the Word and divine Grace. «Inhabited» now, the speaker beholds God. At its simplest, the psychological crisis underlying these poems is that of the passage from alienation to commitment. In this sense, Crémer's dilemma is similar to Alberti's when he writes:[69]

> Angeles buenos y malos,
> que no sé,
> te arrojaron de mi alma.
> Sola
> sin muebles y sin alcobas,
> deshabitada.

To resolve his crisis Alberti chose an ideological commitment antagonistic to Crémer's spiritualized dedication to mankind. Crémer maintains this vital but distant relationship with the Deity in three selections from *Caminos de mi sangre.* «En tus manos» (CS, 11-14) deals with the aftermath of an encounter that filled the speaker with hatred and a need to escape a pursuing God. Doubting he has a purpose, the speaker despairs:

> ¿Para qué soy, Señor, si de la nada vine;
> si me hiciste a Tu imagen y me ensañé en Tu obra,
> si me agoto en un odio inmenso como el mar...?
> ... ...
> guardián y carcelero de mi carne violada.
> ¡Deslígame de Ti!

This doubt is compounded by ambivalence in «¿Por qué?» (CS, 15-19), where the speaker cannot reconcile love for nature and life's victims —widows, prisoners, the bereaved, and the hungry— with hatred for others. The hatred weighs heavily on the speaker, who declares in desperation that God has lost him. However, such declarations do not mark

---

[67] MORATIEL, *La poesía en acción,* pp. 118-22.
[68] MORATIEL, *Ibid.,* p. 118, cites the source as *La Estafeta Literaria,* 10 July 1945: «A veces, me atrevo a suponer que están más cerca del auténtico divinismo los hombres que luchan con Dios —Jacobo, Unamuno, San Pablo, Nietzsche— que los que habitualmente, sencillamente conversan con El y se resignan a su deseada tiranía.»
[69] RAFAEL ALBERTI, «Desahucio», *Poesía (1924-1967)* (Madrid: Aguilar, 1972), p. 321.

the end of his attempts at dialogue. In «Poema» (CS, 20-30) he revives the image of the soul as an empty dwelling entered by God: «¡Es Dios y su llamada! Su crudo aldabonazo / resonando en tus muros su resuelta evidencia.» As before, this leads to an encounter between equals, not a mystic reunion of the soul and its divine source:

> Tú le sientes. Te sientes por su voz y su peso.
> Como un pan en sus manos te elevas a lo alto.
> Y eres tan dios por Él, que le miras al rostro
> sin sacarte los ojos...

Having discovered for himself the natural dignity of man and his worthiness to face God, the speaker shares this truth with mankind. Though fearing misunderstanding, he hopes his poetry embodies the message. In «Quiero» (CS, 48-53), a poetic credo, Crémer writes of his hope for mankind:

> Y yo quiero llegarle con mi verso;
> romper el duro mármol de su frente;
> darme en pan de sus hambres; ser su llanto
> contenido o su muerte.

These lines and others in the same poem characterize the poet as a savior of his fellow men, a persona extensively developed by Blas de Otero. Crémer's commitment to mankind is a humanist view of God, in which transcendental and human planes intersect in the person and message of the speaker. It guides him when he turns for inspiration to the working-class world where he lived. Feeling a bond with workers, the speaker celebrates their dignity, putting into words their inarticulate emotions:[70]

> Yo os canto aquí a vosotros, amigos:
> Hombres de mi raíz, de mi mismo linaje;
> marineros, mineros, labradores...

And, in celebrating their silent endurance, the Christ-like speaker offers sacrifice and communion:[71]

> Llegáis de las regiones del salitre;
> de las constelaciones más amargas;
> del más puro silencio, del más hondo:
> el silencio del hombre desamado.
> ... ...
> Por eso yo quisiera con mi verso
> coronaros de yedras violentas,
> ... ...

---

[70] CRÉMER, «La Espada y la Pared», *Espadaña*, No. 26 (n.d.).
[71] CRÉMER, «Bienaventurados los pobres», *Las horas perdidas* (Valladolid: Halcón, 1949), pp. 64-68.

> y entregarme también a vuestras hambres
> como un pan sin cesar multiplicado.

Many of the poems of *Tacto sonoro* go beyond mere literary protest to criticize bourgeois morality. Crémer offers a harsh judgment in «Diablo mundo» (TS, 39-43), mocking materialist values and the esteem with which they are held. He metaphorically buries this world by over-using capital letters while describing a funeral scene:

> Y el Arte... Gran Cruz de Lata.
> Todo un horizonte tibio
> y amplios pastos siderales
> de papel de oficio.
> Oh, el Mundo —con Mayúscula—,
> y sus hierros enmohecidos;
> y sus losas funerarias
> y sus candiles votivos.

Elsewhere, he personifies «Mundo» with symbols of class status —stiff collar and bowler hat— but degrades the figure by adding a tobacco-stained beard:

> Es una cosa tan seria
> que le imagino:
> duro cuello almidonado,
> bombín de brillos;
> sin una risa
> ni un guiño;
> con barbas de plata, sucias
> de cigarros con arillo.

Social criticism in these poems often occurs through the technique of displacement. Crémer intensifies the impression of human torpor by attributing activity to objects and passive qualities such as despair, resentment, and muteness to humans. He uses this procedure in «Jueves» (TS, 29-30), whose theme is the annual Procession of Silence during Holy Week. In a setting that underlines obedience, barefooted laborers follow the stations of the Cross. By ascribing the penitents' silenced fears to the night, their compliance with Catholic custom to the bell-towers, and their unvoiced cries to roosters, Crémer criticizes the Church's dominion over its followers:

> Centinela de sí misma
> la noche esgrime su miedo
> Sobre los filos del aire
> se empenacha el firmamento.
>
> Y en los altos campanarios,
> maniatados de silencios,
> los gritos de roja cresta
> se suicidan en el viento.

But Crémer also censures the lethargic cowardice of the laborers by dehumanizing them, attributing what should be their own resistance and protest to mere objects and animals. Much the same occurs in «Siesta» (TS, 27-28), where fragmentary dialogue seems to vilify napping workmen. However, embedded comments referring to a diet of chick-peas and harsh working conditions shift blame elsewhere — two hours of rest in a workday lasting from dawn until dusk is little indulgence.

The speaker of *Tacto sonoro* seems a rebellious outsider criticizing all levels of an antiquated system. His criticism of the oligarchy is expected, but that of workers seems to be a nihilist's contempt for weakness and servility. This creates a conflict between different poses of the speaker. On the one hand, the speaker witnesses the effects of economic and religious oppression and, on the other, those of unjust subservience. Crémer alludes to fear and threats of violence in «Paisaje urbano» (PT, 36-38), a poem with images of darkness, silence, and suppressed anger in dusk-invaded urban streets. The speaker implies that darkness only blankets fear and growing despair so that as one night ends with extinguished streetlights, another begins as a night of the spirit. The speaker in «Viajes por el extranjero» (PT, 38-39) transforms persons into expressive synecdoches, «*sombras*» and «*ojeras cárdenas*». He hints at concealed resentment seething in the village by such phrases as «*en ascuas*» and «*de brasas*». Civil Guards and fire images mentioned suggest violent eruption; however, outbreaks are stifled or their force deflected to a safe target: «Jacintón Fernández apuñaló a su cuñada.»

Beyond stylistic echoes of Lorca's *Romancero gitano,* a vein of criticism similar to that of *Poeta en Nueva York* appears in these poems. For instance, Crémer imputes designs upon Spain to Fascists in «Sinfonía marinera» (TS, 79-80), but the reading depends upon knowing that in 1936 Franco airlifted Moorish troops on German planes across the Straits of Gibraltar. These Moors are not those from the age of the Cid, referred to in the epigraph, but rather Franco's forces:

> Castilla —sed de España— sorteando
> audazmente su propio imperativo,
> va empapando su carne —sol y tierra—
> en un hondo designio ultramarino.

Criticism of Franco's complicity in a treasonable plot may be expected of someone jailed and tortured by Nationalists.[72] Less expectedly, Crémer seems to criticize Loyalists who escaped Spain at the end of the Civil War in «Elegía de la muerte en acecho» (TS, 111-15), written in 1944, although references are sufficiently ambiguous to permit a more abstract

---

[72] For an account, see: VICTORIANO CRÉMER, *El libro de San Marcos* (León: Nebrija, 1980).

reading of the poem as addressed to those who through death eluded the suffering and persecution of the living.[73] The structure of the poem is uncomplicated and the speaker commences: «Retornaréis un día.» Then he lists paradoxical conditions that negate his original affirmation, suggesting that the addressees will not return after all:

> Si retornáis un día... Ese día forzoso
> con el grito iracundo meditado a la espera
> y la lenta navaja, azulada de lunas y amarilla de ansias...
>
> ... Oponed cordilleras al ronquido del pecho
> y mares verticales a la urgencia velera.
> Oh, dichosos ausentes, lejanísimos ídolos
> a quienes mar y cielos evitaron la muerte.

Nevertheless, the concluding lines, which echo a nostalgic Alberti poem about exiled *ángeles* now alienated men, persuade a historical interpretation of this poem.[74]

Crémer's poetry in *Tacto sonoro* and *Caminos de mi sangre* is transitional, bridging the period of neoclassicism's popularity. Crémer's poems, written in widely separate periods, synthesize and reintroduce experimental techniques. Their opposition to the neoclassic esthetic is both a literary response to what Crémer judged inauthentic poetry and an ethical challenge, a humanist critique of neotraditionalist values.

Leopoldo Panero, in his review of *Tacto sonoro,* found genuine unity of the work primarily in the author's poetic personality.[75] According to Panero, rather than offering a tranquil reflection on rivers, lilies, statues, and roses or a contemplation of beauty for its own sake, expressed with formal perfection and pleasing rhythm, Crémer sought to leave a lasting impression. His tone of despairing irony juxtaposed the serious and the comic for dramatic effect to better represent the individual's isolation and anguish.

José García Nieto, editor of *Garcilaso,* failed to recognize Crémer's ironic attitude.[76] In his review of *Tacto sonoro* he recommended that Crémer improve his technical control and organizational mastery. García Nieto perceived no more than confused forms and rhythms within single

---

[73] Date cited in a letter from Crémer to Lechner, *El compromiso en la poesía española del siglo XX. Parte segunda,* p. 134, n. 80; and *Ibid.,* p. 37: «Es un poema de difícil interpretación, porque parece referirse a un lejano día en que se realizará el ajuste de cuentas y a la vez al día del Juicio Final (el único modo, quizás, de introducir el primero de los dos términos en su poema).»

[74] See: RAFAEL ALBERTI, «Puertas cerradas», *Poemas del destierro y de la espera* (Madrid: Espasa-Calpe, 1976), pp. 93-94.

[75] LEOPOLDO PANERO, «La poesía de Victoriano Crémer», *Escorial,* 15 (May 1944), pp. 455-57.

[76] JOSÉ GARCÍA NIETO, «*Tacto sonoro.* Un libro de poesías de Victoriano Crémer», *La Estafeta Literaria,* No. 13 (25 September 1944), p. 12.

poems, lines with extra syllables (as if Crémer had miscounted), and undisguised borrowing from Alberti, Espronceda, and Lorca.

De Lama noted that Crémer refused to create imaginary paradises, but rather wrote of reality —naked, wounding, exasperating— as seen from his innermost subjectivity.[77] He compared Crémer to Valle-Inclán and Quevedo, in respect to their alienated view of reality. De Lama's two categories of poetry, the universally human and the dehumanized, drawn from readings of Bergson and Heidegger, stressed the human condition and were clearly suitable for describing Crémer's style, which was «brutally subjective», the essence of *tremendismo*.[78] For years Crémer practised this style, which «sought to develop the rhetorical fervors of the Romantics, or of Hernández at his weakest».[79] Exaggerated rhetoricism diminished in his poetry toward the end of the decade, yielding to the more restrained expression of *Nuevos cantos de vida y esperanza*.

Whether the poetry just discussed was considered *tremendista* or neoromantic, from the horizon of 1945, it differed from predominant styles categorically referred to as pure poetry. Authentic poetry, it reflected the plight of contemporary man and the dilemma of mortality. Its pattern of protest and despair, prior conditions of commitment, disallowed blind acceptance of dogma, but prescribed no solution. Moral inertia, in which death seemed gratuitous and certain, could be surmounted only through belief in some set of values. The major difference between this poetry of protest and other sorts is extent of reference. The former speaks of universal concerns, the latter, of national affairs. Narrower in scope, much later poetry of protest transformed the existentialist dilemma in an unjust universe into protest of an unjust dictatorship and an unfair social order.

---

[77] «Poesía y vida. Objetividad, impersonalidad», *Espadaña*, No. 28 (1947).
[78] For a study of Crémer's *tremendismo*, see: DE LA CONCHA, *La poesía española de posguerra*, pp. 414-20.
[79] J. M. COHEN, «Since the Civil War. New Currents in Spanish Poetry», *Encounter*, 12, No. 2 (February 1959), pp. 44-53.

3

POETRY OF RESISTANCE

Within the widely acknowledged neoromantic tendency initiated in the postwar by the *Espadaña* poets, Dámaso Alonso, and Vicente Aleixandre, developed a category of poetry intended to be read according to quasi-political conventions. This poetry, presaging that of Blas de Otero and Gabriel Celaya, was written between the end of the Civil War and approximately 1947 by poets from places like León, Las Palmas, and Zaragoza, who deliberately avoided publications subsidized by the Franco Regime, instead, depending upon subscribers and private publishers. Such poets shared contempt for Franco with the nation's forty percent the *Caudillo* considered unreliable immediately after the war. This segment of the population —advocates of the Bourbon monarchy, the Republican government in exile, and underground partisans trained by Communists and Anarchists— supported the Spanish resistance movement, part of the European anti-Fascist effort. But hope for immediate liberation was extinguished in 1945 when the Allies did not cross the Pyrenees to rid Spain of Fascism. Undisturbed by foreign intervention, Franco secured his authority, gaining approval in a national referendum to establish an «organic democracy». However, his Regime, which encouraged unfairness, practised oppression, and exploited those least able to defend themselves, was far from democratic and therefore the primary target of protest in resistance poetry.

There are two obvious precedents characterizing the poetry of resistance. John Michael Cohen, noting the similarity between conditions of postwar Spain and those of France a decade earlier, proposed that resistance poetry arose in both cases as a response to the need to speak freely.[1] Moreover, Darío Puccini presented poetry of resistance as a genre in *Romancero de la resistencia española,* anthology with a prologue tracing the historical background and with poems sorted according to whether they were written during the Civil War period, the postwar period within

---

[1] JOHN MICHAEL COHEN, *Poetry of this Age* (London: Hutchinson's and Co., 1960), p. 242.

Spain, or the same period outside of Spain.² By taking *romance* in a general sense, Puccini called attention to poetry centering on the conflict of the Civil War regardless of verse form. The three generations of Spanish poets included substantiate Puccini's claim that Spanish poetry of resistance is as significant as that of other European nations. Both Cohen and Puccini stressed the ideological and political basis of resistance poetry, that is, opposition to the Franco Regime as the chief motive of this tendency.

Different literary tendencies establish different sets of conventions that can contradict but never falsify each other because they are normative rather than empirical systems and, consequently, without common grounds for analytic comparison. Since different systems are not commensurable, Neruda's concept of «impure» poetry, for example, could not disprove that of pure poetry, but only define the purpose and nature of poetry according to its own lights. While different concepts cannot falsify each other, they can replace one another. This process was documented by Juan Cano Ballesta in tracing the ascendency of revolutionary poetry over pure poetry in Spain during the 1930s.³ Consulting well-known periodicals —*El Sol, Cruz y Raya, Octubre,* etc.— he discovered articles by Ramiro de Maeztu, Enrique Azcoaga, Arturo Serrano Plaja, J. V. Foix, Guillermo de Torre, and Antonio Machado about the politicization of art, and another by Juan Ramón Jiménez about the «torpe y feamente llamada *poesía social*». Cano Ballesta also detected echoes from Moscow of Socialist Realism, devised by Stalin and Gorky, promulgated by Zhdanov in «The First All-Union Congress of Soviet Writers» in 1934, and opinions by André Breton, Louis Aragon, and André Malraux about Socialist Realism. Thus it seems that the point of esthetic departure for the poetry of resistance was Socialist Realism from the 1930s, later modified according to the outlook of each poet.

Socialist Realism, the compulsory literary method in the USSR and its dependent nations since 1934, evolved as a tendency in association with the international rise of the working classes, beginning in Russia in the mid-1890s.⁴ It was the extension of Stalinist policies into literature, whereby writers were to create tendentious, party-minded works to transform workers by organizing their thoughts and feelings toward collectivist rather than individualist goals.⁵ According to Zhdanov's version

---

² Darío Puccini, *Romancero de la resistencia española* (1960; México: Biblioteca Era, 1967).
³ Juan Cano Ballesta, *La poesía española entre pureza y revolución (1930-1936)* (Madrid: Gredos, 1972), pp. 149-79.
⁴ C. Vaughan James, *Soviet Socialist Realism. Origins and Theory* (London: Macmillan Press Ltd., 1973), p. 87.
⁵ Terry Eagleton, *Marxism and Literary Criticism* (London: Methuen, 1976), pp. 38-39.

of the Socialist Realist method, writers were not creators of new ideas or seekers of truth, but rather propagandists for the Communist Party and its leaders. For advocates, Socialist Realism was more than a literary style or a question of literary taste, it was the philosophy of the proletarian movement in its battle to create a socialist society, summarized by Lenin's formula: «the truthful, historically concrete representation of reality in its revolutionary development».[6] Convinced that the Socialist Realist method encouraged a crude literary style, opponents tended to disregard the influence Socialist Realism had outside the USSR upon proponents.

The success of Socialist Realism outside the USSR rose in proportion to the influence Marxist views had on writers. In Spain, its growing importance was observable in Alberti's *Octubre,* «Escritores y artistas revolucionarios», and in his revolutionary poems such as this which refers to the prologue to the Communist Party Manifesto: [7]

> ... nosotros lo seguimos,
> lo hacemos descender del viento Este que lo trae,
> le preguntamos por las estepas rojas de la paz y del triunfo,
> lo sentamos a la mesa del campesino pobre,
> presentándolo al dueño de la fábrica,
> haciéndolo presidir las huelgas y manifestaciones,
> hablar con los soldados y los marineros,
> ver en las oficinas a los pequeños empleados
> y alzar el puño a gritos en los Parlamentos del oro y de la sangre.
>
> Un fantasma recorre Europa,
> el mundo.
> Nosotros le llamamos camarada.

The personification of the spirit of Communism as a humble, righteous bearer of good news is characteristic of Socialist Realist poetry, as is the speaker's confessed belief in utimate revolutionary victory. Though Socialist Realist works vary in style and content, all directly or indirectly present the «purpose», in other words, all remind readers of the coming triumph of Communism.[8] In postwar Spain, that triumph would mean the defeat of Franco; thus Socialist Realism was an ideal literary method to convey anti-Franco sentiment as long as hatred of the Regime remained strong.[9]

---

[6] ABRAM TERTZ [ANDREI SINYAVSKY], *On Socialist Realism*. Introduction by Czeslaw Milosz (New York: Pantheon, 1960), pp. 10, 26.

[7] RAFAEL ALBERTI, «Un fantasma recorre Europa...», *El poeta en la calle* (Paris: Librairie du Globe, 1966), pp. 15-16.

[8] TERTZ, *On Socialist Realism,* p. 43.

[9] Compare the use of Socialist Realism in India, related in *Oakland Symposium on Socialist Realism in Literature,* Renate Gerulaitis, ed. (Rochester, Michigan: Oakland University, 1975), p. 77: «... the major reason for the lack of success of Socialist Realism in India after the gaining of independence in 1947 has

The genesis of Socialist Realism was Lenin's program for party theoretical writing, announced in 1905 as the Bolshevik Party was in the process of becoming a mass organization.[10] Means and methods Lenin proposed for tracts, posters, and films, for meetings in cells and village reading rooms, as part of a propaganda campaign monitored by «weather reports» and carried out by «agit-prop» militants, were forced upon imaginative literature. Although Lenin was almost entirely silent on the subject of precepts for literary practice, Zhdanov, Gorky, and Stalin soon required the widespread application of what may be described as a three-step propaganda method.

The first step of the Socialist Realist method is to write from a Marxist bias. Lenin called this the philosophy of «*here* and *now*», as if there were only one correct representation of reality. Since every literary work by a Socialist Realist writer presents the «purpose», if the «*here* and *now*» lead to the paradise of Revolution, praise follows and if not, censure. For proponents, this step discloses a false formerly masked reality; for adversaries, it merely presents a distorted view. The second step of the method is a challenge. Like the showdown in poker, alluded to in the title of Celaya's *Las cartas boca arriba,* the challenge condenses a situation, formulates an opinion, or takes the shape of an either-or choice. Writers skilled in the method are sure that, as in poker, they hold the winning hand and know the outcome. This step infuriates opponents, who dislike its unfair manipulation. While the first two steps of the Socialist Realist method are intended to win converts, the third is to incite them to action on behalf of the Revolution. Even when adapted to particular audiences, poetry readers for instance, the three-step method of Socialist Realism depends upon standard propaganda approaches —outraged innocence, satire, or appeal— and upon such devices as affective language, use of abstract terms like injustice, oppression, and Revolution to elicit emotional reaction and, finally, begging the question or assuming an outcome as certain.

Socialist Realism offers not only a method of writing, but also a corresponding method of reading. The Marxist hermeneutics, or what might be called «Marxism in the eye of the beholder», is an interpretive practice that selects textual details according to a known pattern. In this sense, it resembles the procedure of patristic scholars in search of trinities in sacred writings. Like patristic scholars, adept readers find a message that is simple and unchanging: it is that triumph will come to

---

to do with the fact that Marxism wasn't a strong enough ideology to hold these people together in a group, whereas hatred for the British and British domination was... Socialist Realism and Marxian ideology served as a convenient vehicle for anti-British sentiment, and this sentiment was perhaps more important than Marxism in India...»
[10] EAGLETON, *Marxism and Literary Criticism,* pp. 40-41.

the working classes, the exploiters will be defeated by the exploited. Though the variations that writers might invent to illustrate this pattern are theoretically numberless, the actual range is often limited to a view of society as tidily divided into over- and under-classes: the bourgeoisie and the proletariat. In Socialist Realist works the pattern of social conflict with the tyrannized class ultimately victorious is constant. Thus, a belligerant tone of protest or words like *obrero* and *campesino* do not alone constitute the Marxist message, whose essential element is the «purpose», either explicitly stated or inferred from context.

EUGENIO DE NORA IN THE VANGUARD

The poet most responsible for developing postwar Spanish Socialist Realism was without doubt Eugenio de Nora, whose Marxist beliefs led to involvement with the clandestine Federación Universitaria Escolar (F.U.E.) in association with Manuel Lamana, Nicolás Sánchez Albornoz, Carmelo Soria and others.[11] De Nora, who studied literature in Madrid from 1942 to 1946 and began teaching in Switzerland in 1949, is perhaps best known as the author of a classic study of the contemporary Spanish novel.[12] A precocious writer whose most significant poetry was written before he was twenty-seven years old, De Nora was the author of five collections published between 1945 and 1954, anthologized in 1974.[13] One work received the Premio Boscán, two others were published in the Adonais collection. To these award-winning works may be added *Pueblo cautivo,* whose author was listed as anonymous until recently.[14]

Pueblo cautivo consists of ten poems, preceded by «Explico algunas cosas», reproduced from Neruda's *España en el corazón,* and interspersed

---

[11] JOSÉ MANUEL LÓPEZ DE ABIADA, «Observaciones en torno a la poesía de posguerra. Conversación con Eugenio de Nora», *Insula,* No. 407 (October 1980), pp. 3-4.

[12] Biographical information from CHARLES DAVID LEY, *Spanish Poetry since 1939* (Washington, D.C.: Catholic University of America, 1962), p. 12; EUGENIO DE NORA, *La novela española contemporánea (1898-1967),* 3 vols. (Madrid: Gredos, 1973).

[13] EUGENIO DE NORA, *Amor prometido* (Valladolid: Halcón, 1946); *Cantos al destino (1941-1945)* (Madrid: Editorial Hispánica, 1945); *Contemplación del tiempo* (Madrid: Adonais, 1948); *Siempre* (Madrid: Insula, 1953); *España, pasión de vida (1945-1950)* (Barcelona: Instituto de Estudios Hispánicos, 1954); *Poesía (1939-1964)* (León: Diputación Provincial, 1975). Page references to this anthology appear in the text preceded by P.

[14] The work is mentioned by: GUILLERMO DE TORRE, «Contemporary Spanish Poetry», *The Texas Quarterly,* 4, No. 1 (1961), pp. 69-70; MANUEL LAMANA, *Literatura de posguerra* (Buenos Aires: Nova, 1961), pp. 78-80, 89-90; LECHNER, *El compromiso en la poesía española del siglo XX. Parte segunda,* p. 65; CARLOS BLANCO AGUINAGA, JULIO RODRÍGUEZ PUÉRTOLAS, IRIS M. ZAVALA, *Historia social de la literatura española. (En lengua castellana)* (Madrid: Castalia, 1979), vol. 3, p. 89.

with eleven related engravings by Alvaro Delgado.[15] The colophon attributes the poems to «un POETA SIN NOMBRE» and identifies the year of publication as 1946, «séptima de la tiranía franquista». This unusual book is an important part of De Nora's poetry of resistance, a cycle of poems that despite a complicated publishing history confirms De Nora's significance to Spanish poetry between the Civil War and the mid-1950s. De Nora described the common features of his dispersed poems of resistance in the following manner: [16]

> ... poesía de toma de conciencia, de oposición a una situación y de aspiración a algo que es de tipo extraindividual ya, un tipo de *poesía social,* encarnación de opciones, de sentimientos, de aspiraciones verdaderamente colectivas, multitudinarias...

Prior to the dismantling of the Franco Regime, De Nora referred only indirectly to the fundamental unity of this cycle, first, in the introduction to *España, pasión de vida,* later in that of his anthology.[17]

While clandestine publication was the only path open to a homogenous arrangement of resistance poems during the 1940s, lightly censored publications and heterogenous collections of poems were an alternative De Nora exploited. More than half of the poems of *España, pasión de vida* appeared separately, most long before their book publication in 1954. Eight were printed between 1945 and 1950 in *Espadaña,* two in *Entregas de poesía,* and one original along with three republished poems were included in the *Antología consultada.* De Nora also added four resistance poems to *Cantos al destino,* and two others to *Contemplación del tiempo.*[18]

---

[15] *Pueblo cautivo,* ed. Fanny Rubio, 2nd ed. (1946; rpt. Pamplona: Peralta, 1978); since the work is unpaged poem titles appear in the text. Rubio named him in the introduction to *Pueblo cautivo,* 2nd edition.

[16] LÓPEZ DE ABIADA, «Conversación con Eugenio de Nora», p. 3.

[17] In the first comment, dated 1951, De Nora (P, 267-68) wrote: «Doy esta breve gavilla de poemas con un profundo sentimiento de insatisfacción, con una clara conciencia de provisionalidad, que necesito explicar. Cuando empecé a escribirlos, hace seis años, mi ambición era formar verso a verso un vasto poema en el que la historia viva, el presente y la apetencia de futuro de España se reflejaran, a través de una conciencia joven de español de la posguerra... Pero 'este libro' no se ha escrito. Lo que sigue no son más que fragmentos, preguntas, negaciones de algo que no llega a vertebrar... Por eso éste en un libro provisional, muy sin cerrar aún.» In the later comment, De Nora (P, 8-9) referred to the poems excluded from his anthology in the following manner: «En cuanto a lo no recogido aquí (y que yo mismo no sé si podré optar por publicarlo, o no, en un futuro próximo), debo decir, para satisfacer el interés de los amigos y disipar las reticencias de los desconfiados, que los poemas en cuarentena no son todos recientes, ni tampoco (no siempre) absolutamente inéditos, sino más bien, ¿cómo decir?, desambientados; que sin ser muy numerosos (entre veinticinco y treinta) corresponderían por la extensión a un libro bastante denso, y que si no los ofrezco ahora no es desde luego por tenerlos en menos que los aquí incluidos, sino por motivaciones personales y de circunstancias.»

[18] This listing includes prior publication of poems included in *España, pasión de vida,* arranged by year of first appearance.

De Nora promoted his own views while literary editor of the student publication *Cisneros* in 1943. Before De Nora's appointment, *Cisneros* displayed the neotraditionalist propaganda of the Regime, obvious in a perusal of the first issue. *Cisneros*, No. 1 (January 1943) carries a large photograph of the *Caudillo* accompanied by an offer of tribute. Three religious poems and a review of the major dates of the liturgical year set the tone for two articles: «Singladuras de una nave sin rumbo», condemning the Residencia de Estudiantes, a prewar intellectual gathering place, and praising the Colegios Mayores, postwar educational institutions reminiscent of medieval foundations; and «El problema de la Cristiandad», which forecast a shift in universal history by which Christianity would return to its preeminence. *Cisneros* changed shortly thereafter; De Nora contributed his own essays, poems, and translations, invited poems from Crémer and Otero, and published the essay by De Lama criticizing *garcilasismo*.

One of De Nora's contributions to *Cisneros* (No. 4, April 1943, pp. 65-69) was «Poema en tres tiempos», whose three parts, «Lamento», «Protesta», and «Exaltación», exhibit militant phraseology, heroic manner, and tonal shadings from harangue to self-pity. In sections of the poem De Nora indicated the ideological direction of his later poetry; he combined a shout of protest, a cry for freedom, and a wish for sympathetic addresses in evocation of Spain's isolation during World War II:

> Mi grito no han de oírlo
> estos espacios próximos y bajos;
> no saben escucharlo;
> mi grito ha de ir, clamando
> libertad, sí, por Dios y por la Patria
> más allá de este tiempo y de este espacio.

The politicized protest in this poem is unambiguous. The speaker demands an end to the current situation, «ese paréntesis», and, unexpectedly for Spain in 1943, refers to a controlled press and broadcast system:

    1945: «Presencia», *Espadaña*, No. 14; «España mía: Presencia, Honda es la herida, Galerías profundas», *Cantos al destino*.
    1946: «Pueblos de la meseta», *Espadaña*, No. 20 and *Antología consultada;* «Patria», *Espadaña*, No. 23, *La Isla de los Ratones*, No. 16-17.
    1947: «Recordaré primero», «España», *Entregas de Poesía*, No. 23; «Poesía contemporánea» under title of «Poesía aquí», *Espadaña*, No. 28 and *Antología consultada*.
    1948: «Otoño», *Espadaña*, No. 36 and *Antología consultada*.
    1950: «Encuentros obligados», *Espadaña*, No. 44; «Palabras y palabras» under title of «1949», *Espadaña*, No. 46; «Un deber de alegría», *Espadaña*, No. 47.
    1952: «Canto», *Antología consultada*.
    From *Contemplación del tiempo*, «En la muerte de un amigo» first appeared in *Espadaña*, No. 24 (1946) and «Lo que yo pienso sobre ello» in the fascicle of *Antología parcial* corresponding to *Espadaña*, No. 30 (1947).

> ¡Amigos!
> Hay que cerrar al fin este paréntesis
> que algún cobarde abrió.
>   Quedemos solos;
> si el mundo, tan extenso, está cercado
> de redes enemigas que puntúan
> amables centinelas
> («no pasa nada, nada» por consigna),
> dejemos emisiones y revistas;
> ¡tanta insinuación tibia
> en forma de sonrisa que no cede!
> («... nada, nada:
> el mundo está así bien...»)

Apparently this poem exceeded the ideological limits of *Cisneros;* it was followed by a page-long note stating that, while not difficult to understand, the poem expressed sentiments that might confuse certain readers. To avoid improper readings, a line-by-line paraphrase described the speaker's protest of dehumanization threatening man's morality and endangering worldly peace and beauty. Eventually the revised poem appeared in *Cantos al destino.* Just the first part remained; it denounced hatred, which only led to bloodshed and grief. The shout for freedom, recast as apostrophe, turned the active protest of the earlier version into nostalgia:

> Mi grito ha de ir clamando
> —oh libertad, madre del hombre entero—
> más allá de este tiempo y de este espacio. (P, 27-90)

The unifying theme of *Cantos al destino* is De Nora's concept of *destino* as a simultaneous reference to life and death. In *cantos,* the central poems of the work, De Nora despairs over man's mortality, realizing that time is precious. Using familiar romantic imagery, De Nora casts *destino* as an invitation to self-destruction in the eyes of a femme fatale (P, 105-11); a liberation from the imprisonment of the flesh (P, 124-27); a thirst for demonic immortality (P, 96-105); and, in two poems that soar cosmically, the destruction of the human race, unbeknown to its victims (P, 84-86, 112-13). This imagery, however, forms an effective background to what is novel in *Cantos al destino,* that is, the poems of protest, tenuously united to the rest of the work through occasional allusions to *destino.*

The first of these poems of protest, «Otra voz», interprets the dictum to humanize poetry popularized by Neruda in his 1935 manifesto. It makes clear De Nora's rebellion against neoclassicism and *garcilasismo* and also foreshadows later poems by José Hierro («Para un esteta» from *Quinta del 42),* Gabriel Celaya («Vivir para ver» from *Cantos iberos),* and José Agustín Goytisolo («Los celestiales» from *Salmos al viento),*

Like Neruda, De Nora refuses an evasive attitude toward mankind and mocks the poet of aristocratic pretensions, who writes oblivious to those around him «en artísticas rimas, en símbolos o imágenes / inaccesibles a la profanación bestial de las sedientas multitudes» (P, 75-77). For De Nora, such a poet makes a moral error by neglecting struggle, pain, and death, the lot of all mankind. Rather, the poet ought to illuminate man's destiny, finding inspiration «en la sangre, el anhelo, y la voz de los hombres».

The final three poems of *Cantos al destino* illustrate aspects of Socialist Realism, among them the doctrine of *narodnost*, which calls for the creation of popular national forms of Socialist Realism.[19] Acordingly, De Nora develops the «purpose» with details from Spanish experience to depict the social differences brought about by the outcome of the Civil War, which prevented a true and just peace. No longer focusing abstractly on death, despair, and isolation as existential dilemmas, De Nora refers them to a «*here* and *now*», stressing their political nature. Subtitled «España mía», these poems addressing Spain as the beloved are important both to De Nora's later poetry and as models for other poets; they establish a distinctive personification of Spain and portray the speaker as a devoted troubadour. In the first place, the speaker suggests a personified addressee with phrases such as «tu rostro hermoso» and «cuerpo moreno / que el amor ofreciera» (P, 271, 275). De Nora's idealized Spain is a victim violated by the trenches of war, disfigured by abandoned dwellings, but most of all saddened by her quarreling children, whom she loves equally. The speaker sees beyond these blemishes to the immortal beauty of the Spanish landscape. But this makes him impatient before Spain's unpredictability; she inspires his hope and suffering, his tenderness and fear. In the second place, the speaker offers himself to Spain in order to merge his destiny with hers, to sing of her glory and unfulfilled hope (P, 272, 274). He evokes love and hate by turns, as if patriotic duty were *dulce batalla*. Then, finally, the speaker confesses that his love of freedom, thwarted now, inspires his devotion to Spain: [20]

¡España, España!
¡Pasión de sangre! Amor de vida,

---

[19] JAMES, *Soviet Socialist Realism*, p. 97: «An enormously important though frequently neglected aspect of socialist-realist art is the fact of its multi-national nature, even within the USSR... The *narodnost* of the national form springs from the maintenance of a direct link with the people and should be clearly distinguished from *cosmopolitanism* which, in Soviet parlance denotes the rootlessness consequent on the severance of such a link. Though the art of all the peoples of the USSR must be socialist, the art of each people retains its national flavour by virtue of its 'popular' origin.»

[20] The second line in *Cantos al destino* (Madrid: Editorial Hispánica, 1945), p. 64: «¡Pasión de sangre submergida!».

> amor de libertad te canta
> en una aurora del destino.
> Amor amargo de la patria. (P, 273)

And his devotion to Spain spurs him to victory:

> Te quiere el que en la lucha
> de su amor te va haciendo.
> Sin otra arma combato
> esta guerra en el verso,
> hasta dejar tu forma
> como un sol refulgiendo. (P, 276)

With «otra voz» and «España mía» De Nora began what he planned to be a long poem reflecting the history and future of Spain. He explained the project to readers in the prologue to *España, pasión de vida* in 1954 and much earlier to friends with whom he shared his poems in manuscript.[21] Part of this project to unite politics and literature was *Pueblo cautivo,* of which 210 copies were printed by F.U.E. as an act of resistance.

In *Pueblo cautivo* De Nora recognizes his debt to the revolutionary poetry of the 1930s by placing Neruda's poem as frontispiece and citing verses by Pedro Garfias, with which he dedicates the work to those who: «... aguardan desvelados / con el oído atento bajo la tierra pálida / el disparo de luz de la victoria». Writing of other matters the speaker thereby would evade his moral duty to mankind, failing to rise to the defense when his advocacy was needed, but this does not mean that he is not tempted to write on more delicate topics:

> Acaso yo debiera purificar mis ojos
> en luz de agua o de luna, maravillar mis manos
> en el tacto amoroso de mejillas y flores... (Los días)

---

[21] ANTONIO G. DE LAMA, «Poesía y verdad. El destino poético de Eugenio de Nora», *Espadaña,* No. 19, commented on the project: «Los tres últimos poemas [de *Cantos al destino*] son leve muestra de uno más vasto sobre España, de horizontes inmensos, donde para cantar hay que tener voz potente, con ecos de profunda resonancia. Eugenio de Nora tiene esa voz sin artificios, densa y ancha, porque tiene un alma abierta a todos los afanes de la humanidad y lleva clavados, como flechas, todos los problemas y todas las inquietudes de su Patria y de su época.»

C. LASCARIS-COMNENO, Review of *Cantos al destino, Cisneros,* No. 11 (1946), pp. 115-17 alludes to De Nora's habit of sharing his unpublished poems: «Un compañero nuestro, Eugenio de Nora, acaba de publicar un libro de versos; nos ha dado en bloque lo que conocíamos disperso, ahora lo tenemos entre las manos con la satisfacción de ver la obra consumada de un residente que se lanza al mundo de la poesía con la enseña de su juventud. No es necesario dar a conocer la obra, ya difundida, de Eugenio de Nora, pero sí quiere *Cisneros* hacerse eco de este acontecimiento, quiere coadyuvar en el homenaje a este joven poeta que sale de sus filas y respira su ambiente.»

Rejecting an escapist attitude, the speaker gains authority by relying on personal experience. He sees that there are two classes of people — one wearing military dress, the other mourning. His lament in «Quiero decir» breaks the silence of the streets:

> ... aquí están los años enemigos,
> amargos de odio, abiertos como heridas,
> desfallecidos de belleza aguda.
> ¡Aquí está el alma llena de cadenas,
> el ciego sol sobre la mar sin nadie,
> tanta espada de música en mi pecho!

In this uncensored poem, De Nora then justifies his commitment to resistance by mentioning threats he opposes — volleys of shots, bullets in bloodied walls, and soldiers bearing flags, their arms ready.

The dynamic pattern of *Pueblo cautivo* is created by three attitudes: offended protest, meditative nostalgia, and solemn declaration. All three attitudes may be observed in «Años fuera del tiempo». The personalized speaker is twenty years old, a child when the war began, who longs for age and experience to make credible his declarations and objections. In the first part, he addresses a personified night, whose weeping by pathetic transference plunges him into a river of memories. He is drawn equally to the promised new age and to the shadowy realm of death, to a bright future and to oblivion. In the second part, an impersonal declaratory voice reminds:

> Mas, también de la historia se nutre la esperanza,
> como el rosal de otoño con las hojas caídas.
> Quién sufre su derrota aún no está derrotado.
>
> Dolorosa y tenaz es el recuerdo, vivo,
> de España fusilada.

And then he adds that, despite three years of blood and death, the peace that came was a peace of treading upon corpses. In the final section, taking his cue from Nature's seasons, the speaker remembers that matter is eternal though constantly changing. He vindicates his poetry by claiming as its source what is most enduring in Spain:

> ¡España mía, frágil
> y eterna en cada tallo!
> De tu roca más vieja
> ¡Siento alzarse mi canto!

That Spain is the addressee in «Años fuera del tiempo» marks this poem as a part of De Nora's poetic project. Another poem in *Pueblo cautivo* that apostrophizes Spain is «Testimonio», whose last line repeats the book's title. In early stanzas, the speaker affirms his desire to provide testimony of Spain's distress, to reveal the wretched living conditions within her borders; in the final stanza, he would offer the path to freedom:

> Corral en que vivimos, patria,
> quiero decir la náusea de tus días marchitos;
> quiero soñar y prometer la ruta
> de libertad de tu pueblo cautivo.

In «Paisaje de España», the speaker uses «Tierra de nuestra patria», among other epithets, to refer to Spain. The poem moves from meditative praise, to harsh accusations, and then to declarations in which the speaker claims that nature itself promises an end to slavery, hatred, and exile.

In most of the remaining poems the speaker is a witness as in «Testimonio», but he directs his declarations to various other audiences rather than Spain, in keeping with the simulated presentation of evidence. He reminds fellow Spaniards in «Mandato» that each passing day another opportunity is lost and, as a result, treason and cowardice perpetuate imprisonment and death. As if before a public gathering in «Los días», the speaker begins: «Todo el que pueda, oiga.» And finally, the audience of «La herencia renovada» is composed of the speaker's *compañeros*. Differences between the poems of «España mía» and those discussed from *Pueblo cautivo* show that De Nora expanded the speaker's original role as troubadour to assume attributes of a witnessing spokesman. At the same time, he diversified his audience from the *tú* of his idealized Spain, to *vosotros,* listeners whom he encourages, chides, and tries to convince.

De Nora is probably the first postwar poet to elaborate the role of a witness under oath. His purpose is obviously to gain belief in his declarations, which, by their condemnatory nature, indict the Regime. Phrases placed at the beginning or the conclusion of poems invoke the solemnity of courtroom litigation. Thus, «Quiero decir» ends: «... y entre tantos oficios yo soy aquél que mira, / aquél de quien se pide que atestigüe y declare.» In «Los días», the speaker declares at the beginning:

> ... cada palabra
> que escribo está madura de verdad. Oiga y mire,
> y compruebe las cosas, y su esencia en el verbo.

He concludes the same poem: «Ahí están mis palabras.» The final lines of the last poem in the collection, «¡Libertad!», retroactively enforce this convention for the entire work:

> mientras tanto, las cosas verdaderas:
> sólo canto lo libre. Ved. Mi voz atestigua
> el silencio y la sangre.

De Nora uses the pretense of speaking under oath to claim historically justifiable, yet one-sided, affirmations as objective truth. In *Pueblo cautivo* he freely draws from the stock of anti-Fascist propaganda to correct the equally biased, more powerful propaganda of the Regime. The poem that comes closest to crude propaganda is wordlessly titled with the National Movement's yoke and arrows. The substance of the poem is a gloss on Falangist slogans: «¡España. Una, grande, libre!» and «¡Arriba, España!». However, the speaker subverts their accepted meaning so that each word is another accusation of the Franco Regime: Spain is not unified because the victors sundered it; nor is it great, the victors sold Spain's honor and mortgaged her resources to pay for fratricidal carnage. To illustrate «*libre*», the speaker portrays a march, whose participants were murdered or imprisoned:

> Y a la libre España,
> que seguía su camino de paz hacia el futuro,
> asesinaron por la espalda, y a los supervivientes dieron
> la libertad del plomo y pudrirse en la tierra,
> o de acumular odio entre rejas y estacas.

Having built the poem to bathetic climax, the speaker offers a bitter interpretation of «¡Arriba, España!» claiming that victory went to those who trampled brothers, defamed Spain, and groveled before contemptuous foreign powers. De Nora skimmed the same sources for the vivid images he placed in the first two poems of *Pueblo cautivo*. To represent worldwide depravity in the 1940s, he speaks of festering wounds and men preying on each other in «Mandato»:

> Cada día que pasa
> es otro en que la herida se agiganta y encona,
> en que los criminales digieren su rapiña,
> en que a millones de hombres camaradas del mundo
> se les niega la vida, la ocasión de una muerte
> con honor, combatiendo.

To emphasize the sacrilege of the victors he uses vulgar insults in «Testimonio»:

> ... ...
> patria injuriada por tus mismos hijos
> de perra, los que ensucian
> y mean en tu sagrado...

The complement of this anti-Fascist propaganda is Marxist propaganda on behalf of a heroic proletariat remaking the future. This pattern verges on allegory with its own vocabulary of terms having special meanings. «*Pueblo*» is of course the poetic equivalent of the defeated but someday victorious proletariat. «*Patria*» seldom refers to Spain as a whole, but rather to Spaniards treasonably wronged by the victors. «*Pueblo*» and «*patria*» may be used therefore as equivalents. To signal the optimistic purpose of Marxism, several terms besides «*Revolución*» may be used: *alegría, vida nueva, vida plena, futuro*. The italics De Nora uses in «La herencia renovada» alert readers to these code words:

> En el pulso del pueblo late y sigue la patria.
> ... ...
> pero nuestra mirada busca la vida nueva,
> y una inmensa esperanza
> puebla el aire futuro de cánticos y espigas.
> Alegría es nuestra obra:
> con bautismo de sangre, *alegría* nombramos,
> *vida plena* nombramos en el tiempo que viene.

De Nora confirms the Marxist significance of his goal with the phrase «con bautismo de sangre», which at once alludes to violent change, rites of passage, and mystic communion.

However adept De Nora may be at exploiting common propaganda, he is also skilled at writing poems to be pleasurably read by those not sensitized to Marxist code-words. An example of his skill occurs in «¡Libertad!», where, to project a socialist order, he imagines a free city superimposed upon the real one shackled by chains and in mourning. In the speaker's meditation, spatial and temporal planes cross and he is seduced by his imagination to hear pealing bells and excited shouting, destiny seeking its expression. As he is about to celebrate the arrival of the new age, the vision disappears. This poem and the book thus end with the speaker alone, surrounded by a silence that challenges readers to take a political position.

Despite the number of copies of *Pueblo cautivo,* the only critics apparently noticing its existence were foreigners, and their remarks came years after its publication. Among the first to recognize the work's importance was Guillermo de Torre, who commented that *Pueblo cautivo* spoke out about suffering, but did not carry a quarrel, serve a propaganda purpose, or betray hatred.[22] Manuel Lamana, a fellow leader with De Nora in the F.U.E., quoted poems from *Pueblo cautivo* in his study of postwar literature without referring to its author.[23] Jan Lechner, in his study prepared a decade later, generally agreed with De Torre and Lamana that the work was not truly political.[24] However, in the prologue to the 1978 edition of this work, Fanny Rubio traced the close connection between *Pueblo cautivo* and the student resistance movement, leaving

---

[22] GUILLERMO DE TORRE, «Contemporary Spanish Poetry», *The Texas Quarterly*, 4, No. 1, pp. 69-70.

[23] MANUEL LAMANA, *Literatura de posguerra* (Buenos Aires: Nova, 1961), pp. 78-80, 89-90.

[24] LECHNER, *El compromiso en la poesía española del siglo XX. Parte segunda*, p. 65.

little doubt about the anti-Francoist character of this «anonymous» poetry. The authors of the *Historia social* also called the work political and commented that *Pueblo cautivo* in form and content anticipated the social poetry of the 1950s.[25]

Some of De Nora's poems published under his own name are equally unequivocal. That awakening greatest interest and speculation among readers and critics is probably «Lo que yo pienso sobre ello». First appearing in the *Antología parcial,* then in *Contemplación del tiempo,* it was anthologized several times.[26] The topic of the poem, an execution by terrorizing authorities, is not heavily disguised. The treatment of the topic clearly reveals protest of unjust killings and censure of the «prudent» who condone violence by pretending it did not occur. As in many of the poems of *Pueblo cautivo,* the speaker is a voice of conscience proclaiming truth. Here, he also warns his listeners of the moral consequences of murder, affirming that concealment of such crimes is impossible. Thus, the epigraph from Mayakovsky —«Como suele decirse: 'El incidente ha terminado'»— is used ironically: The speaker asserts the opposite. The political nature of this poem was widely recognized as may be seen in a review of *Contemplación del tiempo* that calls attention to the sociopolitical sense of the poem.[27]

The republication of «Lo que yo pienso sobre ello» seems to show that single poems of protest, but not entire collections, could be published. The fragmenting effect of censorship in the 1940s affected De Nora's *España, pasión de vida.* Finished around 1950, it was published in 1954 only with the unqualified support of José María Castellet and Alfonso Costafreda, judges of the Premio Boscán, and after De Nora made corrections.[28] De Nora called the work provisional, made up of fragments and questions, in the introduction to *España, pasión de vida.* He also omitted some twenty-five or thirty poems from *Poesía (1939-1964),* some presumably comprising *Pueblo cautivo.* Thematic and formal similarities between *Pueblo cautivo* and *España, pasión de vida* aside, the former is an outright condemnation of the Franco Regime, while the latter follows De Nora's intention to write a poem about Spain's past, present, and future through the consciousness of a young Spaniard of the postwar period.

---

[25] CARLOS BLANCO AGUINAGA, JULIO RODRÍGUEZ PUÉRTOLAS, IRIS M. ZAVALA, *Historia social de la literatura española,* III, p. 89.

[26] In fascicule of the *Antología parcial* with *Espadaña,* No. 30 (1947), *Antología consultada,* pp. 161-64, *Veinte años de poesía española,* pp. 189-90, *Poesía social,* pp. 253-55, and in DE NORA's *Poesía (1939-1964),* pp. 166-71.

[27] G[ERMÁN] B[LEIBERG], Review of *Contemplación del tiempo, Insula,* 3, No. 30 (15 June 1948), p. 5: «Entre los poemas sin duda se destaca el que lleva una cita de Mayakowsky: *Lo que yo pienso sobre ello;* las cinco estrofas tienen un profundo sentido político-social —que desde hace algún tiempo asoma en la más reciente poesía española...— y Nora acierta al combinar lo lírico con lo anecdótico...»

[28] LÓPEZ ABIADA, «Conversación con Eugenio de Nora», p. 3.

Pueblo cautivo may be read as a part of *España, pasión de vida;* its purpose is encompassed by that of the longer work. Since De Nora dated the poems of *España, pasión de vida* and arranged them more or less chronologically, they monitor the speaker's ideological development from naive rebellion to clear-cut Marxism.

España, pasión de vida begins with the three poems of «España mía» already discussed. In new poems, the speaker sometimes addresses an idealized Spain, at other times, fellow poets, the general public, and unidentified listeners. An interplay of addressees permits the speaker to vary moral perspective and avoid a tedious denunciatory mode. This work conforms to the practices of Socialist Realism, thus central to its plan is a portrayal of society as composed of antagonistic classes with the expected message that the exploited will one day be victorious. Historical change, reflected in the poems, test the speaker's integrity without undermining the force of his message. De Nora also follows the Socialist Realist convention of *narodnost,* interpreting Marxist doctrine in terms of Spain, emphasizing the profound relation between Spain and its people.

Among the opening poems of *España, pasión de vida* are two that illustrate the psychic damage suffered by the speaker as a result of the Civil War. «Recordaré primero» (P, 277-79) is an idyllic view of Spain through the eyes of «un niño sin memoria», who discovers marvels in a divinely protected land. The following poem, «Patria» (P, 280), portrays the same land through the eyes of an adult who laments the day war broke out, putting an end to his childhood. Unable to fight earlier because of his youth, the speaker is ready to engage in struggle now that he is adult: «Hijo fui de una patria. Hombre perdido: fuerte / para luchar, ahora, para morir, mañana.» This declaration of commitment is the context of the work's second section, a sequence of seven poems.

De Nora shapes the notion of two Spains to his own purpose in «España» (P, 283-86), presenting the Civil War's victors and losers as mutually hostile classes. Each group interprets the meaning of Spain according to its own ideology. For the victors, *«patria»* is a revival of the Spanish Empire, the righteousness of the Counterreformation: «luz de Trento» and «martillo de herejes». However, the speaker declares these titles fitting for orators, but not for «los que a veces trabajan, y otras veces / se pasan con su hambre, los que viven / y duermen / en cualquier parte». For the latter, *«patria»* is the pain and suffering of defeat. The speaker ends with a wish to listen to the «song of life» from the land and people, as if they were inseparable:

> Llegad a la ribera, con los álamos; quiero
> que escuchemos reunidos
> la canción de la vida... como un río.

THE POETRY OF PROTEST UNDER FRANCO

> ... ...
> ¡España! ¿España?
> Un río que se incorpora, un árbol
> que va a hablar.

De Nora's early attempts at Socialist Realism seem to owe inspiration to poster art of the 1930s with graphic realism in black and white. Perhaps the popularity of these poems depends upon the contrast they present to the more customary love sonnets. The speaker of «Canto» (P, 287-88), rejecting a Francoist history of Spain, proclaims the life to come for those who love «with anger and courage», struggle «fiercely happy», and advance «fighting and singing». Beneath a new star of destiny, the freed nation will arise:

> ¡España está en nosotros!...
> ... ...
> en mi alma está el derrumbe de una patria humeante,
> pero arriba una estrella puramente amanece.
> ¡Violadores del Tiempo, la patria no está hecha!
> ¿Quién traicionará el sino de engendrar del presente
> un futuro más bello?
> ¡Ardiente, clara España!
> Tu ancha vida en tus hombres. Tu libertad por siempre.

As spokesman for the exploited, the speaker admires the valor of downtrodden peasants, who suffer «civil extermination», yet still persist. However ingenuous the speaker's admiration, it deserves attention and sympathy in «Pueblos de la meseta» (P, 289-91):

> aún hay la gana dura,
> la gana hasta la sangre de vivir combatiendo,
> la necesidad grave, vegetal, de una hiriente
> pasión de muerte o vida...
> la alegría.

«Sacrificio» (P, 292) is testimonial; the speaker addresses *patria* in a sonnet that is readable, despite its exaggerated pathos by today's standards of taste. Inspired by the Cervantine *Los baños de Argel* referred to in the epigraph, the poem compares martyred Christian captives to the common people and elicits sympathy by such phrases as: «Víctima sin ara», «a culetazos rotos», «[m]ártir eterno». Another sonnet, «La noche» (P, 297-98), is equally sentimental, evoking pity on behalf of the speaker, dejected over the postponement of freedom. Though this tragic pose seems forced, it allows De Nora to gloss an epigraph from Miguel Hernández: «¡Cuánto penar para morirse uno!»

In time, De Nora's artistic preferences mature, he leaves behind war imagery for an impersonal lexicon to describe the elite as «*cifras*», socially select, hierarchically superior figures who look identical, as if they had «uniformes vestidos por dentro, / universales, repetidos, unos». They tip their hats to the speaker, greeting him courteously, but he doubts their sincerity. Unlike the common people these capitalists lack spontaneity; alienated from reality, they do not smile freely, shake hands warmly, feel sad, whistle, offer a caress, or work with pleasure. The speaker feels alienated from them. Ironically, he associates most with the bourgeoisie, though his sympathies lie with the masses.

In the work's third sequence of poems, «Poética», De Nora displays his academic expertise. In «Poesía contemporánea» (P, 304-06) he again criticizes evasive poets, who weave silken illusions to shield disease and deceit, and advocate poetry about square-jawed men, who smile at pain with clenched teeth. According to the speaker, the world needs more poetic revelation; then he defines what true poetry is:

> ... ... La poesía es eso:
> gesto, mirada, abrazo
> de amor a la verdad profunda.
> Ay, ay, lo que yo canto
> miradlo en torno y despertad: alerta.

De Nora's warning in the final line challenges readers to look and act. Thus this poem includes the three elements of the Socialist Realist method: partial view of reality, challenge, call to action. By way of contrast, the same three elements appear in «Otoño» (P, 301-02) as questions and doubts, not about Marxism nor the need for action, but about the efficacy of words, the likelihood that they reach listeners. The dejected speaker evades censors by declaring that his message is proscribed — to affirm he negates, risking misunderstanding:

> ... creímos poder daros
> nuncio del hombre nuevo,
> unas pocas palabras que dijeran
> lo indecible, a rechazos:
> «Eso *no* somos; eso no queremos...»
> y así seguir.
>   Pero seguir, ¿a dónde,
> negando sólo?...

The major concern in «Poeta ignorante» (P, 303-04) is the close identification between words and the world, premise of Socialist Realism. That is, words are not autonomous; they are the substance of the message, pieces of reality. Taking this notion a step further, the speaker contemplates those who shape reality, who «escriben / historia con sus manos, sus cucharas...». He mingles among these people and is able to «regresar con mundo en las palabras». Taking the pulse of life, he reaches out, touches damp blood, then challenges his listener:

> Pero la oscuridad es terca. A tientas,
> ¡qué, qué podré auscultar, pulso de vida!
> Apartar unas ramas, y de pronto,
> ¡húmedas, sí, de sangre! Tú ¿qué dices?

To accentuate the moral evasion of self-consciously beautiful poetry, the speaker of «Palabras y palabras» (P, 307-09) re-creates a *locus amoenus*, then interrupts himself. Impelled by the example of those who sacrificed their lives, by all that is «alerta y mañana», he rejects exquisite language as grotesque and refuses to ornament the walls of a prison, even if powerless to pull them down: [29]

> ¡No seré el que ornamente
> los muros de una cárcel!
> Haré lo que se puede
> decentemente hacer.
>
> —Pero ¿qué puede hacerse?
>
> Ay, desgarrar las manos
> ... sin tocar las paredes.

The most important poem of this section, «Antipoema del cansancio» (P, 309-11), develops a familiar notion when the speaker notes that what he calls poetry has an uncanny resemblance to prose. Rather than claim that his poetry is not art, he declares instead that poets are superfluous. When only the elite read poetry it is a contradiction to write for the masses. The speaker finds his readers unsympathetic, indignant or embarrassed, while his intended listeners have no time for poetry:

> Amigos míos, poetas, nuestro oficio
> es inútil, pensadlo.
> Los que nos oyen no comprenden, y los que entenderían...
> no tienen tiempo de escucharnos.

This problem of poetry directed to the masses preoccupied De Nora, he returned to it in essays and, importantly, seldom wrote poetry thereafter.

As a Socialist Realist, however, he seeks the solution to the problem of inattentive addressees in renewed dedication to Marxist ideals. This is the topic of «Un deber de alegría» (P, 315-17), the hopeful final poem of *España, pasión de vida*. The speaker recasts earlier images to reaffirm his faith in the Revolution, his closeness to the people, and his belief in a better future. Forging a link between this poem and prior ones, the speaker asks, «¿Yo fui triste?». From the example of the common people —hardworking, rich in spirit, yet mustering a smile after a day of back-

---

[29] The earlier version of this poem is different. The second line was originally: «¡... tales rejas con flores!» (*España, pasión de vida* [Barcelona: Instituto de Estudios Hispánicos, 1954], p. 43).

breaking labor— the speaker feels hope, «un deber de alegría». His meetings with common folk are filled with brotherly love, and the certainty that love is the best motive for action —even necessary violence— in the age of man:

>   Nunca sueña quien ama, nunca
>   está solo. La pujanza es idéntica.
>   De la rosa ofrecida
>   al amor, a la piedra
>   fijada con amor, a las balas
>   hundidas y ensañadas
>   por amor, todo avanza
>   y edifica. ¡Despierta!

This saga of the proletarian march to social equality ends with the dawning of the new age as «la aurora iza su bandera rociada».

Modes of Protest

Many Spaniards felt intense disappointment over the refusal of the Allies to topple the Franco Dictatorship at the end of World War II. Their dismay was even greater because the Allies knew the Regime still meted out punishment for alleged war crimes, filling prisons with those who were spared execution. A palpable national mood of pessimism —aggravated by restricted civil liberties, a reduced standard of living compared to pre-1936 levels, and the unlikelihood of a prompt change— unified writers and readers and gave rise to the belief that in literature esthetic value should be subordinate to moral, social, and political values. Yet while writers were united ideologically *against* the Regime, they were not necessarily *for* any purpose other than an end to tyranny. Many who noted a correspondence between the Marxist view of society engaged in class struggle and the Spanish divided citizenry found the Socialist Realist method a useful guide to literary creation.[30] Socialist Realism became a means of taking a stand in opposition to the Franco dictatorship and all it represented. Informed readers knew that general words at the level of parable, allegory, or lament actually referred to Spain of the 1940s. Protest remained a constant among writers of the opposition despite censorship.

---

[30] Compare this observation by ROBERT L. HEILBRONER, *Marxism: For and Against* (New York: W. W. Norton and Co., 1980), p. 145): «... Marxism is the main revolutionary force in the world today, and thereby becomes the natural gravitational center for movements of all kinds that seek to remedy poverty and to express outrage at the manipulation of humanity. Thus, cultlike alienated groups, terrorist organizations, liberation armies and the like rally to the banner of Marxism and use its vocabulary to express their demands and aspirations. As with Christianity in its most zealous days, and for much the same reasons, «Marxism» has become entangled in some of the worst as well as some of the best of human activity.»

Where writers differed was not in whether the dictatorship ought to yield to a more democratic form of government, but in their literary approach toward protest.

The priority of ethical concerns, consequence of sociopolitical conditions, was agreed upon by writers and their intended readers. At the same time, readers often construed political protest in otherwise abstract poems. An example of a work influenced by this reading convention was José Luis Hidalgo's *Los muertos*.[31] The presence of death in the poems of this collection, according to an early review in *Espadaña,* was that of a familiar companion free of threatening or macabre aspects.[32] Yet the presence of this theme in the context of the postwar period along with information that the working title was «La llanura de los muertos» led more than one critic to consider *Los muertos* a commentary on deaths in the Civil War. Max Aub stated that Hidalgo's original intention was to write tragically and apocalyptically about those who died in the Civil War. For Aub, Hidalgo was typical of his generation — resigned to the defeat of the Civil War, yet hopeful for a victorious rebirth of freedom.[33] Another critic, Manuel Teira, reasoned that even if the work was not directly about the Civil War, it had been written in the shadow of national tragedy.[34] The lack of nonconformity in *Los muertos,* however, eliminates it from further consideration here as poetry of protest.

The attitude by which writers expressed protest varies. Without making rigorous divisions, which easily distort the way in which poets combined characteristics across divisional lines, the most frequent attitudes were those of denunciation, allusive irony, and lament.[35] In turn, these attitudes correspond to the techniques of Socialist Realism, moralist allegory, and elegy.

A single work that merits attention for its explicit protest and because it encompasses poems from all three categories is the *Antología cercada*.[36] Two hundred-fifty copies of this brief anthology, illustrated by portraits of its five poets, were printed. Most of the poems in this openly published volume are as frankly critical as those of De Nora's *Pueblo cautivo*. It bears other similar features worth noting. The title, *Antología cercada,*

---

[31] JOSÉ LUIS HIDALGO, *Obra poética completa*, María de Gracia Ifach, ed. (Santander: Institución Cultural de Cantabria, 1976), pp. 63-94.

[32] ANTONIO G. DE LAMA, «Poesía y verdad», *Espadaña*, No. 26 (n.d.).

[33] MAX AUB, *Una nueva poesía española (1950-1955)* (México: Imprenta Universitaria, 1957), pp. 42-45.

[34] MANUEL TEIRA, «El tiempo en *Los muertos*», *Peña Labra*, No. 2 (Winter 1971-1972), p. 8.

[35] These categories match Lechner's, with one exception, «poesía esperanzada» used exclusively for Aleixandre. See: LECHNER, *El compromiso en la poesía española del siglo XX. Parte segunda*, p. 112.

[36] *Antología cercada* (Las Palmas de Gran Canaria: El Arca, 1947). Page references appear in the text, preceded by AC.

with its reference to siege, parallels De Nora's reference to captivity; it addresses protest to foreigners as well as Spaniards; and it situates itself at the confluence of poetry of the French resistance and of the Civil War. Despite these facts, the anthology awoke little overt interest in Spain, although reception was probably not as limited as the small amount of published commentary suggests, in view of the threats of censorship.

The anthology's socio-political implications were recognized by its *Insula* reviewer, who mentioned the influence of certain French surrealists such as Louis Aragon.[37] The work's significance also was recognized in Mexico in an essay of homage on the occasion of its tenth anniversary.[38] In his appreciative article, Gabriel García Narezo related the anthology to its historical context and emphasized that it was in the forefront of the resistance. At the same time, Max Aub praised the poetry of Agustín and José María Millares Sall for «su santo y su seña, su hoz y su martillo», noting that the former poet showed the patriotic influence of Aragon, the latter, that of Neruda.[39]

One device to guide interpretation is a carefully chosen epigraph indicating the provenance of a central image, thesis, model, or other characteristic. The epigraph's reference to a particular tradition, not necessarily literary, is an important contextual element of the optimal reading. Another device serving the same purpose is an introduction orienting readers.

Both of these devices were used in the *Antología cercada*. Agustín Millares Sall heads the two parts of «El martillo del minuto» with significant epigraphs. The first, by Aragon, is an unequivocal blow for freedom and, by implication, against the Franco Dictatorship:

> Une chanson jamais chantée
> Le vin nouveau de la justice
> Et le sang de la liberté (AC, 7).

The second, by Rafael Alberti, refers to the outcome of the Civil War:

> Ese minuto fue el de las balas perdidas,
> el del secuestro, por el mar, de los hombres
> que quisieron ser pájaros. (AC, 12)

Ventura Doreste, contributor to *Insula* and *Espadaña*, wrote the preface to Agustín Millares Sall's *El grito en el cielo,* identifying the author as a *poeta civil* whose imprecatory tone aspired to unanimity at a time

---

[37] G[ERMÁN] B[LEIBERG], Review of *Antología cercada, Insula,* No. 22 (15 October 1947), p. 5.
[38] GABRIEL GARCÍA NAREZO, «*La antología cercada*. Primer aliento del verdadero renacer poético español», *Novedades,* Suplemento literario del domingo, 17 March 1957.
[39] AUB, *Una nueva poesía española,* pp. 108-11.

when lyric poets engrossed in individual vicissitudes were superfluous.[40] Doreste added a pair of quotations: one from Paul Eluard, another from Pierre Emmanuel, holding that poetry of resistance is an offensive for freedom, creating the conditions for a *prise de conscience*. Doreste also wrote the preface to *Canto a la tierra* by José María Millares Sall, a poem in four parts addressed to a personified Spain. The speaker, like that of *España, pasión de vida*, dedicates himself to the land:[41]

> cantando siempre vida hasta la muerte,
> cantando siempre amor para la tierra,
> para ser como un pájaro de fuego,
> anunciando la aurora de tu carne.

Doreste placed this poetry with that of Miguel Hernández, inspired by enthusiasm and hope.[42] The external information in epigraphs and prefaces leads readers to expect political protest.

Focusing upon the effects of oppression, «El martillo del minuto» begins with the speaker's report of anguish, followed by his realization that the anguish is due to historical causes, and ends with his commitment to social change as the proper solution. The various moments of the poem are a meditation on worldwide disintegration that leaves behind fear, mourning, and silence; an allegory based on the *topos* of the world upside-down to refer to the bitter panorama of Spain; a confession by the despairing speaker because his protests meet silence; and finally, an appeal to a foreign audience. In this plea for foreign solidarity, the speaker repeats «*decidme*» with pathos:

> Decidme que hay un pueblo que respira
> y canta más allá de la frontera.
> ... ...
> Decidme que, algún día, el aire puro
> habrá de cancelar tanta miseria.
> Decidme que el amor será la arteria
> de los pasos del hombre en el futuro. (AC, 13-14)

The meditative soliloquy of the first part, becomes in the second part, an address to «Hombres... al lado opuesto» (AC, 13), sympathizers on the other side of the border who might answer the pleas. In the closing lines the speaker vows to reach the corners of the earth: «... la última palabra habrán de oirla, / de mis labios, los ámbitos del mundo» (AC, 14). The latter poem denounces the Regime's corruption by taking a general

---

[40] AGUSTÍN MILLARES SALL, *El grito en el cielo* (Las Palmas de Gran Canaria: Cuadernos de Poesía y Crítica, 1946), p. 5.
[41] JOSÉ MARÍA MILLARES SALL, *El canto a la tierra* (Las Palmas de Gran Canaria: Cuadernos de poesía y Crítica, 1946), p. 18.
[42] *Ibid.*, pp. 5-6.

view. «Labios de acero» by José María Millares Sall protests the unjust execution of a prisoner whose crime was:

> ... defender un sol de causas con sus labios
> de fecundos principios para el hombre,
> la tierra repartida por iguales cosechas,
> los frutos despojados de únicas cortezas,
> por ciudades de luces y apagados infiernos,
> por viñas de esplendores para el alma. (AC, 40)

Like Crémer's «Fábula de B.D.», this poem depends for its energetic effect upon a lexicon of violent terms, rhythmic meters, balladic narrative, and metaphors by which objects are animated and persons dehumanized. Socialist Realist because they present a partial view of reality, these poems are less militant than many by De Nora and are, rather, sentimental appeals.

Before turning to the category of moralist allegory, it is worth remembering that, besides De Nora and the Millares Salls, other poets such as Concha Zardoya and José Luis Gallego wrote denunciatory protest, but encountered restrictions so their work was delayed in reaching the public.

Concha Zardoya, who published her own poetry in the Adonais collection, as well as translations of Walt Whitman during the 1940s, wrote poems of protest during the first two postwar decades, and published them in Buenos Aires.[43] Some later poems are critical of Franco and the Regime, while her earliest poems are of particular interest, because they expand the tradition initiated by Neruda and Hernández.[44] Under the subtitle «En las sombras acechan», Zardoya grouped ten poems: Three evoke the sterility of postwar Spain, four lament the misfortune of the orphaned, poor, imprisoned, and condemned, two deal specifically with the custom of *pasearse* —unannounced detentions and executions carried out at night—, and the last affirms solidarity and the desire for freedom. Other features of this collection, such as the «Nanas españolas» and the «Cancionerillo de la ausencia», place it within the poetry of resistance.

Just as provocative as Zardoya's poetry, *Prometeo XX* by José Luis Gallego was known only to a group of friends until finally published two decades after it was written.[45] The work is composed of twenty-three sonnets interrupted halfway by a long poem in the form of a sonata. This work refers to the first decade of the author's imprisonment as a result of Civil War activities. Second only to Blas de Otero in imaginative cultivation of the sonnet, Gallego proclaims the horror of imprisonment, con-

---

[43] CONCHA ZARDOYA, *Corral de vivos y muertos* (Buenos Aires: Losada, 1965).
[44] *Ibid.*, p. 21: «Los poemas de esta sección fueron escritos entre los años 1939 y 1947, en Madrid. Algunos formaban parte del libro *Dominio del llanto* (Madrid: Adonais, 1947), del cual fueron suprimidos por obvias razones de censura.»
[45] JOSÉ LUIS GALLEGO, *Prometeo XX* (Barcelona: El Bardo, 1970).

trasting a «here», the prison, with a «there», life in the outside world. Denunciation in the poems is intensified by pathos, which the speaker evokes as he develops themes of separation, physical deprivation and decline, and despair.

Allegory, found in the second category of protest poems, is a technique by which a text refers simultaneously to itself as fable and to a set of events or ideas that are its narrative or referential basis. The tone of allegory tends to be serious when the emphasis is on moral issues, satiric when on historical or political events. The presence of allegory in a text prescribes the direction a reading is to follow. This principle is useful to writers under censorship, because it allows them to refer to a known historical situation without actually naming it. Many who wrote and published within Spain encoded their protests as did De Nora, or employed allegory, as did Agustín Millares Sall in *El grito en el cielo*. In this example, Millares Sall criticizes the Regime, chooses Socialist Realism as his literary method, and promises to support the Revolution:[46]

> Quiero asaltar la oculta fortaleza
> que edificó lo que no tiene nombre
> en el triste solar de la pobreza;
> quiero salvarme, liberando al hombre
> ... ...
> Mi puesto está aquí abajo, y no en la luna,
> empeñado en la lucha y siempre activo.

To untangle the signs in these lines, the reader recalls Doreste's introductory remarks discussed above, naming Millares Sall a civic poet. Such information invites a search for political meaning in the poem. Once the reader is prepared to find an allegory with a narrative basis, identifying the allegorical words is simpler. Thus if the «hidden fortress» stands for the Regime, it «has no name» because to write its name would be prohibited, and the «sad ancestral home of poverty» is Spain. The speaker indicates his political commitment by using a religious term «*salvar*». He uses «*hombre*», not to mean the human race, but rather those oppressed by the Dictatorship. The contrast between «*aquí abajo*» and «*luna*» refers to the polemic over Socialist Realism and pure poetry, the former being the speaker's preference. By extension, it refers also to their related ideologies, with Marxism the speaker's choice.

In the *Antología cercada* the poets who use political allegory most are Doreste and Pedro Lezcano. The unwary reader might name the Far East as the setting of Doreste's «Un puerto del Oriente» (AC, 23-25). The informed reader, remembering the title of the anthology, expects it is Spain. This critique of bourgeois capitalism —«Reina invisible y dura:

---

[46] AGUSTÍN MILLARES SALL, *El grito en el cielo*, pp. 11, 13.

el Capital»— may be read as a protest of Far Eastern exploitation based on the poem's assertions: Men do not live by rice alone, they should not live like beasts of burden, and capitalism brutalizes workers by breeding in them envy and the desire for vengeance. Or it also may be read as a Marxist condemnation of the corruption of capitalism. However, read as protest of the Franco Dictatorship, it refers to the Regime's exploitation of workers and political prisoners and moral degeneracy at its highest echelons. Like the final poem of *Pueblo cautivo,* Doreste's «Las dos ciudades» (AC, 28-30) compares a present city with a future one. The two names are plainly allegorical: Sodoma and Libertad. City of the present, Sodoma nurtures violence, exploitation, and treason, but: «Sodoma morirá bajo la llama.» Libertad, a Socialist Realist Arcadia, will have eternal springtime, abundant rivers, innocent maids, and youths as strong as bulls; its cost will be the blood of the wicked, the tireless effort of the virtuous:

> Ven a nosotros, ven, como paloma
> que viene de la altura más hermosa.
> Ven ciudad, con el verbo que enamora.
>
> Y besarán tus pies los libres mares.
> Te regará, libérrima, la sangre,
> oh ciudad de los hombres incansables.

This combination of Biblical tradition and Marxist ameliorism is linked to Spain of the 1940s: «Que Sodoma es el mundo de este tiempo / donde imperan la fuerza y el lamento, / donde la libertad vive entre fuegos.» The explicit connection between the topic of «Guerra en la paz» (AC, 26-27) and Spanish reality is based on the Regime's propaganda that the postwar period is an era of peace. The title therefore invites the reader to think that the declaration of victory in 1939 did not stop conflict but only suppressed it. The poem then condemns Franco's *pax romana,* rather than the perfidy of the human race. Spain's fratricidal strife is the context of this apparently general criticism:

> Donde la sangre cálida se hiela;
> donde no reconoce el hijo al padre;
> donde son los hermanos enemigos
> y Dios casi se olvida de sí mismo;
> son ya los hombres lobos de los hombres.

The same reading procedure, alert to the presence of allegory, enhances the meaning of «Edicto» (AC, 19-20) by Pedro Lezcano. The speaker's irony is not obvious in this poem resembling a proclamation until this unexpectedly exaggerated order —«Queda prohibido terminantemente / morir en calles céntricas.» Without alluding to Spain of the Regime, Lezcano satirizes the mask of serenity to be worn in public and assigns sentiment and passion to a private, tormented realm:

> Cuando, al edicto de la noche, alumbren
> simultáneas estrellas,
> llorad, amad, sufrid, matad acaso,
> calladamente y en tinieblas.
> ... ...
> pisotead los códigos civiles,
> desnudaros de telas.
> Pero al regreso de la luz se exige
> vuestra antifaz, vuestra antialma puesta.

The mention of codes governing citizens' rights, the insinuation of hypocrisy in the word *«antifaz»* and in the neologism *«antialma»* added to a later ban on inopportune dreams and even *«la primavera»* (which in this context carries the meaning of rebirth) build to the climax: an apostrophe to death. By the conclusion of the poem, the overstatements reveal Lezcano's intent to the most unwary reader.

Those accustomed to recognizing allegory in these poems need fewer hints concerning the referential basis. The prevalent view that Franco's triumph interrupted the transition to a more just social order is a message in many allegorical poems of the 1940s, such as that of Gabino-Alejandro Carriedo's *Poema de la condenación de Castilla*.[47] Carriedo combines allegory with elegy to personify Castilla and lament her demise. With language more indirect than De Nora's and with greater pessimism, Carriedo creates a similarly pathetic figure to stand for the other Spain. Without expectation of a better future, the speaker claims that the end of progressive culture in Spain was the end of her history:

> Ya se agotó tu sangre, ya no alienta
> la savia del pensar en tus raíces
> comidas por el topo del suceso
> irrefrenable y del pasar fatídico.
> Ya se acabó tu historia...

Changing civil for religious lexicons, Carriedo implies that Castilla is no longer a symbol of freedom for a new age, but rather a mourning, excommunicated heterodox:

> Castilla excomulgada, estéril, seca
> como estatua de sal, como una madre
> sin fértil alentar, sin el espasmo
> doloroso y feliz de un parto nuevo

---

[47] Examples are from Lechner, who interprets Castilla more narrowly as symbol of the people living there. See: LECHNER, *El compromiso en la poesía española del siglo XX. Parte segunda*, pp. 61-62.

> de extraña madurez y fallecida
> ya en cada herida vieja, ya en el sordo
> recuerdo aterrador, miseria y luto.

The third category of protest, elegaic poetry, is usually a contemplation of life's tragic aspects, receiving consolation in the form of some general principle in action. It contrasts with Socialist Realist poetry in its attitude of sorrowful resignation rather than commitment to action. Yet the elegy too may carry political overtones, expressing opposition to the Regime through despair, while official propaganda optimistically presents the Regime as guardian of tradition, foe of liberalism and Communism. The revival of the elegy began during the Civil War. Two early examples are Rafael Alberti's «Madrid-Otoño» and «El otoño y el Ebro».[48] The first poem, a contemplation of the «Capital de la gloria», its ruined building awash in autumn leaves, ends hopefully as the speaker announces the birth of a more beautiful future, in victory. His second poem comments sadly on the duration of the war as fall passes into winter. The speaker compares the firm resistance of naked trees to that of the soldiers: All await spring to flourish again.

Spreading through the poetry of the 1940s, autumnal themes natural to the elegaic attitude seemed to mirror the tragedy of somber times. In a study of De Nora's poetry, Manuel Mantero called attention to the former's «Otoño», how its questions and doubts portrayed terrible despair, lack of faith.[49] Then, with brief illustrative quotations, he held that this was one of the distinctive notes also in poems by José Hierro, Vicente Gaos, Blas de Otero, Leopoldo de Luis, José Luis Cano, and José García Nieto. The way in which poets employed elegaic themes varied. In De Nora's case, the poetic outlook of despair had its sociopolitical origin in the failure of the resistance movement. In the case of others, despair was associated with the tragedy of man's mortality and therefore was tempered by a stoic acceptance of a universal principle. A third group of poets presented the reality of personal wartime suffering through a distancing elegaic attitude, not protest in the Socialist Realist sense, but rather testimony to irreparable loss.

The last poet of the *Antología cercada,* Angel Johan, deceptively suggested optimism with the title «La eterna canción» (AC, 33-35). Divided into two parts by a change from past tense to present, the poem also changes topic from war's tumult to universal rebirth. After lamenting the war, the speaker describes a period of personal anguish, haunted by silence, hunger, and hatred, sentiments that found their reflection in

---

[48] RAFAEL ALBERTI, *El poeta en la calle,* pp. 67-68, 85.
[49] MANUEL MANTERO, *Poesía española contemporánea: Estudio y antología (1939-1965)* (Barcelona: Plaza y Janés, 1966), pp. 151-55.

barren plateaus and windless seas under a starless sky. Then, suggesting that an eternal process rules human affairs, the speaker describes a world of joyful harmony. Only the last lines of the poem tell the reader that this has been a dream, not reality: «(¡Si fuera todo siempre luz y siempre / mediodía feliz y venturoso!...)»

Also influenced by Spain's tragedy to write elegaic verse, Ildefonso-Manuel Gil declared his mission of remembrance, anguish, and sorrow in «Poética» from *Penas de dolor antiguo*:[50]

> En mi voz, al hablaros,
> carga el dolor la fuerza de su acento,
> y sólo he de dejaros
> esta angustia que siento
> en ritmo entrecortado de lamento.
> ... ...
> Mi verso es así el grito
> que en la más honda entraña me ha brotado.
> Más que en frío granito,
> quiero el nombre grabado
> al pie de un verso en sangre sustentado.

The most characteristic section of the work, «Elegías», includes four elegies, three with dedications: «A mi madre», «Al poeta Miguel Hernández», «Al soldado desconocido». Occasionally events such as war-related imprisonment justify the speaker's sorrow. In the consolatory «Afirmación de la primavera» (PD, 51-53) spring, symbol of rebirth and healing forgetfulness, lessens the burden of sorrow as enjoyment returns. A notable exception to Gil's preference for the elegaic mode is «Los fusilamientos de la Moncloa».[51] Obsessed by Goya's portrayal of the 1808 Spanish rebellion during the French occupation, the speaker vows to turn the painter's visual message into words. For the reader recalling the Civil War, the speaker's version of Goya's message has a double meaning:

> ésta es la muerte vil de los caminos
> cuyos pasos se acercan uno a uno,
> hembra mala de noches sin aurora,
> nodriza del espanto, hija del crimen.

Veiled criticism is subtler in Germán Bleiberg's elegaic poetry of the 1940s, «Trece poemas breves» for instance, in which the speaker's sentiments and the impersonal natural world are bonded by nostalgia.[52] In

---

[50] ILDEFONSO-MANUEL GIL, *Poemas de dolor antiguo* (Madrid: Editorial Hispánica, 1945), pp. 69-70; further pages to this edition are cited in the text, preceded by PD. For a critical study, see: ROSARIO HIRIART, *Un poeta en el tiempo: Ildefonso-Manuel Gil* (Zaragoza: Diputación Provincial, 1981).

[51] ILDEFONSO-MANUEL GIL, «Los fusilamientos de la Moncloa», *Homenaje a Goya (poemas)* (Zaragoza: Ediciones del Pórtico, 1946), pp. 9-12.

[52] GERMÁN BLEIBERG, *Selección de poemas 1936-1973* (London: Grant and Cut-

«Elegía de las hojas otoñales» (SP, 31-34), the speaker seeks a sign of rebirth in autumn leaves and in tombs, legacy of national strife:

> ¿Quién se atrevería a oponer la mirada al destino?
> ¡Que se oculte la mirada en el fondo de los lentos sepulcros,
> donde germina la semilla de la historia!

In this meditation on the past, certain passages invite discovery of a motive for nostalgia and despair more profound than mere personal misfortune. Susceptible to allegorical reading are «*primavera*», season when the war ended, «*violeta*», flower of remembrance, «*aurora*», the Revolution, terms that indicate the speaker's commitment during the Civil War and the postwar consequences:

> ¿Qué pensaréis de mí, hojas muertas,
> al saber que la primavera me ha negado una violeta sencilla?
> Permanece en la nocturna ascensión del deseo
> esa perezosa nostalgia de la aurora.

Another passage using a natural lexicon can be read as an allegory condemning war's victors:

> Pero surgen los jardineros fingidos,
> que no saben regar el césped con agua descendida de los montes,
> sino que siembran de muros la vida y la belleza,
> para asegurar en sus hogares la fugitiva llama del logro.

Conceptually the passage stands out from the rest of the poem. Though the gardeners are unnamed, they are obviously agents of divisiveness in pursuit of personal glory; and in the context of the poetry of resistance their identity is clear.

A fourth category of poetry, taking shape at the end of the decade is what might be called documental poetry. Victoriano Crémer, in a new stylistic period, was perhaps the initiator.[53] His inaugural work was *Nuevos cantos de vida y esperanza,* taking its title from Darío; homogenous in tone and subject, its speaker confirms solidarity with his working-class neighbors of the Puerta-Moneda district of León.[54] The speaker of

---

ler, 1975), pp. 24-30. Additional references to this edition appear in the text, preceded by SP.

[53] Opinion is divided on this point. Crémer said that the publication of his two previous works ended a cycle; see: SERGIO MORATIEL, *La poesía en acción de Victoriano Crémer* (León: Imprenta Diocesana, 1973), p. 38. De la Concha believes Crémer's poetry developed concentrically around the same static reality, rather than in lineal progression. See: *La poesía española de posguerra* (Madrid: Prensa Española, 1973), p. 393.

[54] VICTORIANO CRÉMER, *Nuevos cantos de vida y esperanza* (Barcelona: Instituto de Estudios Hispánicos, 1952). Page references in text are to this edition, if preceded by NC or to *Poesía total (1944-1966)* (Barcelona: Plaza y Janés, 1970), if preceded by PT.

«Regreso» explores motives for his feeling of community by reviewing what he values in his humble neighborhood. With semi-religious awe he mentions quiet evening streets, a convivial cup, simple adobe walls. Among his own people he finds spiritual renewal:

> Aquí contemplo vida...
> ... ... Siento
> que soy un hombre más entre los hombres.
>
> ... ...
> Frío tengo en el alma, pero canto,
> ahora que estoy aquí de nuevo y veo
> tanto gozo y dolor, tanta miseria
> y tan clara esperanza compartida. (NC, 42)

«Nana del hijo» (PT, 152-59) seems a fanciful lullaby until the speaker reveals that the child he addresses was born in poverty and silence «como nacen los perros, / sobre unos trapos viejos o unas pajas podridas». Then, lest the child one day reproach him, he turns from illusion to reality to be truthful with the child: «Por eso yo no debo cantar ni inventar nada, / sino decirte cosas / del mundo que vivimos; / cosas desnudas como el aire.» The reality he presents includes death and the exploitation of laborers: «millones de hombres escupen los pulmones por la boca.» The values of Love and Beauty, prized by the bourgeoisie, are dangerous deceptions for a member of the working class. Furthermore, the speaker warns of a cataclysmic social change threatening European civilization. This message, however, takes a decidedly un-Marxist view of the revolutionary masses; instead of militant proletarians they are patient ants:

> algo sucede lejos...
> ... ...
> Sucede que ya Europa es un ídolo viejo
> rodeado de muertos;
> como una larva inmóvil, arrastrada
> por pacientes hormigas.

Beyond continental Europe mass movements for economic justice answer a clarion of new beliefs to mobilize but Crémer neither gives a Marxist countersign nor tries to convert his listener. His social philosophy takes second place to exotic images:

> con bocas de sequía, avanzan multitudes
> obstinadas.

The provisional title «Cancionero de Puerta-Moneda» was used when «El Pipa» appeared in *Espadaña*, No. 44 (n.d.). Other poems with prior publication are «Niebla», *Espadaña*, No. 42 (1949); «Niños», before revision, called «Futuro», *Espadaña*, No. 46 (1950); «Friso con obreros», *Laye*, No. 15 (September-October 1951); and «Regreso», *Espadaña*, No. 48 (1950).

> Ya el desnudo indonesio,
> con sabor de raíz submarina y mirada de almendra,
> quiere gozar los frutos de la tierra que labra,
> y endereza los humos de sus nuevos altares.
>
> ¿Qué campana convoca
> los relucientes ojos del Camerún, de Libia,
> de Angola o de Rodesia
> en los fértiles valles del tigre y gacela?

Converting the experiences of the poor into words, the speaker affirms his own existence and that of his fellow man. His mission of portraying reality instead of illusion is a moral obligation in the name of life:

> Si mi voz no existiera, tu luz se desharía
> en este oculto cielo de la alcoba.
> Por eso te retengo y te hablo...

This mission, declared in the work's final poem, ethically justifies the rest of the work as a compassionate view of the working class.

Crémer rescues individuals from forgetfulness, portraying them in words they lack to present themselves. «Dulce amor» (PT, 145-47) contrasts the bourgeois and working-class worlds, charitable intentions and gestures versus rounds of hurried, silent meals of dark bread, overburdened wives and men working long hours then raucously drinking at night. As the speaker shows, this life is the opposite of bourgeois domesticity with its nightly gatherings, children reading quietly and parents listening to the radio. Crémer shows the way money determines way of life without making it a pretext for the Marxist message, which he dislikes for its emphasis on political domination.[55]

Crémer believes that labor is man's authentic relation to the world, a view propagated earlier by Arturo Serrano Plaja, particularly in the poem «Estos son los oficios».[57] In this view, the work ethic is the way to a better future; and workers, indispensible members of any society, have the power to lead the way.[57] Clothed in blue they pour into the dawn

---

[55] Compare CRÉMER's statements in «Esquema para un cuadro sinóptico sobre poesía y trabajo», *Poesía Española*, No. 8 (August 1952), p. 3: «En ningún momento aparece inserto el espíritu verdadero del trabajo en nuestra Poesía. Cuando más se la aproxima es con estrepitoso rechinamiento político... Existe un momento en nuestra Literatura en que el concepto del trabajador se mixtifica grotescamente: es el triunfo de lo que se dio en llamar literatura social...»

[56] ALICIA M. RAFFUCCI DE LOCKWOOD, *Cuatro poetas de la «Generación del 36»* (Universidad de Puerto Rico: Colección UPREX, 1974), pp. 89, 91.

[57] Compare CRÉMER's commentary on «Friso con obreros», in «El trabajo y la poesía (Esquema para un Estudio)», *Humanidades*, 2, No. 2 (July-December 1960), p. 387: «Es que hemos llegado al momento en que el trabajo ha dejado de ser ornamento lírico, para convertirse en sustancia humana. Es que, de pronto, los poetas han descubierto que el trabajo tiene una intimidad superior a la del temblor de los astros. Es que, al fin, ha sido percibido el latido verdadero del mundo.»

Relevant to this observation is the following statement from C.B., Review of

streets on their way to mines and construction sites like a surging river in «Friso con obreros» (PT, 144-45):

> Son —desteñido azul— agua profunda,
> río de frescas márgenes que busca
> su mar de cal y de ladrillo, su hondo
> pozo mineral que hierve y canta.

«Soportando futuro a las espaldas», they neither look to a vanguard for leadership nor claim to possess a unique moral sensibility. They dispense with small talk, are oblivious to the beautiful gardens and parks they pass; absorbed in their own survival, they plod known paths like oxen:

> Si quisieran gritar, lo harían, porque
> no están muertos, conocen la palabra
> que sólo se pronuncia desde el sueño
> y es como un toro, violenta y ácida.

The remaining poems of the collection are lyric sketches of tenacious characters who contradict stereotypes of *pueblo*. Crémer focuses on their everyday life, catching unique visions and desires, showing the variation that terms like proletariat hide.

Espadaña, which began and ended amid controversy, documented the polemic over commitment. After attacks on *garcilasismo, Espadaña* criticized complacent moral drift that encouraged an attitude of provisionality, a view that Spain was in a temporal hiatus.[58] To *Espadaña* this seemed a cowardly retreat from moral duty since the «provisional situation» was already an institution. Rather, the situation demanded that people take one of two positions: «perfeccionarse en *valor* o acrecentarse en *eficacia:* hombres éticos u hombres políticos». The publication also took issue with complacency in the literary world, where any poem or opinion was blandly received, whether provocative or not.[59] An excess of «good taste» was a breeding ground for innocuous verse and opinion that smothered valuable work. *Espadaña* wanted controversies in which genuine criticism occurred; polemics, concluded the publication, were signs of life, interest, enthusiasm, and creativity.

Alluding elsewhere to the question of commitment, De Nora wrote

---

Nuevos cantos de vida y esperanza by VICTORIANO CRÉMER, *Laye,* No. 19 (May-July 1952), p. 72: «A menudo el adjetivo *social* califica a... cualquier tipo de manifestación con resonancias en lo colectivo; poesía de programa, de arenga, de sujeto plural —el nosotros o vosotros de tantos poemas contemporáneos— o de simple vivencia mayoritaria... Pero el término social tiene un sentido, un carácter impreso por el uso histórico-político que de él se viene haciendo durante un siglo que recorta un valor significativo en el léxico de todos. En ese sentido se puede decir precisamente de la poesía de Victoriano Crémer que tiene un contenido social.»

[58] «Poesía y vida: Situación provisional», *Espadaña,* No. 33 (1948).
[59] «Blandura», *Espadaña,* No. 40 (1949).

of poetry vacilating at a crossroads, not of different styles but of how to express a «chaotic» reality.[60] This crisis of commitment of course was between two outlooks, both favoring social justice and democracy while differing on the issue of Marxist commitment. De Nora submitted an open letter to *Espadaña,* sparking the publication's final burst of polemic.[61] In the battle between ethically persuaded intellectuals and politically committed Marxists, De Nora sided with the latter. In his letter he analyzed *Espadaña,* No. 45, according to Marxist procedures, sorting items for approval and censure. He liked the inclusion of Vallejo's «Masa» and Figuera's poems, was glad that Otero's *Angel fieramente humano* was reviewed, but thought the poet of Bilbao deserved higher praise. By contrast, he objected to Pemán's «Presencia de Dios» and Anglada's article, which belonged in a humor magazine. Furthermore, he disputed the claim that *Espadaña* was addressed to all social classes, challenging Crémer and De Lama to a showdown:

> ... si Vds. quieren hacer una poesía, una literatura humana, eficaz y popular... Habrán de no olvidar que los posibles lectores, público o pueblo, están divididos en clases de ideas, gustos, intereses y concepciones de la vida divergentes u opuestos, y que es preciso decidirse por unos o por otros (en el caso de que su mismo ser y personalidad no los haya situado ya de hecho, previamente a toda decisión).

Espadaña was not destined to emulate the PCE's *Nuestra Bandera.* De Lama clarified that dialogue supposed agreement over premises that would take the matter from the realm of poetry into such areas as philosophy, sociology, and politics, turning *Espadaña* into a political or ideological publication at the sacrifice of poetry.[62] De Nora's challenge, later regretted publicly, led to a decision by De Lama, Crémer, and Castro Ovejero to suspend publication indefinitely.[63]

---

[60] EUGENIO DE NORA, «Machado ante el futuro de la poesía lírica», *Cuadernos Hispanoamericanos,* No. 11-12 (September-December 1949), p. 583.

[61] JUAN MARTÍNEZ, pseud., «Poesía y verdad. Carta abierta a Victoriano Crémer», *Espadaña,* No. 46 (n.d.).

[62] ANTONIO G. DE LAMA, «Sobre una carta», *Espadaña,* No. 47 (1950). JOSÉ ANGEL VALENTE, «Poesía para el pueblo», *Cuadernos Hispanoamericanos,* No. 18 (November-December 1950), pp. 471-72, made a representative statement concerning the social function of poetry that unconditionally rejects De Nora's belief in poetry as an instrument of direct social change as misguided.

[63] Other accounts of this polemic are in: FANNY RUBIO, *Las revistas poéticas españolas* (Madrid: Turner, 1976), pp. 270-71; LECHNER, *El compromiso en la poesía española del siglo XX. Parte segunda,* pp. 51-52; VICTORIANO CRÉMER, «Para una biografía de *Espadaña*», *Peña Labra,* No. 14 (Winter 1974-1975), pp. 2-6. De Nora attributed the suspension of publication to difficulties with censorship over texts by Neruda, Otero, and himself in: «Eugenio de Nora desvela todos los secretos de la discutida revista leonesa», *Diario de León,* 12 October 1973, pp. 20-21. An article in Crémer's short-lived *Espadaña II,* «Revista de la Vida Leonesa», cited by MORATIEL, *La poesía en acción,* pp. 39-40, seems to blame vested personal interests in the literary world for *Espadaña*'s demise: «Existen actualmente en España

THE POETRY OF PROTEST UNDER FRANCO

To writers in Madrid, the episode between De Nora and *Espadaña* seemed to test the issue of commitment. Disturbed by what he considered a «vogue», José Luis Cano informed readers nation-wide that commitment meant imposing themes upon the poet, giving him a direction to follow, making him write with a purpose in mind, in short: «poniendo la poesía *al servicio de*».[64] Cano's preferred view was that of poetry as unconditioned by outside control, heeding only the poet's own sentiment, passion, solitude, or dream. In principle, he said, he was not against any poetry, whether popular, social, or patriotic, but believed the likely outcome of this challenge would be a hasty retreat to the ivory tower by poets who would write only for themselves.

The poetry of resistance no longer was a common literary front against the Regime; Socialist Realist poetry —against the Regime but for the Revolution— gained momentum.[65] The code words of *existencialista* and *tremendista* ceded to *social* and *engagé*, indicating a new perception of poetry of protest. The former terms stressed the role of the poet as an individual, the latter emphasized the role of the poet as part of a collective with obligations and loyalties. While writers of humanist persuasion shared some goals with Marxists, they became uneasy when forced to take a political stand. Ramón de Garciasol, for example, colorfully rejected the Marxist challenge:[66]

> ... nuestra poesía ha de ser agoniosa, luchadora, cordial y al servicio del hombre que no se resigna a volver a lo cuadrúpedo, a castrarse la voz y a mover el rabo a golpe de consignas, abdicando de eso que define la virilidad...

—quizá con mayor fuerza de intereses que nunca— núcleos de definidores, interesados en eliminar del ámbito literario toda competencia. Es una especie de mercado negro que lucha con toda la ventaja de su posición de privilegio, aunque con el grandísimo inconveniente para el futuro de su gran manifiesto.

Para imponer sus productos utilizan el medio desleal de las definiciones anticipadas, de los peligrosos encuadramientos. No les basta su posición de monopolizadores de premios, categorías, distinciones y otras públicas zarandajas. Necesitan quedarse solos y no para entendérselas cara a cara con el gran toro literario, sino para que no exista ni la más remota posibilidad de que cualquier subalterno pueda pisarles el terreno.»

[64] JOSÉ LUIS CANO, «Poesía y polémica», *Correo literario*, 2, No. 16 (15 January 1951), p. 3.

[65] Commenting on the new taste, CHARLES DAVID LEY wrote, in *Spanish Poetry since 1939*, p. 109: «That more than half the poets included should be definitely left-wing, makes the book [*Antología consultada*] partly political. which may have been what the editor intended. In the years immediately after the Civil War, writers who actively supported the regime were in the ascendent, and this unfortunately resulted in certain poets coming to the fore whose political prestige was greater than their poetic gifts. By 1951 the situation was almost reversed. It had become fashionable to admire poets who, though living and working in Spain, were professedly of the left in ideas. The poems they published referred fairly openly to their political ideas and yet passed the censorship; this would not have happened if they had written in prose.»

[66] J. L. G., «En torno a la poesía social», *Ambito*, No. 2 (1951), p. 15.

In a similar vein, Leopoldo de Luis upheld the value of poetry directed toward others as emergency poetry without a program, necessary poetry addressed to mankind:[67]

> ... quiero hacer una poesía *necesaria*. Una poesía de cura de urgencia. Sobre la marcha. Porque el destino que cumplimos inexorablemente, es el de caminar. Homo viator. Pretendo escribir cumpliendo un deber de fidelidad íntima y de fidelidad a lugar y tiempo... Sin llegar a defender lo que generalmente se entiende por «poesía social», la vida del momento en que el poeta habla, exige que su poesía sea eficazmente intercomunicación.

Marxists, on the other hand, reasoned that the more entrenched the Franco dictatorship became, the more aggressive their posture had to be in response, particularly since Franco sought international respect and investments to develop Spanish trade and industry. The Marxists wanted to prove that the intellectual opposition was not as ineffectual as the *Caudillo* assumed.

These circumstances transformed the publication of a modest anthology into a cause generating charges of partiality. Francisco Ribes, editor of the *Antología consultada,* planned to correct a distorted image of Spanish poetry nurtured by the Regime's publications and awards.[68] Thus he polled sixty knowledgeable people, listed in the anthology, to discover whom they judged the ten best poets emerging in the postwar period.[69] He excluded from consideration poets who were deceased or who were known before the Civil War. This meant the omission of Miguel Hernández, José Luis Hidalgo, Dionisio Ridruejo, Leopoldo Panero, Luis Rosales, and Carmen Conde. As a result, De Nora, Otero, Celaya, and Crémer were prominent and the absence of José García Nieto was obvious. Nevertheless, the term «known» was flexible. Panero did not published a book until after the war and Ridruejo's work *Plural,* though published earlier, was completely unnoticed. On the other hand, Crémer supposedly published *Tendiendo el vuelo* in 1928 and Celaya published *Marea de silencio* in 1935 under his legal name Rafael Múgica.

Perhaps misunderstandings concerning the *Antología consultada* were

---

[67] Leopoldo de Luis, «Una poesía de cura de urgencia», *Correo Literario,* 2, No. 25 (1 June 1951), p. 13.

[68] Francisco Ribes, ed., *Antología consultada de la joven poesía española* (Santander: Hermanos Bedia, 1952).

[69] Speculative discussion of Ribes' procedures began before the anthology was compiled. Compare the following from Joaquín Zuñica, «A cada cual lo suyo», *Ambito,* No. 2 (1951), pp. 19-20: «Este nuevo —y al parecer sensato— editor, pretende realizar una especie de antología con referéndum... ¿Existirá, sin embargo y a pesar de todo, cierta unanimidad en la elección de esos diez poetas? ¿Y por qué diez y no cinco o veinte?... Otra cuestión que inevitablemente se nos plantea es la de si entre los diez mejores líricos de la posguerra puede incluirse a Carmen Conde, pongo por ejemplo de figura dada a conocer, como tal figura, en este período, pero ya con obra publicada antes del 36.»

inevitable. The issue was more fundamental than whether the selection of poets was representative, it centered on the relationship between poetry and reality. For committed Marxists, poetry was inextricably entangled with the reality in which it existed, as were all other fields of endeavor. Marxists evaluated poetry first in terms of whether it advanced Marxism, them for its esthetic value.

The Socialist Realist esthetic, according to statements by De Nora, Celaya, and Otero in the anthology, was practised by poets who left the seclusion of an ivory tower for the tumult of city streets. Not aristocratic men of letters seeking the quintessence of beauty, they were intellectual producers contributing «una obra necesaria», «un trabajo más». The status of poetry changed too; freed from rigid poems, poetry «pasa a través de éstos como una corriente». Communicative poetry was addressed to «un nuevo tipo de receptores espectantes... unas desatendidas capas sociales que golpean urgentemente nuestra conciencia llamando a vida». Poetry was social, seeking readers everywhere: «la poesía es 'algo' tan inevitablemente social como el trabajo... no ya para la mayoría, sino para todos, para todos sin excepción». When poetry directed to humanity was unheeded, the burden fell to the poet: «Bien sabemos lo difícil que es hacerse oír de la mayoría... Pero comenzad por llamarlos, que seguramente la causa de tal desatención está más en la voz que en el oído.» The urgent messages of Socialist Realist poetry dealt with mankind's future, not just that of Spaniards: «nos educamos y vivimos en una cultura lánguida, apocada, medio muerta de desnutrición y asfixia. No pienso en España, sino en Europa entera.» Accordingly, if one felt nostalgia, it was «una nostalgia infinita, pero jamás del pasado, siempre de lo futuro y desconocido». To overcome culturally conditioned pessimism: «Hay que lanzarse con alegría, y el que no la tenga que se calle, a una gran ofensiva poética contra todo eso. Debemos y *podemos* tener aquel viejo buen empuje de los poetas renacientes y de los primeros románticos.» The program to be followed: «Tarea para hoy: demostrar hermandad con la tragedia viva, y luego, lo antes posible, intentar superarla. Naturalmente, esto es lo más difícil. No hay creador capaz de levantar unas ruinas si no dispone de un ideal positivo.» This was a positive ideal, against the literary current, but with the winds of social change: «Hay que escribir a favor del viento, pero contra corriente.» Poetry was a tool to transform the world: «La Poesía no es un fin en sí. La Poesía es un instrumento, entre nosotros [otros] para transformar el mundo.»

Traditionalists thought the conventions of Socialist Realism illogical, artificial, and unesthetic; and the Marxist division of poetry into mutually exclusive categories of good and bad, an insidious falsification of the world's richness. Poetry, they believed, was subject to its own system of values within a realm separate from others like science, philosophy, religion, and politics. Consequently, the primary value of poetry was esthetic quality, to which other values were subordinate, whether communicative, inspirational, or propagandistic. Traditional critics were interested in expressivity, form, rhythm, lyricism, and the associations these had with abstract qualities. Such critics either overlooked political meaning or regarded it abstractly as the presence of ideology.

Joaquín de Entrambasaguas reprimanded Ribes, a non-academic in the territory of literary criticism, for the peculiar methods he employed.[70] He claimed that readers seeking orientation would be misled by this anthology, which failed to reflect poetry actually written. Equally unkind was a reviewer in a Barcelonan student publication who disputed the premises of Socialist Realist poetry.[71] First of all, the man of letters devoted to art seldom existed in a poor country like Spain, second, no one questioned the supremacy of life's virtues, lastly, the pretense that poetry was addressed to the masses in possession of the secret of life was undermined by what was, for those lacking the tools of literacy, an inaccessible literary language.

Ricardo Gullón made a deliberately unbiased evaluation of the anthology.[72] He noticed Carlos Bousoño, José Hierro, Vicente Gaos, Rafael Morales, and José María Valverde, as well as their controversial peers — De Nora, Celaya, Otero, and Crémer. Seeking to harmonize apparent differences among the poets, Gullón found all nine in agreement on three important points: solidarity with mankind, intention to communicate with others, and intention to express themselves clearly to all. He thought differences a matter of degree and not, as Ribes asserted, evidence of two different attitudes. Then Gullón attacked the idea that there was an uncrossable abyss between love of beauty and rejection of injustice. Those who supported the idea, he believed, provoked false separations by presenting political issues as if they were universal moral imperatives. The poet of humanist conscience, devoted to beauty, should not have to apologize to others for immersing himself in a search for the profound resonances of the poetic word instead of the eddies of partisanship. Imaginative richness, he asserted, was compatible with ethical commitment to mankind; but to serve an ideology was to renounce artistic duty for the facile, the trivial, the propagandistic. José Luis Cano, sharing Gullón's position, insinuated that the poets of the Generation of 1936, with the exception of Crémer and Celaya, were purposely left out; however, he agreed with Ribes' division of the poets into two groups, though he

---

[70] JOAQUÍN DE ENTRAMBASAGUAS, Review of *Antología consultada*, *Revista de Literatura*, 2, No. 3 (July-September 1952), pp. 237-44.

[71] J. G., Review of *Antología consultada*, *Laye*, No. 21 (November-December, 1952), pp. 89-91.

[72] RICARDO GULLÓN, «La joven poesía española (en torno a una Antología)», *Insula*, No. 81 (15 September 1952), pp. 1, 5.

described the groups from a traditionalist bias.[73] In the wake of these reviews followed rumors. Some centered on the fact that Ribes asked for ten poets but published nine. Ribes claimed that the tenth poet received significantly fewer votes and he included a graph with a dip from 50 percent for the holder of the ninth position to 30 percent for that of the tenth to justify his decision. The distrustful, however, suspected that the tenth poet was José García Nieto and made preposterous accusations of a «secret police» of poetry.[74]

---

[73] José Luis Cano, «Una 'Antología consultada'», *Cuadernos Hispanoamericanos*, No. 38 (February 1953), pp. 245-47: «Una es la de aquellos poetas que han reaccionado severamente contra cierta poesía esteticista de las generaciones anteriores y se esfuerzan por lograr una poesía que hable directamente al hombre de hoy, e incluso sepa expresarlo en sus versos, en los que quieren cantar no sólo bellos motivos o hermosos sueños, sino la tragedia desnuda del hombre actual y la injusticia de un mundo agotado. Otra es la actitud de aquellos que siguen creyendo en que la poesía no tiene por qué encerrar un fin social, sino que debe limitarse a expresar sentimientos humanos, por sí mismos, no por lo que puedan ayudar a transformar el mundo y la condición del hombre, tarea que es de la política, no de la poesía.»

[74] Jacinto López Gorgé, «Poesía y polémica. Los que hablan mal de la *Antología consultada*», *Sigüenza*, No. 4 (1953), p. 11: «En cuanto a la 'particular clase de policía secreta de la poesía' que Pérez Valiente inventa, mejor sería no hablar, como nos propusimos al principio. Digamos, sin embargo, que si esa *policía* existe, no será fácil encontrarla en la tertulia provinciana y sí en Gijón, donde todos hablan mal de todos... Siempre que no estén delante los interesados, y sin atreverse, desde luego, a exponer sus opiniones por escrito. De ahí la procesión de cartas y juramentos verbales a García Nieto y compañía, asegurándoles que les dieron su voto. La hipocresía y el resentimiento abundan en la vida literaria española, pero no en la revista o el escritor de provincias que se atreve a decir lo que honradamente piensa y lo firma, además, con su nombre.»

4

POETRY OF POLITICAL PROTEST

Spanish intellectuals favoring alternative policies to those of the Regime looked north to France, asylum for political refugees of the Civil War, and nation where world affairs were discussed freely. Following the lead of French counterparts, Spaniards believed the USSR the homeland of communism without examining the consequences of «historical materialism» for the Russian people, who suffered purges, slavery, and oppression. From the onset of the Cold War in 1947 until 1956, when Khruschev discredited Stalinist practices, both Spanish and French Marxists held an uncritically favorable view of the Communist Party. Because the Regime was inflexibly opposed to the Communist Party, Spanish Marxists maintained an equally intolerant stance toward the Regime. Thus Marxists and neotraditionalists sought the political allegiance of a public which neither favored the Regime nor a Marxist revolution and for whom the question of commitment was fraught with complications.

Commitment, or *engagement,* came to prominence during the late 1940s when it was directed toward the dissolution of the Franco dictatorship and the formation of a democratic government. By 1950 the Cold War drew this issue beyond national confines; the world seemed at the crossroads of socialism and capitalism, radically different visions of man and society. Thus intellectuals no longer weighed commitment in terms of an end to the Regime, they considered as well which kind of society would be best, not just for Spain, but for all Europe. The differences between traditional liberalism, of which capitalism is the economic expression, and Marxism, requiring a socialist economy, are apparent in their comparative views of man, society, culture, and literature.

According to the liberal outlook man is free to become whatever he makes of himself in a life that is a continual project. Isolated by nature, man enters into relation with others on a contractual basis. The liberal social order, based on the supremacy of the individual, rewards personal achievement. Consequently, excellence of taste is admired in both art and intellect, which are considered the expression of man's highest aspirations. In contrast, the Marxist view holds that man is the «ensemble of social relations», a creature inescapably enmeshed in an ever-present sociality, which suppresses the effect of individual personality. In this kind of society where human exploitation is theoretically impossible, human activity fuses *theoria* and *praxis,* that is, knowledge or thought merges with actions in the experience of life. Marxists believe the bourgeois social order is flawed by conflict of interests between the few, who control the means of production, and the many having no direct ownership of those means and who are obliged to exchange their labor for wages. Because this seems unfair, Marxists support the proletarian movement to replace the rule of the few with that of the many, to establish a society based on the collective moral purpose of the greatest good, in which the free development of each person is the condition of the free development of all.

The aims and tasks of the arts under these two views are equally at odds. The major question to be answered is whether the arts are the affirmation of individuality, an apolitical expression of the eternal verities, or an expression of the economic and social relations among men, a tool used by the dominant class in order to reinforce the reigning social order to its own advantage and to the detriment of its adversaries. Each view of the arts has its own ideological direction, preferred topics, and specific creative methods. These methods and topics that serve bourgeois reality are usually unfit for the Marxist reality and vice-versa. For the writer trained in one ideological tradition, conversion to the other entails not only a change of political loyalty, but also an artistic metamorphosis not easily achieved. For writers at mid-century, such consequences required pondering.

In weighing alternatives, many intellectuals agreed that something was dreadfully wrong with Spain and perhaps even the Western world. Some chose Marxist commitment as the only honorable path when Franco, as they would say, wooing Western economic interests, became an accomplice of monopoly capital, making Spain one more nation to fall before oligarchies with a master plan of world conquest. Only the establishment of socialism, they believed, assured a government guaranteeing social justice. Others sincerely desiring social justice feared Marxism as a direct route to another authoritarian regime as abusive as that of Franco. Favoring humanitarian goals, they protested what they considered wrong, but vacillated before what seemed a narrow political program. Regarding the problem of commitment from an intellectual stance, they examined causes, conditions, and consequences by means of systematic doubt. However, from this procedure, limited to the realm of cognition, they derived no final conclusions; at best they could offer only provisional commitment. Their non-authoritarian attitude, by which conclusions were subject to revision in the face of new information, meant that they usually had mixed feelings about commitment, always wondering if moral certainty was worth the loss of independent judgment. Yet Marxist commitment was a tempting alternative, offering intellectuals a place of honor and a duty to fulfill. As the *intelligentsia* of the Spanish Communist Party, they were to provide the consciousness of Spain's proletarian movement. Honorable position and purposeful activity were strong antidotes to the usual maladies of intellectuals — despair, inertia, and a persistent feeling of uselessness.

The Partido Comunista de España (PCE) was the first Communist Party outside the USSR to enter into governing power when it participated in the Popular Front electoral victory of February 1936. From that moment, the PCE presented itself as the advocate of cooperation between middle-class liberals and the working class.[1] At the outbreak of the Civil War in July 1936, party membership increased threefold to over 300,000 with claims made of over one million. Some of this growth was owed to gratitude for Russian aid in the defense of Madrid, a struggle compared at the time to the 1905 defense of Petrograd. But much of the increased enrollment resulted from the conviction that the Communists were well organized: their troops were disciplined under fire, they informed the public of the political and military significance of their actions, they had the most efficient system of communication, supply, and medical aid. Outlawed at the end of the Civil War, the PCE went underground, most of its members executed, imprisoned, or exiled. Among the last was Dolores Ibárruri, deputy during the Second Republic and front-line orator during the Civil War known as La Pasionaria, the personification of maternal Spanish spirit. Living in Moscow after the Civil War, she was named Secretary-General of the PCE in 1942. Under her direction during the early postwar period, the PCE engaged in such clandestine activities within Spain as guerrilla attacks, organization of prisoners, and distribution of propaganda — *Mundo Obrero* in Madrid, Andalusia, and northern Spain; *Verdad* in Valencia; *Unidad* in Málaga; *El Obrero* in the Canary Islands; *Nuestra Palabra* in the Balearic Isles.[2]

When France curtailed overt activities of the PCE within its own borders between 1950 and 1956, making guerrilla incursions almost impossible, the Party infiltrated existing groups and organizations within Spain to form coalitions of power. The PCE primarily sought two groups with established roles in party thinking: students, the *intelligentsia* of the future, and workers, the proletariat.[3] The PCE was quick to take advan-

---

[1] GABRIEL JACKSON, *The Spanish Republic and the Civil War 1931-1936* (Princeton: Princeton University Press, 1965), pp. 360-61.
[2] *Historia del Partido Comunista de España* (Varsovia, Poland: Ediciones «Polonia», 1960), pp. 215-23.
[3] *Ibid.*, pp. 247-48.

tage of any evidence of opposition to the Regime and welcomed as beneficial to the Party such documents, for example, as one printed in Spanish, English, and French by the Unión Federal de Estudiantes Hispanos and the F.U.E.[4] And the PCE encouraged exposés like one Manuel Tuñón de Lara delivered in Paris, stating that between 1942 and 1950 not a single literary work of any depth was produced in Spain, nothing representing the moral vibration of the Spanish people.[5] The PCE also sent militants into Spain to meet with intellectuals. For instance, Jorge Semprún, author and screenwriter, organized a network of contacts among groups in Madrid, Barcelona, and San Sebastián during the 1950s under the pseudonym of Federico Sánchez.[6] Among workers, the PCE agitated for better wages by organizing existing unrest to secure maximal impact. One of the most successful efforts was a boycott and general strike in March 1951, which paralyzed Barcelona despite the fact that strikes were considered seditious and were punishable by death.[7]

Santiago Carrillo assumed leadership of the PCE in all but title in 1956, the year in which World Communism as a single party was dissolved. Already pursuing goals that went against the rigid Stalinist-Leninist policies of Ibárruri, Carrillo rejected armed revolt against the Regime and instead encouraged general strikes and efforts to create coalitions: «the peaceful way to socialism». To give one result, in 1957 the «Estudiantes Comunistas de Madrid» was founded, one of numerous student groups in opposition to the Regime's student syndicate (SEU).[8] By entering the Regime's labor syndicates to form *ad hoc* committees that later became permanent, the PCE managed to establish the effective working-class organization called the Comisiones Obreras, tacitly recognized by the Regime after 1962. Party propagandists demanded on behalf of workers wage increases to meet rises in the cost of living, equal pay for equal

---

[4] Reproduced as «Etudiants étrangers que venez en Espagne», *Les Temps Modernes*, No. 55 (May 1950), pp. 2075-76. The U.F.E.H. published a clandestine periodical beginning in May 1946; the F.U.E. was a prewar student organization, revived secretly during the 1940s.

[5] Reported by ALFONSO AYENSA, «La Culture espagnole sous le régime de Franco», *Les Temps Modernes*, No. 55 (May 1950), p. 2050.

[6] See: JORGE SEMPRÚN, *Autobiografía de Federico Sánchez* (Barcelona: Planeta, 1977), pp. 54-59; PAUL PRESTON, «Quarrelling with Carrillo», *Times Literary Supplement*, 9 June 1978, p. 646: «Semprún was something of a world-famous figure. More importantly, he was a party hero. From the age of seventeen until his capture in 1943, aged twenty, by the Gestapo, Semprún fought in the French Resistance. In Buchenwald, his linguistic abilities not only helped him to survive but also allowed him to organize the communist network within the camp. As Federico Sánchez, he carried out clandestine work in Spain with courage and intelligence, eventually being coopted on to the PCE's politburo.»

[7] *Historia del PCE*, p. 238.

[8] SERGIO LEÓN, «Notas sobre el movimiento estudiantil en España», *Horizonte Español 1972* (Colombes, France: Ruedo Ibérico, 1972), p. 166.

work, an eight-hour workday, unemployment insurance, and the implementation of safety regulations.

While some party militants propagandized the proletariat, others gained influence among artists and writers. Their theory, SocRealism (Socialist Realism), was more than the mechanical application of a style, it was, to use characteristic language, the literary arm of a worldwide movement associated with the rise of a politically conscious industrial proletariat, a reflection of the struggle to establish a socialist society.[9]

The purpose of SocReal literature is what distinguishes it most from traditional literature. The Soviet writer, Andrei Sinyavsky, stresses the teleological purpose that underlies every Marxist endeavor:[10]

> It was the genius of Marx that he proved the earthly paradise, of which others had dreamed before him, was actually the Purpose which Fate destined for Man. With the aid of Marx, Communism passed from moral efforts of isolated individuals —«Oh, where you, golden age?»— into the sphere of universal history...

By this policy, writers who speed the coming of socialist society help as much as sculptors, musicians, soldiers, agronomists, and engineers, or as institutions, such as the theater and the press, or as objects, such as machines and guns. All efforts must be subject to the higher destiny of securing the new age of man; from that, they all gain nobility. This is the political implication of Celaya's statement: «... mi concepción del mundo y mi marxismo se hallan latentes en cualquiera de mis poemas — aun de aquellos cuyo tema no es socio-político».[11] And De Nora's: «Yo trato de hacer poesía, simplemente, pero creo en la trascendencia humana, social y hasta política de la poesía, y no me opongo en principio, a 'utilizarla' con fines exteriores, como arma incluso, a veces».[12] The militant need not search for truth, it is manifest in the pronouncements of party leaders. He sets aside the anguished inquiry of the bourgeois intellectual to spread Marxist ideas as revealed truth, in accord with the principle of *partiinost,* that is, loyalty to the Communist Party, its leaders, and their policies.[13] Compatible neither with open-mindedness nor historical accuracy, *partiinost* discourages interest in ideas other than those directly related to life as a march toward socialism. What a liberal considers a reckless disregard for truth is, for the Marxist militant, the presentation

---

[9] Czelaw Milosz uses the term «Socrealism» in: ABRAM TERTZ [ANDREI SINYAVSKY], *On Socialist Realism* (New York: Pantheon, 1960), p. 10.

[10] *Ibid.,* pp. 30-31.

[11] GABRIEL CELAYA, *El hilo rojo* (Madrid: Visor, 1977), p. 7. Further references to this book appear in the text, indicated by HR.

[12] Cited by: CHARLES DAVID LEY, *Spanish Poetry since 1939* (Washington, D.C.: Catholic University of America, 1962), p. 215.

[13] C. VAUGHAN JAMES, *Soviet Socialist Realism. Origins and Theory* (London: Macmillan Press, Ltd., 1973), p. 101.

of what should be as what is: the Party's achievements and aspirations are glorified, its defects and failures, misrepresented or forgotten.

To skeptics, the SocReal utopia seems an ingenuous montage of sentiment and slogan, a modern version of the myth of the Golden Age; and expectedly, they wonder how it captured the imagination of multitudes because there is no *prima facie* plausible reason for the collapse of capitalism or its replacement by socialism. The «design of history», based on an evolutionary vision of historical events, is a tacit teleology, rather than the prediction of dialectics, which cannot speak about finality.[14] Nevertheless, for believers, the Revolution is a prophesied utopia where happiness and plenty are the right of all men, not just the few. As Marx said: «The proletarians have nothing to lose in it [a Communist Revolution] but their chains. On the other hand, they have a world to gain.»

In the literary portrayal of the message, since action leading to socialism is heroic, those actively participating on behalf of the Revolution are heroes. Workers and peasants are automatically heroic because of their class origin and way of life. For intellectuals, class background is less important than actions. Marxists recognize that the *intelligentsia* is politically heterogeneous with eclectic views, unstable principles, and vague social ideals. They know that an intellectual, even of worker or peasant origin, may not advocate proletarian interests. On the other hand, a bourgeois intellectual may earn the heroic literary treatment ascribed automatically to the proletariat provided he commit himself to «building socialism».

In literature the proletariat is idealized; this allows values associated with an unsophisticated way of life to receive favorable emphasis. Manual labor, comradely relations, reverence for children, pleasure in simple joys, stalwart courage, and good cheer are customary proletarian traits. The representation of the bourgeoisie, depending upon the psycho-sociological concept of the «other», is less clear-cut. Thus no traits are necessarily bourgeois, but all portrayals of the bourgeoisie describe otherness. Yet, because this class opposes the interests of the under-class by making use of hidden or overt violence, Marxists hold that the proletariat may use violence in its own interest. Lenin, who himself found violence distasteful, abolished for once and for all the notion of personal guilt when he said during the Revolution that «without systematic and merciless repression of the exploiters' opposition, without being unhesitant before any bourgeois-democratic formulae, not only a socialist but a democratic revolution is unthinkable, just as there are no serious measures

---

[14] ROBERT L. HEILBRONER, *Marxism: For and Against* (New York: W. W. Norton, 1980), pp. 85-88.

which it would be unthinkable to use in the fight against the crisis and the devastation caused by the war».[15]

The melodramatic Communist line, with its struggling social classes, is only raw material for Spanish poets converted to winning the Revolution. Usually born to the white collar of the petty capitalist, obsessed by class guilt, they risk the Regime's displeasure, to say nothing of occasional fines, in order to spread the «Good News». However, unwilling to relinquish a lyric speaker for what logically should be a collective speaker, these poets adopt the personae of revolutionary rebel, bourgeois martyr, proletarian bard, or agitprop militant depending upon the anecdote at hand. They make the most of impoverished themes with infusions of strong sentiment — despair, exaltation, pride, guilt. As dedicated militants they seek recruits among their listeners by inspiring emulation or threatening shame. They themselves are new men, who bond *theoria* and *praxis* in a life devoted to the Revolution. Thus the speakers' journey from bourgeois alienation to Marxist consciousness tends to overshadow the proletarian march. A quest, it passes through lands of ideas, terrains that are correlatives of ideologies. Like moralist allegories these works maintain a serious tone with irony only at the expense of class enemies. A skeptical reader, however, sees the speaker, not as the voice of truth, but as a proselytizer and may reject the poetry or fall into an ironic reading at the speaker's expense. For all but the most committed readers, the Communist line thrives best when the theme is subtly handled.

Blas de Otero's Epic for the Age of Man

Blas de Otero may be remembered with good reason as Spain's foremost poet during the Franco Dictatorship. After an early period during which he wrote religious poetry, he entered what is generally considered the first period of his mature poetry — existentialist protest enhanced by an imaginative use of the sonnet form. The second period, which includes his most characteristic poetry —that of commitment— began after he joined the PCE in 1952.[16] More than any other fact this led, first, to a virtual critical silence around his works and, second, to an identification of Otero the poet with the persona of his poetry. Otero's position as

---

[15] S. FEDYUKIN, *The Great October Revolution and the Intelligentsia* (Moscow: Progress, 1975), p. 57.
[16] The date is cited in: «Una lírica al servicio de la inmensa mayoría», *El País*, 30 June 1979, p. 20. The PCE publicly acknowledged his role in a note cited by ROSA MARÍA PEREDA, «Ha muerto el poeta Blas de Otero», *El País*, 30 June 1979, p. 20: «El PCE ha hecho pública una nota de duelo por él, militante del partido desde los tiempos atrás de la clandestinidad. 'Supo aunar', dice la nota, 'la mejor tradición poética española con la poesía de vanguardia y revolucionaria. Sus obras y su vida de militante comunista son conocidas en el mundo entero...'.»

party propagandist, at a time when the PCE was illegal in Spain, made prudent critics avoid public comment on his committed poetry while gossips dismissed him as a *maldito* whose best poetry was written before 1950. Not until the end of the Dictatorship was it possible to find his major works easily available in Spain, so that his own countrymen could read them. Furthermore, the silence surrounding Otero was intensified by his own personal reticence; thus little was publicly known about his life.[17] Unlike Celaya, who frequented literary circles, Otero was a reluctant participant. Then too, the travels that took him as far as the USSR and China, including a four-year stay in Cuba, added to his legendary quality. It is no surprise, therefore, that the poetic persona should seem essentially the same as the poet in person and, further, that the life told in poetry be thought that of the author.[18]

Pablo Neruda has been considered an autobiographical poet as well. The speaker of *Residencia en la tierra,* overcome by melancholy despair, who is reborn a Marxist in *Tercera residencia,* makes the same ideological transit as Otero's speaker. Neruda's imagery, referring to his exchange of bourgeois pessimism for Marxist confirmation of life, hope, and the ideals of Russian socialism, derives from the same Socialist Realist inspiration:[19]

> Yo toqué con mis manos la camisa
> del crepúsculo azul y derrotado:
> ahora toco el alba de la vida
>   naciendo con el sol de Stalingrado.
> ... ...
> Yo pongo el alma mía donde quiero.
> Y no me nutro de papel cansado,
> adobado de tinta y de tintero.
>   Nací para cantar a Stalingrado.

---

[17] «Una lírica al servicio de la inmensa mayoría», *Ibid.,* p. 20, mentions that Otero fought the Civil War with the Nationalists after having been on the side of the Second Republic; following the war he worked as a legal advisor for a Vizcayan business, then took only occasional jobs to allow time for writing. He may have received financial assistance as well; CARLOS BARRAL, *Los años sin excusa* (Barcelona: Barral, 1978), p. 183, names as Otero's «Maecenas» Alberto Puig Palau.

[18] Compare these statements: MORAIMA DE SEMPRÚN DONAHUE, *Blas de Otero en su poesía* (Chapel Hill: North Carolina Studies in the Romance Languages and Literatures, 1977), p. 13: «Con el propósito de conocer más profundamente al hombre y al poeta, reconstruiremos ciertos aspectos de su vida y manera de pensar, mediante el estudio y el análisis de sus poemas autobiográficos...» And JOSÉ LUIS CANO, «En la muerte de Blas de Otero», *Insula,* No. 392-393 (July-August 1979), p. 7: «Ahora que se nos ha ido un gran poeta y un gran amigo, nada más inútil que intentar escribir una sintética biografía de Blas. Porque su vida, su vida entera, está en sus poemas, en sus libros, y a ellos debemos volver para sentirle vivo.»

[19] PABLO NERUDA, «Nuevo canto de amor a Stalingrado», *Tercera residencia (1935-1945)* (Barcelona: Seix Barral, 1977), p. 79.

In this sense, both poets record the most representative intellectual metamorphosis of this century, each from the vantage point of a particular moment and place. But their poetry is intentionally of wider significance than personal confession, it is tacitly epic. They present the speaker of their poems as a symbol for all men of good conscience, a figure whose fate is involved with that of the nation or even of mankind. Both Neruda and Otero cultivated a genre variously known as lyric epic, anti-epic, or personal epic, which places an emphasis on narrating the successive mental or emotional states of the speaker as a representative figure.[20] The genre was created by Walt Whitman, who sought a unique form of epic vision to express what he called the moral revolutions of his age.[21] He thereby created a speaker incarnating the people, spirit, and geography of his nation, a bard commensurate with all. Otero, like his precursors, created an integrated speaker within an evolving corpus of poems, to speak for a specific ideological outlook, drawing persuasive force from the use of set phrases, maxims, euphemisms, and regionalisms. Only in this restricted sense is Whitman's, Neruda's, or Otero's poetry autobiographical.

I. *Quest for Salvation*

The first cycle of Otero's poetry, including *Angel fieramente humano, Redoble de conciencia,* and *Ancia,* explores man's quest for relatedness in a disintegrating civilization.[22] In each work, Otero uses the same themes arranged in similar narrative order. The speaker searches through storm-tossed seas, along bottomless precipices, and up dizzying heights, determined to find God, yet always failing. He then tries to reach the divinity through a Neoplatonic ascent that is to no avail either. In great despair, the speaker finally turns his attention from his individual plight

---

[20] JAMES E. MILLER, Jr., *The American Quest for a Supreme Fiction. Whitman's Legacy in the Personal Epic* (Chicago: University of Chicago Press, 1979), pp. 34-36.

[21] Otero professed his admiration for Whitman with tribute and emulation. He admired Whitman's love for mankind and nature, his faith in freedom and equality:

> Amo a Walt Whitman por su barba enorme
> y por su hermoso verso dilatado.
> Estoy de acuerdo con su voz, conforme
> con su gran corazón desparramado. (PPP, 30)

Two lines from Whitman's «So Long» impressed Otero: «Camerado, this is no book, / Who touches this touches a man.» He used them as the epigraph to his anthology *Esto no es un libro* (Río Piedras: Editoria Universitaria-Puerto Rico, 1963).

[22] BLAS DE OTERO, *Angel fieramente humano. Redoble de conciencia* (Buenos Aires: Losada, 1977); *Ancia* (Madrid: Visor, 1975). References to these editions are in the text, preceded by the appropriate abbreviation: AFH, RC, An.

to mankind's. Here he finds a secure basis for commitment, which he affirms at the conclusion of each work with increasing fervor.

The opening poem of *Angel fieramente humano,* with its echoes of Darío's «Lo fatal», captured the imagination of a generation that remembered the Civil War, feared the atom-bomb, and thought the impasse in Korea sufficiently dangerous to worry, not just about its own survival, but about that of the human race. Mankind lost its glory to the past without retaining any hope for the future:[23]

> Una generación desarraigada,
> unos hombres sin más destino que
> apuntalar las ruinas. (AFH, 11)

Stricken by mortality, filled with dread, but unwilling to renounce life, man is a paradox of existence:

> Es que quiere quedar. Seguir siguiendo,
> subir, a contra muerte, hasta lo eterno.
> Le da miedo mirar. Cierra los ojos
> para dormir el sueño de los vivos. (AFH, 12)

For the universality of his themes, Otero dedicated the work to the immense majority.[24] At the outset of his metaphysical journey, the speaker evokes Neoplatonic doctrine, which considers man's soul to exist as emanation from a single principle with which it seeks to be reunited through trance or ecstasy.[25] In the poems of «Desamor» this quest for the Godhead merges erotic and sacred images, a search described as an encounter between man and woman. Just as physical union is brief when measured against a lifetime, so too that of man's soul in ecstasy with the deity. Forgetful that duality of soul and body limits perfect union to fleeting moments, the speaker blames woman for failure rather than human nature:

> Cuerpo de la mujer, fuente de llanto
> donde, después de tanta luz, de tanto
> tacto sutil, de Tántalo es la pena. (AFH, 22)

---

[23] For exegesis of this poem, see: EDMOND L. KING, «Blas de Otero: The Past and Present of 'The Eternal'», *Spanish Writers of 1936. Crisis and Commitment in the Poetry of the Thirties and Forties,* Jaime Ferrán, Daniel P. Testa, eds. (London: Tamesis, 1973), pp. 125-33.

[24] «Autocrítica de libros. Lo que dice de *Angel fieramente humano* Blas de Otero», *Correo Literario,* 1, No. 2 (15 June 1950), p. 9: «El libro es, en el buen sentido de la palabra, subjetivo... Pero casi todo lo que se dice en ellas [las tres partes] tiene validez para todos los hombres. Por eso —y por otros motivos— va dedicado *A la inmensa mayoría.*»

[25] Contemporary opinion recognized this as the Platonic theory of beauty. See: ANGEL VALBUENA BRIONES, «Ultima poesía de Blas de Otero», *Alcalá,* No. 10 (10 June 1952).

Feeling his life consumed by death, kiss by kiss, the speaker still blindly follows his desire into the nothingness of total night:

> Porque quiero tu cuerpo y lo persigo
> a través de la sangre y de la nada.
> Porque busco tu noche toda entera. (AFH, 26)

Left «en un charco de lágrimas» (AFH, 30) and exhausted by his arduous effort, the speaker requests humiliation befitting his self-loathing. The poems of «Hombre», divided into two subsections, chronicle the speaker's over-hasty plunge into Marxist commitment. A humanist sensibility tempered by frustration and despair increases tension as the speaker stands at the brink of self-destruction. Attacked by vertigo, he balances unsteadily between fascination with and terror of death, doomed by a desire impossible to fulfill. He is a tragic contradiction, a creature of mixed natures:

> Esto es ser hombre horror a manos llenas.
> Ser —y no ser— eternos, fugitivos.
> ¡Angel con grandes alas de cadenas! (AHF, 42)

By all that he is, feels, and knows, the speaker realizes that he is mortal, a lightning bolt that disappears without a trace after a fearful noise: «La vida es ese ruido / del rayo al crepitar... y luego, consumido, / no queda ni el desastre de su estela» (AFH, 50). At his psychological nadir the speaker finds a modicum of divinity within, sufficient to propel him across the depths to the safety of commitment. Though God betrayed him, he hopes his fellow men will be more trustworthy; and, since dealings among men are dignified, he will kneel and grovel no longer. As if walking on the waters of mankind's aspirations, the speaker confidently commits himself:

> ... avanzo
> sin dudar, sobre abismos infinitos,
> con la mano tendida: si no alcanzo
>
> con la mano, ¡ya alcanzaré con gritos!
> Y sigo, siempre, en pie, y así me lanzo
> al mar, desde una fronda de apetitos. (AFH, 52)

Yet his confidence weakens, he vacillates at the threshold of dread, a figure of living death beset by the vertigo of being human, wondering whether he is only a plaything of God after all. He came close to the revolutionary realm of freedom without actually entering, but now retreats to climb a ladder to nowhere:

> viene
> el vértigo a todo correr desde el vacío
> y, cerrando los ojos,
> nos asimos a nuestro ser más íntimo,

> y seguimos
> y seguimos subiendo la trágica escalera
> colocada
> creada, por nosotros mismos. (AFH, 55-56)

Without further explanation, the speaker opens the last part of «Hombre» with a euphoric burst of song celebrating his newly acquired purpose. In one ambiguously worded stanza, which humanitarians might find inspiring, a skeptic sees only traditional images with dashes of propaganda for the credulous; addressing mankind, the speaker states that he brings dawn, water and light. Then he points to himself as mentor and harangues his listeners with insults and orders:

> ... Soy. Luego es bastante
> ser, si procuro ser quien soy. ¡Quién sabe
> si hay más! En cambio, hay menos: sois sentinas
> de hipocresía. ¡Oh, sed, salid al día!
> No sigáis siendo bestias disfrazadas
> de ansia de Dios. Con ser hombres os basta. (AFH, 60)

The remaining poems in this section explore a new terrain for Otero: Marxist propaganda. One dedicated to De Nora and another to Alberti alert knowledgeable readers to the ideological nature of Otero's humanist commitment.[26] The speaker addresses De Nora confidentially, praising their mutual efforts to propagandize. De Nora used *Espadaña* as a platform to accomplish this. Otero, more inclined to theory than practice, continued his study of *Capital*. One of his favorite passages was Marx's image of the collapse of capitalism as the bursting of the «integument». He adapted this in the poem «A Eugenio de Nora» (AFH, 61-62) by portraying De Nora as the mast of a sinking ship, who splits the hull to reveal the promised heaven where the expropriators are expropriated. When addressing the exiled Alberti, Otero objects to the former's statement that he was no longer an angel, but rather an empty man, written out of the annals of history. Otero believes that Alberti and his fellow emigrés are the «best angels». Then, indulging in poetic play, he scrambles coded words —*blanco* (Traditionalist), *azul* (Falangist), *manos* (terrorist squads), *peces* (members of the PCE)— in a political conundrum that passes muster as a lyrical seascape:

> Las aguas maternales.
> Blanco y azul, si carmen, pescadores
> de carmines ponientes enredados.

---

[26] After 1949, De Nora found Switzerland more congenial than Spain, where he risked imprisonment; Alberti waited forty years for a change of government and a senate seat.

> Las manos, redes, y los peces, flores
> submarinas. Los peces de colores. (AFH, 64)

In «Crecida» the speaker rises, like Marx's ghost thirsty for justice, on a tide of blood innundating the earth.[27] The lines of this poem exceed in horror those of «Explico algunas cosas», where Neruda repeats: «Venid a ver la sangre por las calles.» In Neruda's poem there are rivers of blood, but in Otero's the seas themselves run red. The speaker repeats the word «*sangre*» in hypnotic distress:

> voy sobre Europa
> como en la proa de un barco desmantelado
> que hace sangre,
> ... ...
> Traigo una rosa en sangre entre las manos
> ensangrentadas. Porque es que no hay más
> que sangre,
> y una horrorosa sed
> dando gritos en medio de la sangre. (AFH, 68-69)

The scene changes abruptly in the third section, «Poderoso silencio»; the speaker rethinks his commitment, returns to the ladder, and makes another appeal to God. He tries reverse psychology by ordering: «Oh, cállate, Señor, calla tu boca / cerrada» (AFH, 75). When insolence fails, he tries to get even by declaring himself God's equal: «Mira que, dentro, desde ahora, luego, / somos, no somos —soledad— iguales» (AFH, 80). With these words the speaker figuratively washes his hands of the matter in order to dedicate himself to finding joy and hope by another path. Therefore in one poem he offers a psalm for the new man, in another he lyrically reviews the important events of his life, and he concludes, in a poem directed to Ibárruri *et al.*, with a wish for a helping hand to find the path ahead:

> Alcanzadme la mano, ay, alcanzádmela
> la mano.
> Madre.
> Puede ser que mi calle esté más arriba,
> más
> adelante. (AFH, 92)

Redoble de conciencia is the sequel to *Angel fieramente humano* only insofar as it concludes with a definitive commitment to Marxism, the speaker renouncing forever the anxiety and commotion of bourgeois society. Otherwise, the work remaps the same metaphysical and ideological domains as its predecessor. The speaker, fettered angel, bears the additional

---

[27] For a stylistic analysis of this poem, see: EMILIO ALARCOS LLORACH, *La poesía de Blas de Otero* (Salamanca: Anaya, 1966), pp. 117-21.

signs of a savior. As a Christ figure, he proclaims in the dedicatory poem: «¡Ay, ese ángel fieramente humano / corre a salvaros, y no sabe cómo!» (RC, 100). A flawed redeemer, the speaker is a doubting Christ, antagonistic son of God, who dedicates his work to the immense majority, which —being the underclass of society— cannot rise of its own accord, as the saying goes, without overturning the superstructure formed by official society. Not yet a Marxist by conviction, the speaker returns to the austere regions of existentialist anguish in poems such as «Voz de lo negro», «Mar adentro», and «Tierra», which could be easily from the earlier work. In other poems however, the speaker overcomes his urge for masochistic surrender. He suggests that, if God did not exist to torment man, death would still be sufficient. Then with anger he demands that God, first, renounce the religious paraphernalia that mask the nature of death and, second, give mankind eternal life:

> Entonces ¿para qué vivir, oh hijos
> de madre; a qué vidrieras, crucifijos
> y todo lo demás? Basta la muerte.
>
> Basta. Termina, oh Dios, de malmatarnos,
> O si no, déjanos precipitarnos
> sobre Ti—ronco río que revierte. (RC, 106)

Adding retaliation to blasphemy, the speaker then wishes to return in kind the treatment meted out by God — strangulation, starvation, murder:

> ... ¡Si pudiese yo matarte,
> como haces tú, como haces tú! Nos coges
> con las dos manos, nos ahogas. Matas
>
> no se sabe por qué. Quiero cortarte
> las manos. Esas manos que son trojes
> del hambre, y de los hombres que arrebates. (RC, 114)

With this poem Otero managed to upset the superstructure of León, who penetrated the poem's allegorical imagery and promptly punished Otero's lack of respect.[28] They failed to recognize Otero's sincere interest in the issue of the silent God or the profound, if frustrated reverence of the speaker as savior. The speaker indeed is the forsaken son calling out to his Father, first with voice, which becomes incoherent, then with gestures:

---

[28] LECHNER, *El compromiso en la poesía española del siglo XX. Parte segunda*, p. 57, quotes a letter from Crémer stating that the poem: «Había suscitado muy enconadas polémicas de ortodoxia religiosa. Antonio G. de Lama, sacerdote, tuvo que hacer confesión pública de insolidaridad.» FANNY RUBIO, *Las revistas poéticas españolas (1939-1975)* (Madrid: Turner, 1976), p. 271, writes: «Este poema le costó a la revista grandes y serios disgustos (esta vez en el campo eclesiástico)... En conversación con Blas de Otero, éste me relató que en el Sínodo Episcopal se llegó a hablar de excomunión.»

> ...Mudo soy. Pero mis brazos
> me alzan, vivo, hacia Dios. Y si no entiende
> mi voz, tendrá que oír mis manotazos.
>   Abro y cierro mi cruz... (RC, 116)

Feeling faint, dying or dreaming, the speaker suddenly witnesses the heavens caving in to entomb his soul. While excavating the rubble, the speaker hears God's call but, rather than answer the voice from the tomb, lets Him rest in peace:

> A toda luz, el cielo se derrumba,
> arriado de raíz, sobre la tumba
> donde mi alma vive sepultada.
> ... ...
>   ... A son de azada
> llama Dios en mi alma. Y, aquí yace. (RC, 118)

In «Gritando no morir» the speaker combines more Christological references —calling God «*Yavé*», mentioning a wound in his side, beseeching the heavens for salvation— to narrate his own crucifixion:

> ¡Quiero vivir, vivir, vivir! La llama
> de mi cuerpo, furiosa y obstinada,
> salte, Yavé, contra tu cielo airada
> pluma de luz. En el costado brama
> la sangre... y el pecho, desolado, clama. (RC, 119)

Haunted by the spectre of a death whose time, place, and means have not been disclosed, the speaker reflects that he is thirty-three years old and on the verge of an identity crisis. He suffers the usual symptoms of this class-specific bourgeois illness — disorientation, anxiety, isolation, and anomie. With a misguided hope of finding his way, he compulsively returns to the Neoplatonic ascent. When the interlude ends in disaster, he dies.

«Tabla rasa» opens immediately following the death of the speaker. In a voice from beyond, he reports his entry into Nothingness after the recent apocalypse in which everything exploded:

> Posteriormente, entramos en la Nada.
> Y sopla Dios, de pronto, y nos termina.
> Aquí, la Tierra fue. Aquí, la grada
> del mar. Aquí, la larga serpentina
> de los planetas. Ved. La Nada en pleno.
> No preguntéis. Estaban. Se aventaron. (RC, 133)

No longer tormented beyond endurance, the speaker imaginatively reenacts with Irenka a highlight of pre-Revolutionary history.[29] He relates the

---

[29] The poem is dedicated to Irenka N. K. See: BLAS DE OTERO, *Ancia*, p. 166.

last living moments of Rubén Ruiz, a captain in the Red Army, who suffered a cruel death while saving the world from Fascism in the Battle of Stalingrad. In honor of Ruiz's sacrifice, a monument was raised on the banks of the Volga river. There his mother, Dolores Ibárruri, often grieved over her son's tragic sacrifice to the birth of the new age:

> Posteriormente. Irenka, Irenka. El caso
> es grave. Vamos, sopla esta pelusa
> de la muerte, este hilo del fracaso;
> esa alga, esa nada, esa medusa...
>
> ¿Sientes? La sangre sale al sol. Lagarto
> rojo. Divina juventud. Tesoro
> vivo. ¿Te apartas? Oh Rubén. Me aparto.
> Besas y lloras. ¿Ves? Yo beso, lloro.
>
> Es el final, el fin. La apocalipsis. (RC, 134)

After wiping the slate clean, the speaker leaves behind his morose despair to seize reality. He eschews anguished diction to speak with sage-like humility of momentous but seemingly trivial affairs. He only reports what he knows in «Que cada uno aporte lo que sepa» (RC, 139-40); nevertheless this is considerable. For instance, he theorizes that the proletarian movement, which spread like wildfire for twenty years after the Revolution of 1917, was blocked by bourgeois reaction mouthing ambiguous words like «suspensión de hostilidades». In matters of war and peace, he prefers peace of course, but only if it is not another name for war. «Mundo» (RC, 143-45) is an exceptional credential of philosophical erudition. The speaker holds that the chaotic state of the twentieth century is a result of the Traditionalist world view as represented by St. Augustine's writings. He dramatizes the crisis —which many recognize, but whose solution is known only to Marxists— by nonchalantly alternating the titles of the Agustinian *opera omnia* with the consequences of *translatio imperii* to bite with irony the hegemonies that have run Spain to ruin since the Punic Wars.

Otero then prepares for the speaker's transition to new man from his dual role as human angel and humanized Christ by discarding remaining vestiges of iconography in «Aren en paz». The doctrine he adapts holds that Christ, Second Person of the Trinity, is associated with the notion of Logos: divine wisdom manifest in the world. Otero transfers the Logos from the humanized Christ unable to save man to its new situation in the persona of the Social Logos. Appearing for the last time as a Christ, the speaker ponders how he might assure peace for all men. Should he lay his heart atop a mountain? Let his severed hands pray for the desolate? Or should he allow his body to wander the countryside proclaiming «la paz del hombre, el hambre de Dios vivo, / la represada sed de libertad» (RC, 150)? He decides that he can best serve mankind by being buried forever. The final poem confesses Marxist faith. Reborn as the Social Logos, the speaker accepts the fundamental unity of life and death. He thus ends the first cycle, challenging life and its dangers as if he were a bullfighter defying death, wishing to be remembered for having lived life fully rather than for his ephemeral writings:

> Digo vivir, vivir como si nada
> hubiese de quedar de lo que escribo.
>
> Porque escribir es viento fugitivo,
> y publicar, columna arrinconada. (RC, 153)

Ancia, whose title unites the first syllable of *Angel fieramente humano* with the last of *Redoble de conciencia,* consolidates poems from the earlier works within familiar thematic categories and refines their narratological progression. This alone would not make *Ancia* worth commenting here. However, the collection of eighty-nine poems includes forty-eight new ones, which accentuate the speaker's transition from metaphysical doubt to ideological certitude. The poems of *Ancia* are divided among three sections with «Es a la inmensa mayoría» as the poem of dedication, «Digo vivir» and the new «Conmigo va» as epilogue. In the first and longest section, Otero combines poems from the earlier works without distinguishing the persona of human angel from that of humanized Christ. This composite is further integrated by three new poems —«Epitasis», «Ecce homo», «Encuesta»— in which Otero inserts his name, thus merging the early personae into a single one called Blas de Otero. Stylistic evolution is noticeable; Otero includes two prose selections, «Otra historia» and «La Monse», similar to those of *Historias fingidas y verdaderas* and a sub-section called «Parábolas y dezires», epigrams of the sort found in *En castellano*. The reading arrangement of *Ancia* differs most from that of *Angel fieramente humano,* which interpolates poems of existentialist doubt prior to the poems of commitment. It is closer to that of *Redoble de conciencia* in that both proceed directly from poems of social commentary to those of Marxist commitment. Among new poems of social commentary is «15 de diciembre de 1950», addressed to Gabriel Celaya —complement of earlier poems to De Nora and Alberti— and «Virante». In the latter poem, the speaker offers a hand, inviting listeners to follow him because he knows the way. Then he represents his change of heart in a punning allegory. He, who used to spin off balance now spins the threads of hope:

> Eché la noche por la borda. Al borde
> del vértigo, viré y cambié de sitio.
> Hoy hilo, hilo a hilo, la esperanza
> a ojos cerrados, sin perder el hilo. (An, 160)

Importantly, as the Social Logos, he spins the threads of hope without losing «el hilo rojo que atraviesa toda la Historia y sirve de guía a aquellos que quieren comprenderla».[30] This reference to the Marxist tenet of the interdependency of economic, political, and cultural relations clarifies the meaning of *esperanza* in the stanza cited, it is the hope for a new society, for a Marxist Revolution.

II. *Social Logos*

The speaker as new man is protagonist of a trilogy that includes *Pido la paz y la palabra, En castellano,* and *Que trata de España*.[31] In contrast to a formal structure of separate thematic categories, typical of the first cycle of works, *Pido la paz y la palabra* and *En castellano* lack textual divisions. The speaker figuratively sets aside pen and paper to broadcast his message through the streets. Different types of poems —social criticism, artistic tribute, pledges of solidarity, appeals, explanations, witticisms, testimony, pleas, harangues, challenges, confessions, and elegies— are intermingled, intuitively clustered, according to various associations. A line may have from one to sixteen syllables or more, poems may be as short as two brief lines or run for pages. The tone modulates from gentle pleas to scathing indictment. From sonnets —«cárceles de mis sueños»— Otero turns to rhymed and unrhymed couplets, tercets, quatrains, and free verse. Just as disparate are his themes. Solidarity, oppression, protest, and the Spanish landscape are accentuated by motifs such as children singing, bells tolling, the Eiffel Tower, the Tree of Guernica, and Tibidabo. All are fragmentary elements to be identified, enumerated, tabulated, interpreted to confirm the range of Otero's interests.[32] Without the Marxist hermeneutics to guide interpretation, the meaning of these poems might go in many directions. This is because allegory and affectivity —Otero's predominant modes— are not literal but abstract. The speaker, attributing his suffering to Spain's social disorder, for example, makes vague references to hatred, bloodshed, and fratricide and to his physical state, correlative of his state of mind: «Mis ojos hablarían si mis labios / enmudecie-

---

[30] Engel's phrase is cited by CELAYA, HR, 8.
[31] BLAS DE OTERO, *Con la inmensa mayoría (Pido la paz y la palabra. En castellano)* (Buenos Aires: Losada, 1972); *Que trata de España* (Madrid: Visor, 1977). References to these editions appear in the text preceded by the appropriate initials: PPP, EC, QTE.
[32] «Blas de Otero y Muñoz», *La Estafeta Literaria*, No. 4 (30 April 1944), p. 9: «... raramente lee novelas, como no tengan un gran contenido de valor puramente literario... Ciencia, Historia y Filosofía, jamás: le parecen frívolas y poco serias. Su alimento predilecto lo constituyen los clásicos españoles... También frecuenta a los místicos y lee sobre ellos. En este momento tiene en trance de lectura *San Francisco*, de Chesterton; la tragicomedia lopesca de *Peribáñez* y todos los libros de poesía del mundo, porque Blas, al revés que la generalidad de los poetas, lee siempre las poesías de los demás, y nunca las suyas.»

ran... y mi mano derecha seguiría / hablando» (PPP, 15). Such poetry belongs to Socialist Realism because it promotes the doctrines of the PCE. But, at the same time, it avoids crude esthetic practices often associated with this literary doctrine. The unitary character of the trilogy is achieved, not by a symmetrical arrangement, as in the first cycle, but rather through the speaker as the personification of the Marxist ethos.

The impression of a single protagonist in Otero's corpus is contrived from a few details that maintain the speaker's integrity through successive reincarnations. The fettered angel, suitable image for existentialist anguish, was unable to help mankind. The humanized Christ, dubious Logos, was unable to promise eternal life, his ability put in doubt by an unheeding God, thus he helped mankind by doing away with himself. Unlike the angel, unsure of his message, or the Christ-figure, unsure of the value of the message, the Social Logos is himself the authentic message. The speaker surmounts the separation between bringer and word by being the living text. In the first poem of this cycle, the speaker reports that he tore up his poems. This tactic erases distinction between such terms as writer and text, message and action; it also dramatizes the speaker's process of integration with his fellow men. Rejecting a false sense of uniqueness that yielded only anguish and alienation, the speaker becomes universal, finding terrestrial salvation in mankind. The textual details by which this illusion is maintained appear at infrequent, yet crucial points in the reading order. Thus both works under discussion begin with lines that remind readers of the pretense that this is oral poetry. The poem «A la inmensa mayoría» gives a brief history of the persona and concludes as the speaker's last will and testament is delivered «en carne y hueso» (PPP, 10). The dedicatory poem of *En castellano* keeps the metonymic convention, opening with: «Aquí tenéis mi voz...» (EC, 79). Immediately following, «Papeles inéditos» is a prose reminder that the speaker has set aside pen and paper to save the world «por publicar con el ejemplo lo que ya silencié con los papeles» (EC, 82). This procedure, admittedly a falsification, is further enhanced when, in «Juicio final» (PPP, 36-37), the speaker declares that he is an unrepentant sinner, an angel fallen to earth where he belongs. The reverse of heaven, earth is the starting mark of his journey to the homeland of mankind. Therefore this final judgment is pronounced not by God, but by the Social Logos.

Spain, the speaker's admitted obsession, is the arena for his struggle in the name of peace and social justice. The nation's beauty inspires his lyricism, its faults his censure, and its backwardness his grief. The ties that bind him to Spain are beyond rational explanation: «Creo en ti, patria... aunque hoy hay sólo sombra / he visto / y he creído» (PPP, 71). Like writers of earlier generations whom he echoes, he is quick to denounce Spain:

> España, espina de mi alma. Uña
> y carne de mi alma. Arráncame
> tu cáliz de las manos. (PPP, 44)

The speaker is not simply quarreling with Spanish censors, who refused to allow publication of *Pido la paz y la palabra* without corrections or *En castellano* in any form.[33] Like his idealistic forebear, Don Quijote, who tilted with giants that were windmills, the Social Logos tilts with the Regime, which is not what it appears either. Though he suffers blows, he casts the Marxist message to the winds absolutely sure that his beliefs will eventually triumph and that the people, his Dulcinea, will prevail:

> Por más que el aspa le voltee
> y españa le derrote
> y cornee,
> poderoso caballero
> es don Quijote.
>
> Por más que el aire se lo cuente
> al viento, y no lo crea
> y la aviente,
> muy airosa criatura
> es Dulcinea. (EC, 109)

The speaker unites the convention of his own changing identity in the image of the phoenix with a vow of solidarity in «Yotro», whose title itself represents the unity of speaker and people : «... un hombre. ¿Solo? Con su yo soluble / en ti, en ti y en ti... Nosotros. Ancho mar... Es el bosque. Y es el mar...» (EC, 176-77). The speaker is one with the sea of humanity and, switching metaphors, with those who are rooted in belief like trees in the earth.

Otero's medium imposes the conventions of print, thus the pretense that his poetry is oral creates cognitive tautness, a clash of conventions he exploits to esthetic advantage. By requesting readers to pretend they are listening not reading, Otero implies that writing falsifies the authenticity of experience, and that his «oral» poetry, therefore, is more authen-

---

[33] Referring to censorship, J. M. COHEN, «Since the Civil War. New Currents in Spanish Poetry», *Encounter*, 12, No. 2 (February 1959), p. 53, states: «Meanwhile, as I write, the censorship has made a sudden attack on the poets, selecting Blas de Otero as the first victim. From a collected volume of his early poems [*Ancia*] two pieces were struck out as it went to press. Then a reprint of a later book [*Pido la paz y la palabra*] was forbidden, and his newest collection [*En castellano*] likewise prevented from appearing. None of his work in the last six years, in which its social content has become a little more pronounced than before, can be bought in Spain. It is, however, to be published in Buenos Aires.» Concerning the censorship of *Pido la paz y la palabra*, MARIO HERNÁNDEZ, «Su obra: la reordenación permanente», *El País*, 30 June 1979, p. 21, writes: «Previamente había publicado *Pido la paz y la palabra* (1955), uno de sus libros más perfectos. La censura obligó a marcar con puntos suspensivos los versos 'impublicables' y condujo al poeta a buscar neologismos que ocultaran referencias explícitas.»

tically sincere. Further, the speaker must project sincerity if his political propaganda is to be believed.

As works of propaganda, *Pido la paz y la palabra* and *En castellano* are evidence of changes in party thinking during the mid-1950s. As the Regime gradually relaxed stringent cultural control, the PCE took the initiative of calling for a national reconciliation based on the argument that the postwar division of Spain into two ideological camps had changed to a division based on wealth alone. That is, the rich were getting richer and the poor, poorer. Therefore the Party declared: «Una política de venganza no serviría a España para salir de la situación en que se encuentra. Lo que España necesita es la paz civil, la reconciliación de sus hijos, la libertad».[34] Otero's project anticipated the Party's announcement of the doctrine of peace. Otero, as a militant, observed the temper of the Party and the people as he traveled through Spain, giving lectures or poetry readings. Additionally, he was in Paris around 1952 in voluntary exile to write an «explosive» book of poems.[35] And, while neither *Pido la paz y la palabra* nor *En castellano* are pure propaganda, they are the esthetic representation of the new policy, they plead for the Party and its doctrine of peace.[36]

Peace, the central theme of the cycle's first work, is mentioned in two poems that are prayer-like: «Pido la paz y la palabra» (PPP, 56-57) and «En el nombre de España, paz» (PPP, 64-65). The theme continues in the second work via the dedicatory poem, whose last stanza is a vow of peace mindful of Lenin's rationalization of violence: «Labraremos la paz, la paz, la paz, / a fuerza de caricias, a puñetazos puros» (EC, 80). More interesting is a poem of peace that incorporates the matriarchal figure of Dolores Ibárruri. Doubtless, «Hija de Yago» may be read as addressed solely to a personified Spain. But since the Social Logos is a sincerely committed Marxist, as devoted to his political mother, La Pasionaria, as to his nation, Spain, he repeats to both the party message he is to deliver:

> Madre y maestra mía, triste, espaciosa España.
> He aquí a tu hijo. Ungenos, madre. Haz
> habitable tu ámbito. Respirable tu extraña
> paz. Para el hombre. Paz. Para el aire. Madre, paz. (PPP, 20)

---

[34] *Historia del PCE*, pp. 255-57.
[35] Jorge Semprún, *Autobiografía de Federico Sánchez*, pp. 95-96.
[36] Carlos Blanco Aguinaga, «El mundo entre ceja y ceja: releyendo a Blas de Otero», *Papeles de Son Armadans*, No. 254-255 (May-June 1977), pp. 159-60: «Diálogo clandestino, pues, con todas las limitaciones inherentes a la clandestinidad... puede ocurrir que se encuentre el poeta hablando desde arriba, tan oscura y arbitrariamente como quienes sólo quieren dirigirse a la 'minoría'; sin conocer, la respuesta a la mano dialogante que extiende... Riesgo: que las más sencillas palabras se vean arrastradas por la expresión indirecta cuyo secreto pertenece sólo a los iniciados.»

«No espantéis el ruiseñor» in a Marxist reading also yields a message to Ibárruri, who must open the door to the new age: «Abre / la puerta al alba, / madre. / Mira, / madre, que viene / herida» (EC, 142). Otero and Ibárruri are Basques, he from Bilbao, she from Gallarta, which is the title of an enigmatic poem evoking the mystique of the masses: «corto en palabras, pero en olas ancho» (PPP, 25).

These works of propaganda propose to strengthen solidarity among party members and sympathizers by emphasizing their common bonds. One of the warmest messages is «Aceñas», which joins an embrace of friendship with a pleasant vista of waterwheels turning in the swift current of the Duero. The repetition of the vowel «o», perfect sound and form, encircles the shapes the speaker remembers:

> Hoy que estoy (dilo en voz muy baja) solo.
>
> ... Es hermoso oír la ronda
> de las letras, en torno
> a la palabra abrazadora: C-o-m-p-a-
> ñ-e-r-o-s. Es como un sol sonoro.
>
> El Duero. Las aceñas de Zamora.
> El cielo luminosamente rojo. (PPP, 23-34)

The speaker extends these bonds of brotherhood to an entire people on the side of peace, harbinger of the new age dawning: «He salido a la luz de la esperanza. / Hombro a hombro, hasta ver un pueblo en pie / de paz, izando un alba» (EC, 128) But, as he implies elsewhere, peace must be fought for by common effort: «Roja bandera herida por el alba... sé que es bello combatir unidos» (EC, 165). Unfortunately, not everyone the speaker addresses takes the messages to heart.[37]

The bourgeois notion of freedom, usually defined negatively as the absence of constraints on action, contrasts with the Marxist, which insists that a prior state of economic equality is an indispensable condition of freedom. In the *Manifiesto,* Marx described the new society as «una asociación en que el libre desenvolvimiento de cada uno será la condición del libre desenvolvimiento de todos». It was obvious to Marx that to secure equality open struggle might be necessary. One of Otero's titles reminds readers of this doctrine: «Libertad supone o significa igualdad de condiciones para el desarrollo de todo hombre» (EC, 116-17). Following

---

[37] These verses by «Punto redondo», «A Blas», *Champa,* No. 8-9 (May-June 1954, p. 5), indicate to understand the message is not to accept it: «¡Ah, Blas! / A brazo partido / luchaste y ahora / dices que vences, / que has vencido. / Hablas / con los amigos / y dices 'la vida', / 'hay que seguir', / 'es lo que digo'. / ¡Ah, Blas! / Te lo dijimos: / si pones tu fe / frente al mar / estás perdido. / ¡Ah, Blas! / A brazo partido. / Te fuiste. Y después / de todo, ¿quién es / el que ha perdido? / Además / que más da. / 'Aquí no hay más / Yo respondo'. / Tú lo has dicho'.»

Marx's reasoning, the speaker of «Zurbarán 1957» alludes to the lack of freedom and equality in Spain when he asks: «dónde / está el trapo, / la Libertad tirada por el suelo» (EC, 174-75); and when he states: «España / libre. (Violentas / carcajadas.)» (EC, 113). Therefore, in the name of future freedom Otero satirizes Spain in poems of protest such as «Hija de Yago» (PPP, 19-20), «Biotz-Begietan» (PPP, 49-50), «Condal entredicho» (EC, 122-23), «Muy lejos» (EC, 124-25), «Caniguer» (EC, 170-71).[38]

By satirizing unsatisfactory conditions, Otero builds his case for revolutionary change. Properly biased assertions, a point of view free of mixed feelings, and laughter at the expense of the opposition form the strategic basis from which Otero launches his poems of pleading. As the Social Logos in action, he sincerely delivers familiar messages: Spanish solidarity in «Juntos» (PPP, 39-40) and «Entendámonos» (EC, 146-47); foreign solidarity in «Me llamarán, nos llamarán a todos» (PPP, 41-42) and «Quiero» (EC, 148-49); a polite call to rebellion in «Proal» (PPP, 43-44), and finally, a generous number of credos, of which the best-known is certainly «En la inmensa mayoría» (PPP, 72-73), a confession of endless faith.[39] Written from a Marxist viewpoint, these poems form part of a tradition Otero shared with Neruda, Vallejo, Alberti, Hernández, and De Nora. But that tradition, in Otero's eyes, was not limited to these Marxist writers.

Antonio Machado, neither Communist nor Socialist, was adopted by the PCE as the «poeta del pueblo» since his views and actions did not impede the social revolution.[40] Otero, who admires Machado as the greatest Spanish poet, includes three poems of homage in these collections. In «Con nosotros», with its allusion to solidarity, he salutes Machado's populism:

> En este Café
> se sentaba don Antonio
> Machado.

---

[38] For rhetorical analysis of these poems, see: GEOFFREY R. BARROW, «Some Otero Satires of Hypocrisy», *Neophilologus*, 64, No. 2 (April 1980), pp. 227-43.

[39] Otero described the intention behind *Pido la paz y la palabra* in an interview with Claude Couffon, cited by JOAQUÍN GALÁN, *Blas de Otero, palabras para un pueblo* (Barcelona: Ambito Literario, 1978), p. 71: «Abordo lo que podríamos llamar un tema histórico. Una vez más es el hombre lo que me interesa, pero no ya el hombre considerado como individuo aislado, sino como miembro de una colectividad inserta en una situación histórica determinada. Los problemas evocados son los que se plantean hoy a toda la humanidad: asegurar la paz y obtener una libertad auténtica. Esta libertad, como he dicho en uno de mis poemas, supone o significa igualdad de condiciones para el desarrollo de todo hombre. Naturalmente, mis poemas se refieren sobre todo a los hombres de mi patria: España.»

[40] For the definitive recuperation, see: MANUEL TUÑÓN DE LARA, *Antonio Machado, poeta del pueblo* (Barcelona: Laia, 1975).

>   Silencioso
> y misterioso, se incorporó
> al pueblo... (PPP, 29)

He develops the allusion in «Palabras reunidas para Antonio Machado», portraying the foremost poet of the Generation of 1898 as communion host for the people — «*el mar*» in Otero's metaphor:

> El mar
> se derrama hacia Francia, te reclama,
> quiere, queremos
> tenerte, convivirte,
>   compartirte
> como el pan. (EC, 154)

Machado's verses are so familiar to Otero that they surface as he writes «En el corazón y en los ojos» (PPP, 27-28). On the other hand, he feels obliged to withhold allegiance when Machado states that the future is unmapped territory: «no hay camino, / se hace camino al andar». Otero believes in the Revolution — and the new age it promises. Both poets look to the future, but Machado does so with uncertainty, while Otero with doctrinal sureness:

> Sol en los hombros, avanzan
> unidos.
>
> Hay. Siempre. Hay
> caminos. (PPP, 38)

«Ahora», title of this poem, invites readers to ponder the circumstances that invalidate Machado's doubt and explain Otero's commitment.

By the same principle of prefiguration, Otero claims as part of his heritage the poetry of Rubén Darío.[41] The author of *Cantos de vida y esperanza* wrote in the preface of that work: «Yo no soy un poeta para las muchedumbres. Pero sé que indefectiblemente tengo que ir a ellas.» This statement describes Otero's own position with such accuracy that he used it as the epigraph of *Angel fieramente humano,* modifying the phrase by substituting «de mayorías» for «para las muchedumbres». In recognition of the good intentions Darío shares with him, Otero echoes another line from the same preface in the title: «Yo soy aquel que ayer no más decía...» (PPP, 34-35). The despair Darío felt before death, since he believed we do not know where we are going nor from whence we come, in Otero's poem is pessimism doubly felt, first before death, then before the chance he would not see a Revolution in Spain.

Otero's most important poem concerning other writers is the penul-

---

[41] Compare also: BLAS DE OTERO, «Rubén Darío y la poesía española contemporánea», *Champa,* No. 15 (March 1955) p. 5.

timate of *En castellano* dedicated to a certain Nicolai Vaptzarov and worth citing in its entirety for comment:

> La soledad se abre hambrientamente,
> ah todo alrededor es hombre y fronda
> de hombro arraigado en la raíz más honda:
> la tierra, firme, descieladamente.
>
> Ah noche, y noche y noche en pecho y frente,
> tapia del mar, barrido a la redonda
> por ola y ola y ola en ronda y ronda
> azul y blanca: roja de repente.
>
> Todos los nombres que llevé en las manos
> —César, Nazim, Antonio, Vladimiro,
> Paul, Gabriel, Pablo, Nicolás, Miguel.
>
> Aragón, Rafael y Mao—, humanos
> ángeles, fulgen, suenan como un tiro
> único, abierto en paz sobre el papel. (EC, 178-79)

Before listing the names of Communist poets who are his ideological and artistic mentors, Otero reviews the motives of his own poetry. In the first stanza, he notes that on the edge of the abyss he chose solidarity with men, who like trees were rooted firmly to the earth, rather than the isolation of an «uprooted» individual reaching to the heavens. Yet, as he indicates in the second stanza, he was still anguished because the besieged masses, like a walled-off sea, were surrounded by Falangist (blue) and Traditionalist (white) forces. Finally, a Communist (red) force gathers strength perhaps to break through the encirclement. Otero places his loyalty with this force and with its poets, whose verses in the name of peace «crack like a pistol shot». United in goals and outlook with his guides, he calls their names one by one —Vallejo, Hikmet, Machado, Mayakovsky, Eluard, Celaya, Neruda, Guillén, Hernández, Aragon, Alberti, and Mao Zedong— in reply to random conjectures that his poetry is not written primarily in the Marxist cause.

The fluid arrangement of *Pido la paz y la palabra* and *En castellano* yields to orderly sequence in the last part of the trilogy, *Que trata de España*. Like *Ancia* this work condenses a decade of Otero's poetry; unlike *Ancia* only a few of the poems are from previous collections. Consistent with the title, this work is a treatise; the topics are in logical succession with each explored at length.[42] In reading order the chapters deal with the biography of the speaker, Marxist hermeneutics, songs inspired by Spanish folk music, lyric paintings of Spanish landscapes, revisionist

---

[42] Otero was quoted by ANTONIO NÚÑEZ, «Encuentro con Blas de Otero», *Insula,* No. 259 (June 1968), p. 3, as saying that the theme of this work too was «ante todo el de la paz, una paz activa, y la lucha de los pueblos llamados subdesarrollados y colonizados o neocolonizados, etc.».

Iberian history, and finally, the history of Marxist revolutionary progress. This systematic exposition, based on a total of more poems than the two previous collections combined, adds extraordinary force to Otero's views.[43] If the stylistic innovations are few and the themes customary, this work is still important because it develops a line of writing to its perfect form.[44]

In *Que trata de España,* the Social Logos preserves the integrity of his persona as he reveals new information about himself, furthering the impression of autobiography. The speaker incorporates the crisis of doubt and commitment with images that suggest the awakening of a somnambulist: «Desperté / tarde. Me lavé (el alma): en fin, bajé / a la calle» (QTE, 159). He also interweaves family memories, details of schooling, names of towns, cities, rivers, and nations he has visited. However, these details simply create a space and time for his nostalgia and criticism, offering him a springboard to general issues. They do not recount a biography in the customary sense. In «Noticias de todo el mundo» (QTE, 51), the speaker confesses that at forty-seven years of age he is rather frightened at being no more than a Spanish poet of the twentieth century, unread by illiterates, workers, or children. The confession becomes an avowal to combat their fear in the name of peace and better wages. Similarly, the speaker lists his major works in «Impreso prisionero», each characterized allusively. References to his most recent work gave him an excuse to denounce censorship, for Otero first published *En castellano* in French, under the title *Parler clair:* «Hablo / en español y entiéndese en francés. / ¡Oh que genial trabucamiento / del diablo! / ¿Hablar en castellano? Se prohíbe» (QTE, 32). The speaker is already a habitual traveler in Spain, a trait emphasized in «Perdurando» (QTE, 19), where he lists major cities of the Peninsula. The socialist nations of the world are vistas he adds to his itinerary in this work, usually as a foil to Spain. In Moscow, Leningrad, Georgia, and Shanghai, the speaker nostalgically recalls the Cantabrian ports of his natal region, topic of two poems (QTE, 27-29). An eastern journey from the Neva river at Leningrad to Peking is motive for the speaker's reaffirmation of faith in the immense majority, despite some sad stories he might relate (QTE, 174). Three other poems —«Historia de la reconquista» (QTE, 160), «Cuando venga Fidel se dice mucho» (QTE, 182-83), «Poeta colonial» (QTE, 184)— disclose his solidarity with the Cuban Revolution. Clearly, the speaker is committed to the Party.

---

[43] For a thematic study, see: EMILIO MIRÓ, «España, tierra y palabra, en la poesía de Blas de Otero», *Cuadernos Hispanoamericanos,* No. 356 (February 1980), pp. 274-97.
[44] EMILIO ALARCOS LLORACH, *La poesía de Blas de Otero* (Salamanca: Anaya, 1966), pp. 151-54.

It is a truism of Otero criticism that the poet's ideological progression is observable in the prepositions he uses with the phrase «*la inmensa mayoría*»; from «*a*» to «*con*» and then to «*en*», indicating a progressively closer identification with the masses. This stylistic manifestation of his evolution culminates in *Que trata de España*. The Social Logos not only speaks to, with, and in the immense majority, he also speaks from the immense majority using its own words. He is *vox populi* in the phrase's most literal sense.

Popular wisdom is support and source of Otero's word. Popular language, composed of words that can be touched and felt —«*voz bordada*», «*pedazos de palabras*», «*sílabas de tierra*» (QTE, 46-47)— is a language for talking about matter of *this* world. The speaker refers to stylistic renewal found in oral language when he says: («*Escribo / hablando,* escucheando, caminando») (QTE, 47). The masses are like an open book to be read by the speaker, who transfers their words to paper with a minimum of intervention. The interwoven metaphors mentioned in the title of «Voz del mar, voz del libro» allow the speaker to protest the burden of the superstructure, which like heavy ships, weighs down the sea of humanity:

> Yo le ayudo...
> ... ...
> a levantar las olas entre las líneas
> que el mar alzó desde su mudo abismo.
>
> Si me pongo a gritar, es que el mar grita
> desde hace siglos algo tan sencillo
> como «¡Me pesan mucho los navíos!
> ¿Quién me ayuda a quitármelos de encima? (QTE, 62)

Otero adopts this metaphor in «El mar suelta un párrafo sobre la inmensa mayoría» (QTE, 63), an experiment in personification. The speaker is the sea, encircled by reclaimed land, which it partially recovers from time to time. Though illiterate, the sea nevertheless claims to speak more eloquently than poets, merchants, or mercenaries. Laughing at false redeemers, it preaches with its waves, which inspire fear among the powerful. To authenticate the pretense of an illiterate speaker in this poem, Otero omits all punctuation except the final period, using capital letters to begin thoughts and uncomplicated syntax to indicate structure. The Social Logos uses this technique again in «Una carta» (QTE, 147-50), employing the literary device of a found document. The speaker «transcribes» a letter he encountered on the rugged rise above Alicante. According to the letter, it was written by a certain Carmen in Orihuela to her recently inducted brother, Manuel, who sent her a snapshot of himself in uniform. The speaker alternates «transcriptions», revealing imperfect orthography that tacitly condemns the level of Spanish literacy, with his own parenthetical asides concerning the misguided, but good-intentioned, behavior of the underclass.

Passing the watchword of the Revolution is as important in this collection as in Otero's earlier works. Sometimes the poet inserts propaganda indirectly, as in the poems just discussed, other times he is explicit. Otero dedicates one poem to the PCE celebrity Marcos Ana, sentenced twice to death and finally released after serving twenty-three years. His anthology, *Las soledades del muro,* written while in prison, gained an international reputation, affirming the ideological temper of the 1960s.[45] Otero celebrates their friendship, muses on the years of servitude, and asserts his *compañero*'s importance as one who helps spread the watchword of freedom:

> La libertad por el suelo.
> Tú te levantas, la apoyas
> en el hombro del obrero.
>
> El olivo y las espigas
> te dan la mano, se pasan,
> brisa a brisa, la consigna. (QTE, 120)

The sign of propaganda takes various forms. In one musical poem, it is simply the repetition of «*alegría*» and the mention of «*campo de amapolas*», «*centro del fuego*», and «*pañuelo rojo*» (QTE, 113). Or it may be the promise of a better future to replace the dismal present:

> aventura truncada, orgullo hecho pedazos,
> lugar de lucha y días hermosos que se acercan
> colmados de claveles colorados, España. (QTE, 121)

And it is an order directing an unadorned Spain to don the symbolic color of progress:

> incomprensible España pupitre sin maestra
> hermosa calamidad
> ponte tu traje colorado danza ataca canta (QTE, 184)

Occasionally the countersign is a witty phrase, a rejuvenated cliché: «Quiero una España mañanada / donde el odio y el hoy no maniaticen» (QTE, 158). On the other hand, the term may be developed elaborately through several poems, as in a series concerning Don Quijote, whom the speaker criticizes for lack of solidarity, for being ruled by illusions. However, the speaker too has known the exalted despair of Cervantes' hero, thus he confides:

---

[45] MARCOS ANA, *Las soledades del muro* (Madrid: Akal, 1977), back cover: «... traducidos a todos los idiomas de los pueblos en lucha, aparecen por vez primera en una editorial española para que puedan ser conocidos, tras años de prohibiciones, por sus compatriotas.»

> Debajo del cielo de tu idealismo,
> la tierra de arada de mi realismo.
> Siéntate a mi lado, señor Don Quijote.
>
> Junto al pozo amargo de la soledad,
> la fronda de la solidaridad.
> Sigue a Sancho Pueblo, señor Don Quijote. (QTE, 127)

Cervantes, creator of the ideologically failed Don Quijote, is censured also: «En su pluma nadie medra» (QTE, 125). By far the longest poem of the series is «La muerte de Don Quijote» (QTE, 131-35), a collage of putative quotations involving Cervantes, Don Quijote, and Sancho, which builds to a climax where Don Quijote on his deathbed surrounded by mankind, slowly rises, embraces the closest person, and begins to walk. Otero, in effect, changes Spain's best-known literary figure into a new man as part of a plan to revise perceptions so that Spain might enter the age of socialism where all will thrive.

Otero's works experienced a pattern of reception that was far from conventional. After an initial flurry of critical reviews between 1950-1952, his new poetry was neglected by leading critics until the late 1960s, and his later works were discussed widely in Spanish publications only during the last years of his life. To what extent this pattern was forced by censorship, or was adopted voluntarily by prudent critics, is unclear. However, it would be exaggerated to believe that Otero experienced the sort of censorship known in countries such as the USSR or Cuba by writers like Andrei Sinayavsky or Heberto Padilla.

Those who reviewed *Angel fieramente humano* were aware of Otero's heterodoxy according to observations they made about the work. Bleiberg indicated that the poetry was not a mere statement of position, though it shared Celaya's approach, because it joined a refined poetic technique with a true concern of the times.[46] Crémer called notice to the fact that in the Adonais contest for 1949 *Angel fieramente humano* aroused so much attention without receiving an award that one member of the panel, unnamed in the article, publicly declared Otero deserving of the prize.[47] *Redoble de conciencia,* which won the Premio Boscán, was admired for its technique and content. Bousoño, for example, judged Otero one of the few excellent poets in Spain, as expressive as Quevedo.[48] Noting that Otero addressed the great majority, Bousoño described a single technique used to this end, the transformation of set phrases and clichés. A young

---

[46] GERMÁN BLEIBERG, Review of *Angel fieramente humano, Insula,* No. 54 (15 June 1950), pp. 4-5.
[47] VICTORIANO CRÉMER, Review of *Angel fieramente humano, Espadaña,* No. 45 (1950).
[48] CARLOS BOUSOÑO, «La poesía de Blas de Otero», *Insula,* No. 71 (November 1951), p. 2.

reviewer for *Laye,* publication of the SEU in Barcelona, identified Otero's position as one of nonconformist rebellion and objected to the excessively imprecatory tone.[49] Perhaps one of the most influential essays about Otero's early poetry was that by Dámaso Alonso, where he commented upon their shared «uprootedness».[50] Alonso, after arguing that Otero's principal themes are those essential to mankind —God, love, and death— suggested that his poetry was a rich source of material for future stylistic analysis. This essay reappeared as the preface to *Ancia* in 1958. Yet, the public attention enjoyed initially by Otero's poetry was short-lived.

Between 1951 and 1958, Otero published new poems in various places: *La Isla de los Ratones* («Gallarta», No. 24-26); *Cántico* («Arboles abolidos», No. 1); *Champa* («Pido la paz y la palabra», «En el nombre de España», No. 3-4, p. 5). The last publication also held an interview with José García Nieto, asking him about Blas de Otero.[51] The editor of *Garcilaso* stated that he understood the motivation and esthetic provenance of Otero's poetry, but hesitated to judge it for his own lack of serenity. Avoiding the issue of orthodoxy, García Nieto classified Otero as fundamentally a romantic, religious poet. Then, without allowing that Otero was the best Spanish poet, «as some have said», he agreed that Otero was the most interesting, yet warned: «Pero Blas de Otero sabe que la misión de la Poesía, como la palabra de Aquél, no es la de venir a traer la paz.» After this interview, Otero's poetry was seldom discussed publicly.[52] A review of *Pido la paz y la palabra,* by José María Caballero Bonald, sensitively analyzed Otero's stylistic art, «[a]l margen de su aparente condición didáctica...»[53] *Insula* published «Juntos» from *Pido la paz y la palabra* under the title «Desterrado hijo de occidente» in No. 121 (15

---

[49] A[LFONSO] C[OSTAFREDA], Review of *Redoble de conciencia, Laye,* No. 17 (January 1952).

[50] DÁMASO ALONSO, «Poesía arraigada y poesía desarraigada», *Poetas españoles contemporáneos* (Madrid: Gredos, 1952), pp. 370-80.

[51] «Tres poetas vizcaínos: Jaime Delclaux, Blas de Otero y Javier Bengoechea. José García Nieto habla para *Champa*», *Champa,* 3, No. 17-18 (May-June 1955), pp. 4-5.

[52] Apparently Otero entered contests despite rebuffs, if a curious article from 1956 is at all accurate. Published in *La Estafeta Literaria,* No. 52 (14 July 1956), p. 8, it reported that in the competition for the «Tomás Morales» prizes —8000, 6000, and 3000 *pesetas*— with a panel composed of Florentino Pérez Embid, Rafael Balbín Lucas, Pedro de Lorenzo, and José Hierro, 126 works were judged. The semi-finalists for each prize were: first, Pino Ojeda and García Nieto; second, Pino Ojeda and Blas de Otero; third, Blas de Otero and Garciasol. The winners were announced as: first, Rafael Morales, *El alba;* second, García Nieto, *De cara al Atlántico;* third, Pino Ojeda, *La piedra sobre la colina.* No explanation of the discrepancy between finalists and winners was offered. The awarded works seem to have escaped critical acclaim.

[53] JOSÉ MARÍA CABALLERO BONALD, Review of *Pido la paz y la palabra, Papeles de Son Armadans,* No. 1 (July 1956), pp. 118-22.

January 1956), p. 5; but the next reference to this work in *Insula* appears two years later, parenthetically, in Cano's review of *Ancia*.

Ancia of course dealt with poetry from Otero's first period, a relatively «safe» topic. An extraordinary work, it earned the Premio de la Crítica for 1958. Representative reviews focused upon Otero's enrichment of the original collections with new poems, the condensed refinement of the single entity, and the contrast between *Ancia* and *Pido la paz y la palabra*. José Luis Cano claimed that Otero protested an unjust society, but asserted that his poetry was not to be confused with partisan poetry or poetry of propaganda.[54] In support, Cano cited Otero's statement in the *Antología consultada* to the effect that social poetry was acceptable as long as the poet regarded social themes with the same sincerity he felt for traditional themes. In *Acento Cultural* Carlos Vélez, while reviewing *Ancia*, mentioned as his favorite work *Pido la paz y la palabra*.[55] Then, drawing implications from the same statement cited by Cano, concluded that «si puede existir una revalorización de la poesía ante el público en general, sólo puede estar en este camino, el del cuerpo limpio, el de la lucha directa con las armas sobre la mesa». Both critics mentioned their anticipation concerning Otero's forthcoming volume, *Con la inmensa mayoría*, to be published by Losada in Buenos Aires.

Around the same time, several poems that would be part of *En castellano* were published in *Cuadernos Hispanoamericanos* and *Papeles de Son Armadans*.[56] In a comparison of these versions with those of the Losada edition, illuminating differences gauge what was allowed by the Regime's censors. For example, the final stanza of «Poética» was modified by one word: *martillo* was rewritten as *cuchillo*. The Losada version contains sensitized words — hammer and sickle:

> Apreté la voz.
> Como una mano
> alrededor del mango de un martillo
> o de la empuñadura de una hoz. (EC, 85)

In «No salgas, paloma, al campo» (EC, 113-14) words with ideological connotations were changed. They refer to the color associated with the

---

[54] José Luis Cano, «La poesía de Blas de Otero», *Insula*, No. 145 (15 December 1958), pp. 6-7.
[55] C[arlos] Vélez, Review of *Ancia*, *Acento Cultural*, No. 2 (December 1958), pp. xxxii-xxxiii. Celaya, HR, 85, mentioned that Vélez was «[u]n poeta falangista, al que en cierto momento yo creí recuperable.»
[56] Blas de Otero, «Entre 1948-1955», *Cuadernos Hispanoamericanos*, No. 91-92 (July-August 1957), pp. 157-63. Poems from *En castellano*: «Pato», «Poética», «Sol de justicia», «Nómina», «Entendámonos», «Copla del río», and «Letra». «En castellano», *Papeles de Son Armadans*, No. 27 (June 1958), pp. 329-34. Poems from *En castellano*: «Patria aprendida», «Libertad supone o significa igualdad de condiciones para el desarrollo de todo hombre», «Quiero», «Aire libre», «No salgas, paloma, al campo», «Pluma que cante».

Falangists (*azul*), and the color of the stripe added to the Spanish flag during the Second Republic (*morada*). The alternate words, *añil* and *molada* maintain the rhyme scheme so that adept readers can guess what the original words were, and savor deciphering a censored poem about censorship:

> Anda
> jaleo, jaleo,
> No dejan ver lo que escribo,
> porque escribo lo que veo.
> Sé que Castilla
> es ancha.
> Cómo decir añil, ayer,
> molada.
> Ayer.
> Mañana.

The restrictions that forced Otero to find publication abroad —Paris, Mexico City, Buenos Aires, Puerto Rico— seemed to loosen in 1963 when he arranged for *Que trata de España* to be issued simultaneously in Paris, Havana, and Barcelona. In anticipation of this event, *Insula* featured ten poems from the Spanish edition prepared by Editorial RM of Barcelona.[57] Nevertheless, when Otero examined this edition he discovered that over seventy poems, more than half, had been suppressed. Consequently he repudiated the Spanish edition, citing the French one by Ruedo Ibérico as authentic. When asked at that time what position he thought the Regime ought to take concerning art —«liberalismo, 'dirigismo', 'orientacionismo'»— Otero dryly observed that the state can censor the writer and, importantly, the writer can censor the state:[58]

> En vez de referirme a la posición del Estado respecto al arte, lo haré a la inversa. Pienso que la actitud del escritor con respecto al Estado debe ser de colaboración y servicio siempre que el Estado, a su vez, sirva realmente al pueblo y a la cultura. De no ser así, debe hacer uso de la censura. El escritor.

Despite José Luis Cano's reticence during the 1950s, the editor of *Insula* obviously admired Otero's poetry; Otero was the most represented poet in Cano's anthology of patriotic poetry, which included others such as Machado and Unamuno.[59] Cano dedicated the work to Pierre Emmanuel «que ama y sueña a España», but indicated that he had omitted «la

---

[57] BLAS DE OTERO, «Que trata de España», *Insula*, No. 197 (April 1963), p. 3.
[58] SERGIO VILAR, *Manifiesto sobre arte y libertad. Encuesta entre los intelectuales y artistas españoles* (Barcelona: Fontanella, 1964), p. 257.
[59] JOSÉ LUIS CANO, *El tema de España en la poesía contemporánea* (Madrid: Revista de Occidente, 1964).

poesía política propiamente dicha, es decir, de la que pone una clara intención de propaganda política, sea la que fuere». He selected four poems each from *Pido la paz y la palabra* and *Que trata de España,* and two from *En castellano.* Thereafter, Cano prepared an entire anthology of Otero's poetry, called *País.*[60] Half the poems of this work are from *Que trata de España,* another third from collections not published in Spain previously.

By the time *País* was published Otero was known world-wide. When interviewed in 1968, he stated that editions of his works in Spain ran from 3,000 to 5,000 copies each and were completely sold out.[61] Furthermore, the three jointly published editions of *Que trata de España* totaled 19,000 copies while editions of his works destined for Latin American audiences totaled 27,000 copies. A decade later, he was quoted as saying that he sold more than two million books in his lifetime, some in editions of 30,000 copies that were republished six and seven times, thus reaching the mass readership he sought.[62]

Gabriel Celaya and Agitprop Poetry

Celaya, in collaboration with Amparitxu Gastón, founded a small press called «Cuadernos de Poesía Norte» to indicate to the world his dedication to the pursuit of literature. Animating this publishing venture, begun in 1947, was a circle of friends Celaya attracted to San Sebastián that included Blas de Otero, Leopoldo de Luis, José Suárez Carreño, Eugenio de Nora, Miguel Labordeta, and Camilo José Cela.[63] Forgetting that other groups existed earlier and elsewhere, Celaya claimed that, with visitors such as PCE cadre Jorge Semprún after 1952, Norte was «uno de los primeros nidos de la *poesía social*».[64] Initially lacking a supply of manuscripts by other writers, Celaya maintained the rhythm of one issue per month by publishing his own works under different names to disguise the fact that all works were from his own pen.[66] Of the first six, three were poetry —*La soledad cerrada* signed with his legal name, Rafael Múgica; *Tranquilamente hablando* under the pseudonym, Juan de Leceta; and *Movimientos elementales* with his *nom de guerre,* Gabriel Celaya, assumed to avoid embarrassment to employers— alternated with translations of Rilke's *Cincuenta poemas francesas,* Blake's *El libro de Urizen,* and Rimbaud's *Una temporada en el infierno.* After the success of Norte was assured,

---

[60] BLAS DE OTERO, *País,* José Luis Cano, ed. (Barcelona: Plaza y Janés, 1971).
[61] «Encuentro con Blas de Otero», *Insula,* p. 3.
[62] «Una lírica al servicio de la inmensa mayoría», *El País,* p. 20.
[63] PIERRE-OLIVIER SEIRRA, *Gabriel Celaya* (Paris: Seghers, 1970), p. 34.
[64] GABRIEL CELAYA, *Itinerario poético* (Madrid: Cátedra, 1977), p. 22.
[65] GABRIEL CELAYA, *Las cartas boca arriba* (Madrid: Turner, 1974), p. 10.

Celaya revived the heteronyms occasionally, as in a poem Juan de Leceta addresses to Celaya:[66]

> A veces, como entonces, te recuerdo,
> Celaya, entrechocado,
> con tu furia retenida y palpitante
> desde una distancia extraña
> parecida al ensalmo,
> y con dientes reales mascando un ritmo cuadrado.
> Entonces tú cantabas a tu modo,
> y bailaba Leceta como un oso,
> y el señor Múgica pagaba todos nuestros excesos.

Inevitably critics assigned a different personality to each name in analyzing the Celaya *oeuvre:* to Múgica was attributed the surrealist poetry written prior to 1936, to Celaya the serious work after 1939, and to Leceta «el escándalo de una poesía lisa, llana y prosaica que en su amanecer unos llamaron existencial y otros social».[67] What for Celaya was a bow to editorial expediency turned out to have profound interpretive significance.

A characteristic of Celaya that weighs heavily on critics is his tendency to explain his own work through essays, declarations, and literary studies. A self-conscious poet, aware of the role he plays in the literary tradition, Celaya more than once cites Thierry Maulnier's image of the poet as a tapestry weaver, unseen behind his work, but always thinking, calculating, and maneuvering, so that threads of the design produce the desired effect on spectators.[68] Celaya places his poetry written from 1947 to 1954 in esthetic opposition to *garcilasismo* for reasons discussed earlier in reference to De Nora. But, whereas in theoretical writings De Nora emphasizes the ideological motivation of his direct poetry, Celaya tends to focus upon linguistic aspects, such as semantics, the nature of literary change, and the communicative function of literature. Among Celaya's contributions to literary debate is the theory resulting from his stylistic search, that of *prosaísmo*.

Prosaísmo is concerned with explaining why an informed choice of commonplace topics and expressions, and the use of simplified structures is not only esthetically defensible, but the only way to supplant cliché-ridden, over-embellished styles supported by the Regime's subsidized publications (Inq, 105-07) Since the official styles depended upon an aristocratic lexicon, traditional meters, and classical forms, to Celaya's mind the most obvious way to rejuvenate poetry would be to cultivate

---

[66] GABRIEL CELAYA, *Las cartas boca arriba*, p. 109.
[67] [ANGEL CRESPO], «Gabriel Celaya», *Poesía de España*, No. 1 (1960), p. 4.
[68] GABRIEL CELAYA, *Poesía y verdad* (Barcelona: Planeta, 1979), p. 49; *Inquisición de la poesía* (Madrid: Turner, 1972), pp. 55-56. Subsequent references to these editions appear in the text, preceded by PV or Inq.

a bare style. In this sense, far from sponsoring a deterioration of quality, *prosaísmo* sought quality by introducing complex simplicity. Celaya traces this theory to Zhandovism, and the coincidence between the rise of the proletarian movement and the literary preference for human themes (Inq, 221-28). Thus, he concludes, the poet's duty is to create a public «y algo más que un público», namely, the socialist Revolution. When poetry and politics intersect, Celaya believes no one can abstain from taking a position, since the appropriate analogy is not a parliamentary debate, but a struggle between different conceptions of the world.

Although Celaya and Crémer both opposed *garcilasismo,* the poet of León took issue with Celaya because of what Celaya called «ideological discrepancies».[69] In a review of Juan de Leceta's *Tranquilamente hablando* (*Espadaña,* No. 33, 1948), Crémer announced that the work was not poetry, its speaker was complacent, sarcastic, and unresponsive to his surroundings. Then, in an editorial, «Prosaísmo» (*Espadaña,* No. 38, 1949), Celaya's style was judged an inappropriate corrective for abuses by earlier poets; it only opened the door to literary dangers: ordinary language, clichés, conversational idiom, and careless rhythm and rhyme. *Espadaña* preferred a poetic attitude toward reality, one that reaped the poetry scattered along furrows sown with prose. Celaya replied by open letter to Crémer (*Espadaña,* No. 39, 1949; Inq, 64-6). He argued that he was not merely against pure poetry, surrealist poetry, and *garcilasismo;* he opposed all «poetic» poetry as a whole for its fastidious over-refinement. Consequently, he searched the poetry of the Middle Ages for new techniques, thereby discovering the value of narration, description, and argument. At this point, De Lama entered the fray with a review of *Las cosas como son* (*Espadaña,* No. 40, 1949). Conceding that it was an interesting experiment, a rambling meditation on the death of a friend, he denied that the theme qualified it as philosophy, or the varied line lengths, as poetry. Celaya's reply was a lecture, delivered in Bilbao in 1950, published the following year (PV, 37-65). He objected to the artist using his work like a well-lit shopwindow to display an ego. For Celaya, self-sacrifice to art is a moral obligation that implies a duty to reach others. Only by dedicating himself completely to his work, can the artist be rewarded by extending the limits of his being to live collectively. The true artist does not offer his work as a finished object: «La dispara fuera de sí como algo que fundamentalmente está pensado y dirigido hacia otro» (PV, 49).

---

[69] Compare Inq, 63: «El primer ataque, o por lo menos el de más resonancia dentro de nuestro pequeño mundo poético, fue en un artículo editorial de la revista *Espadaña*. Incurría en muchos tópicos porque, no ya mi poesía, sino mi ideología, le caía mal al autor de aquel texto...»

I. *Praxis of SocRealism*

The notion that the poem is an act of communication rather than an object confirms the aptness of the epistolary from of *Las cartas boca arriba*.[70] Despite the presence of letters to Otero and Neruda, the political nature of this SocReal work, surreptitiously indicated by the title's double meaning, passed without comment by censors of the Adonais collection, first publisher of the work. The letter to Otero, which opens the work, explains Celaya's vision of the ego as a kind of biological consciousness that in its higher form merges with other aspects of reality without itself disappearing and in its lower form is the strange, decadent entity, referred to in *Lo demás es silencio*. Celaya hesitates ambivalently before straightforward Marxist commitment, indicated by his use of the past tense rather than the verbal present and future:

> Y vi que era posible vivir, seguir cantando.
> Y vi que el mismo abismo de miseria medía
> como una boca hambrienta, qué grande es la esperanza.
> Con los cuatro elementos, más y menos que hombre,
> sentí que era posible salvar el mundo entero,
> salvarme en él, salvarlo, ser divino hasta en cuerpo. (PC, 354)

Obvious slogans materialize when Celaya addresses Neruda about the collective glory of proletarian life, the joy, the hope, and «la vida en un puño que golpea la hueca / cultura de una Europa que acaricia sus muertos». The final stanza of the poem is a declaration of resistance in the name of those who struggle against a decadent culture:

> Te escribo desde un puerto,
> desde una costa rota,
> desde un país sin dientes, ni párpados, ni llanto.
> Te escribo con sus muertos, te escribo por los vivos,
> por todos los que aguantan y aún luchan duramente.
> Poca alegría queda en esta España nuestra.
> Mas, ya ves, esperamos. (PC, 390)

The widely cited «A Andrés Basterra» celebrates the communion of suffering and creation Celaya feels with workers: All use their hands, transforming raw materials, realizing a promethean task, whether with lumber, steel, cement, or words. After an awkward first stanza, where Celaya comments the class difference between himself, an owner, and Andrés, a worker, the catalogues of natural resources, foreign ports, manufacturing operations, trades, and finished products roll to a grand finish in a handshake between equals: «La mano, Andés. Tu mano, medida de la mía»

---

[70] Unless otherwise indicated, references to Celaya's poetry appear in the text, preceded by PC for this edition: GABRIEL CELAYA, *Poesías completas* (Madrid: Aguilar, 1967).

(PC, 380). Other poems addressed to personal friends are typically celebrations of friendship and propaganda vehicles. Specific names mean little, as Celaya stresses: «¿qué importan los nombres? El hombre habla con el hombre».[71] It is not anymore necessary to know who Joaquín Gurruchaga is than who Andrés Basterra is. To the latter Celaya explains his notion of fraternity, to the former, he confesses his elation at having renounced bourgeois egoism, using an allegorical immersion in the sea of humanity to portray symbolically his experience:

> Al hundirme en el mar ya no fui nadie.
> Nadar es ondular, ser también agua,
> confundirse con ella, serpentino.
> ....
> Vanos fueron mis gritos personales,
> mi yo de escaparate, mis ideas,
> mis lindos sentimientos de hombre herido. (PC, 356-57)

To Jesús Olasagasti, Celaya rebelliously scorns bourgeois society in the name of a new world. He mocks the bourgeois code of moderation that stifles joy:

> Todo está prohibido: fumar, beber, reír a locas,
> disfrazarse de arcángel, entrar por los espejos,
> llamarle guardia al guardia y a una rabia, alegría,
> o dar fuego al cohete con una rosa roja. (PC, 360)

These letters indicate the direction Celaya takes in *Lo demás es silencio* and *Cantos iberos,* written during a period of «fecundity and enthusiasm» (PC, 21).

The messages of fraternity and political resistance in *Las cartas boca arriba* might seem signs of an imminent ideological metamorphosis for Celaya. In fact, this change is not complete until Celaya writes *Cantos iberos.* Thus, *Lo demás es silencio,* rather than a document of commitment, is a crucial work in Celaya's personal development as a Marxist writer, the artistic manifestation of an episode in the transformation of his consciousness.[72] It is representative, as well, of the dilemma experienced by bourgeois intellectuals who esteem their individualism, yet

---

[71] GABRIEL CELAYA, *Las cartas boca arriba,* p. 11.
[72] GABRIEL CELAYA, *Lo demás es silencio* (Madrid: Turner, 1976), p. 9. Compare, GABRIEL CELAYA, *Poesía y verdad (Papeles para un proceso)* (Pontevedra: Ediciones Litoral, 1959), p. 66 [Though sharing title with the 1979 edition, the two are not identical in content]: «Mi cantata de aquella época explica mi situación. Por un lado, me sentía identificado con el dolor del pueblo, y me parecía ver claro en qué sentido podían orientarse las soluciones. Por otro lado, llevaba en mí sin remedio unos problemas de intelectual que no podía dar por nada sin simplificar o mentir. Y así, a falta de solución limpia y lindamente dialéctica, planteé mis contradicciones como un conflicto trágico, dando voz independiente a los tres impulsos que en mí luchaban.»

who are sympathetic to Marxist notions about the nature of man and society. In Celaya's view, his own poetry is a bridge between the antecedents of social poetry in French surrealism and the politicized poetry of the 1950s (PV, 70-71). Adding plausibility is the fact that Celaya pursued university studies in Madrid and lived in the Residencia de Estudiantes, becoming acquainted with Lorca and Neruda, among others; and, during 1935-1936, he wrote two works, *Marea de silencio* and *La soledad cerrada,* the latter of which was noticeably surrealist with a Freudian emphasis.

Specific autobiographical content is scant in *Lo demás es silencio,* rather Celaya explores the general reactions suffered by the liberal psyche —ambivalence, shame, anguish over wasted ambitions and opportunities— caught in the interplay of bourgeois individualism and Marxist socialism. Therefore Marxist propaganda is subordinate to the acute dilemma of the liberal protagonist. To accentuate the tension of conflicting goals, Celaya revives the dramatic choral poem, a form with roots in the epic, which he chose for its emphasis on the auditory mode. That is, if the contest between the Medieval *mester de clerecía* and *mester de juglaría* were translated to this age, Celaya would select the latter over the former (Inq, 191). Accordingly, he chooses popular poetry over learned, a «*mester audio-visual*» that emphasizes acoustical phenomena over the visual qualities of the printed page (Inq, 161).

Given this work's subversive aspects, Celaya wisely concealed fragments in progress under the innocuous-sounding title, «La buena nueva».[83] Doubtless for similar reasons he selected a Shakespearean allusion for the title of the book; Spain has not suspected England of full-scale treachery since the times of Sir Francis Drake and his pirates.

In Celaya's description of *Lo demás es silencio,* the Protagonista represents the poet's ideological position prior to Marxist commitment, the Mensajero speaks from a rigid Stalinist outlook, and the Coro in the background is the indecisive *pueblo-mar,* composed of the silenced victims of oppression, for whom the poet feels morally obliged to speak (IP, 23). To impart depth to this ideological material, Celaya draws upon Freudian psychic components; thus, the Protagonista functions as the deliberating ego, the Mensajero as the rigid superego, and the Coro as the instinctual, unconscious id. By employing these divisions of the mind to underpin characters, Celaya gives the sympathetic edge to the Protagonista, who wavers between the admonishments of the Mensajero and the invitations of the Coro; he is a tragic hero torn between duty and chaos.

---

[73] Fragments appeared in the following: *El Pájaro de Paja,* No. 2 (February 1951), No. 5 (August 1951); *Deucalión,* No. 5 (March 1952). FANNY RUBIO, *Las revistas poéticas españolas (1939-1975)* (Madrid: Turner, 1976), cites: p. 206, *La Calandria,* No. 2 (February 1951); pp. 222-23, *Doña Endrina,* No. 2 (1951), No. 4 (1952).

The Protagonista, in the mind of the Mensajero, is what is known to Marxists as a «superfluous man».[74] Neither clearly good nor evil, he proclaims his neutrality on any issue, his understanding and sympathy for both sides. His pretentions baffle a member of the Coro:

> Ni verdadero ni falso,
> eres tan sólo un poeta
> que si vive de mentiras,
> también siente lo que inventa.
> No sé por dónde cogerte,
> Gabriel Celaya Leceta... (PC, 431-32)

Vague, ambiguous, suffering the pangs of conscience, he is filled with pity for the downtrodden Coro and seeks mystic communion to escape his obsessive terrors, to save himself from a strange mutant consciousness evolving from bourgeois decadence:

> Vamos a convertirnos en algo no pensable.
> Va a surgir del abismo no agotado un ser nuevo,
> un ente colectivo, cenagoso, nocturno,
> ... ...
> Tendrá nuevos sentidos, nuevos miembros y un nuevo
> modo de desplazarse, palpitar con el tiempo
> y apreciar donde empiezan y acaban sus fronteras. (PC, 481-82)

This solipsistic vision is a wild imagining of the Protagonista, as even he realizes, though he doubts there is a way out of his existentialist dilemma. What he fears most is the annihilation of his identity, probable consequence of commitment. But he listens courteously to the Mensajero's schematic description of the socialist way.

Taking advantage of the Protagonista's hesitancy, the Mensajero, an «Engineer of Souls», praises the virtues of reason and justice:[75]

> Yo, ingeniero del alma colectiva,
> yo que entiendo tus íntimos problemas
> de mínima y preciosa luz herida,
> te exijo más conciencia. (PC, 475)

With a steel-like grip on his theory and a dogged optimism in action, the Mensajero is a perfect example of an agitprop (agitation-propaganda) cadre. He subdues vacillators like the Protagonista, whose superego cedes to self-indulgent urges, with weapons from his psychological arsenal. For instance, he tells the Protagonista to stop thinking for himself, which

---

[74] TERTZ, *On Socialist Realism*, pp. 65-66: «Between the positive hero, head proudly lifted, cheerful and the clear straightforward enemy intent on hindering the purpose, is the superfluous man... He is neither for the Purpose nor against the Purpose — he is outside the Purpose.»

[75] TERTZ, *On Socialist Realism*, pp. 11-12: «After the 1917 Revolution in Russia, writers were given the honorary titles of 'Engineers of Souls'.»

provokes stark terror. Shame is another effective weapon. The Protagonista values his manhood and understandably dislikes comments like this: «Los hombres, cuando son hombres, / no cultivan su inconsciencia, / ni se abandonan al flujo / de su inmanencia secreta» (PC, 454). The Mensajero's decisive weapon, however, is the enticement of revenge. Offered this, his subjects gladly turn their backs on capitalism; the certainty of revenge by Revolution more than compensates guilt at destroying a familiar social order. Having suffered the usual humiliations at the hand of meddling priests and money-grubbing entrepreneurs, the Protagonista is eager to be free. The Mensajero, finding this an opportunity for harangue, panders to the petty-capitalist's desire to wipe the slate clean:

> Aventad el incienso
> de lo tradicional.
> Romped el mecanismo
> de interés-capital.
> Los amos que os humillan
> y el hijo de tal cual
> sólo son monigotes
> de un viejo carnaval.
> ¡Golpead!
> La riada del pueblo
> va hacia el bien por el mal
> y, entre escombros, levanta
> el nuevo hombre social. (PC, 461-62)

Unfortunately, when the Mensajero describes the perfect society to convince the hesitant Protagonist, he paints a world of gray uniformity few discerning individuals would find appealing:

> Pequeño es nuestro reino, pero es nuestro
> y en él nos descubrimos con sentido,
> trabajamos humildes y contentos,
> construimos con gloria lo concreto.
> No existe un más allá de este dominio. (PC, 490)

It is difficult to imagine who might take this as the promised paradise on earth.

Early in the work, Celaya draws a metaphorical analogy between the masses of humanity and the sea. Lacking definition, the populace usually conforms to imposed limits, being timelessly the same though in continual movement. Occasional turmoil seldom lasts, customary rhythms soon return; the masses are inconstant, loyal to whatever seems to answer their immediate needs. The first portion of *Lo demás es silencio* is an interchange between the Coro and the Protagonista, in which the former tries to convince the latter that his personal problems are trivial. By comparison, the difficulties they chronicle are tragedies. Celaya makes use of this opportunity to insert several examples of personal oral history, which contrast with the version of Spanish history purveyed by the Regime. Celaya's obvious intention to redress historical errors of omission extends through successive works, based on episodes from the Civil War and the period of resistance.[76] In the final case history, a farmer relates that both his sons were killed in the Civil War and his daughter became a prostitute. This convinces the Protagonista of his potential usefulness as their representative. He offers to become the troubadour of their revolutionary march, the symbolic clapper of their bell of silence:

> Campesinos, obreros, trabajadores broncos,
> mujeres soterradas, varones cara al viento,
> en vosotros, arcaicos, descubro mi firmeza.
> Quiero cantar el noble silencio golpeado,
> quiero ser un badajo de campana en la ausencia
> y un dolor martillado que se clava en el centro. (PC, 429-30)

Where the Protagonista expected gratitude for his offer to immortalize them, he awakens only suspicion. The simple people of the Coro, believing the Protagonist is trying to enhance his self-importance at their expense, become excited and fail to pay attention. The Protagonista, weary of trying to reason with the Coro, throws care to the wind and sheds three millennia of civilization. Without delay, what was a reasonable exchange of views becomes a celebration of total freedom:

> ¡Belleza! Es la belleza: la fiesta, el ocio, el libre,
> feliz e inconsecuente cantar en lo inmediato
> con que acaba en suspenso la larga asignatura
> de ser un europeo cristiano y archiculto.
> ¡Que restalle la vida! ¡Que se encienda la fiesta!
> ¡Con tiros, con consignas, con *slogans,* con huelgas...!
>
> (PC, 441)

The Protagonista is as joyful as the Coro at this festive revolution, but his initial euphoria dissipates in the face of chaos — inevitable result of an undirected revolution. In a spiral of anxiety, he delivers incoherent, telegraphic entreaties, searching for confirmations of his identity. Midway through this metamorphosis, he issues indecipherable oracular verses:

> El mar se llama «Siempre» y el hombre «Ese», Ninguno.
> La muchacha que duerme mientras crece la hierba se llama «Todavía».
> La esperanza alisando sus plumas de luz larga se figura que piensa.
> Y el mar se llama «Nunca» si refleja ese exceso. (PC, 451)

Without the mysterious verses being deciphered, the Mensajero interrupts, cutting short the melée and organizing the Coro into squads.

---

[76] Some examples: «Las resistencias del diamante», «Vías de agua», «Episodios nacionales», *Parte de guerra* (Barcelona: Laia, 1977).

The Mensajero insists that the Coro needs discipline to suppress natural anarchic tendencies. Then, to win over the Protagonista, he delivers, with Stalinist integrity, a peroration enumerating the benefits of socialism: fire, potting, plows, basket-making, metallurgy, wheels, poetry, agriculture, and more of course. During the final moments of *Lo demás es silencio,* the Protagonista still wavers before this massive Marxist challenge and states to no one in particular: «Mentiré santamente que aún les queda esperanza, / callaré lo que sufro porque sólo es miseria» (PC, 490).

Celaya acknowledges that *Lo demás es silencio,* which ends in complication rather than denouement, is structurally flawed and represents an ideological pause in his Marxist transformation (IP, 23). Psychologically, Celaya had to await an integration of fragments represented by the caricatural militant and the indecisive Protagonista. This integration in commitment is registered programmatically by Celaya's seven points entitled «Poesía eres tú», where he affirms that: «Hay que apostar al 'ahora o nunca'» (PV, 73). Poetically, it is obvious in such poems as «En lo mío, con todos», in which the speaker recalls a safe-house where he and fellow Communists would meet in a circle of warm camaraderie:

> Con los míos,
> voy al futuro tranquilo,
> porque amigos y enemigos
> quedaremos reunidos
> en la Casa, en lo que digo,
> como peces o no peces
> coleteando el abismo. (HR, 136)

Celaya's most impressive credentials of commitment, however, are his *Cantos iberos.*

II. *The Red Thread*

Cantos iberos was prepared during 1953-1954, years of «rage and hope» for Celaya.[77] Life and literature intersected as Celaya's profession, political activity, and poetic advocation collided explosively. Commited to the PCE, but still employed by a family-owned and operated business, Celaya sided with workers in their strike against the company.[78] At the

---

[77] GABRIEL CELAYA, *Cantos iberos* (Madrid: Turner, 1976), p. 9: «*Cantos iberos* fue escrito en los años de furor y esperanza, pero a pesar de eso, o quizá por eso mismo, es el libro más calculado para producir un determinado efecto de cuantos he escrito en mi vida.»

[78] PIERRE-OLIVIER SEIRRA, *Gabriel Celaya,* p. 38: «En 1954 des movements de grève ont lieu à Saint-Sébastien. Celaya prenant fait et cause en faveur des revendications des ouvriers de l'enterprise familiale, se brouille définitivement avec sa famille, avec laquelle le climat était déjà plus que tendu de fait de sa vie affective.»

same time, he was in contact with Jorge Semprún, whom he met for the first time in June 1953.[79] Then too, PCE members were looking forward to the fifth PCE congress, originally scheduled for August 1936, but postponed for nearly two decades because it was impossible to gather a large representation from within Spain.[80] The reunion scheduled for 1-5 November 1954 in Prague was the congress in which Carrillo's policy of Reconciliación Nacional —renunciation of violent overthrow for infiltration of existing associations— would be unveiled. A few months earlier, Celaya rehearsed the new policy of infiltration at the *III Congreso de Poesía* held in Santiago de Compostela.

As part of the cultural awakening permitted by Ruiz-Giménez, Education Minister, an annual Congreso de Poesía was established with the intention of gathering major Peninsular poets and attracting poets from other parts of the world, particularly from Spanish-speaking countries. The first, in 1952, «fue la primera vez que se hizo un canto a la libertad, públicamente».[81] Highlights of this gathering in Segovia were reports by Claude Rupert on Swiss poetry and Roy Campbell on English poetry, a masterly synthesis of modern Catalan literature by Carles Riba, and «La generación poética del 25» by Ricardo Gullón.[82] The anthology published as testimony of the second congress in Salamanca gathered together poems by José Luis Cano, Gerardo Diego, Ildefonso-Manuel Gil, Charles David Ley, Blas de Otero, Leopoldo Panero, José Angel Valente, and others.[83] The third congress, scheduled for July 1954 in Galicia, began for most participants after a twelve-hour bus ride through the mountains from Madrid. Reports of the congress vary considerably. Ricardo Molina celebrated the spiritual elegance and exquisite modesty of Mediterranean cultures, which made possible such convocations: «Son nada más y nada menos que symposium, convivium, convivencia en poesía.»[84] He called attention to the total lack of rhetoric, mutual recitals of poems, political watchwords, or veiled purposes that might have disfigured the essence of this gathering. Alfonso Canales recalled speeches by Ramón Menéndez Pidal, Joaquín Pérez Villanueva, and Carles Riba as well as excursions to Padrón, Pontevedra, La Coruña, and the coastal islands.[85] He summarized the import of the congress: «Se han complementado grupos y tendencias, se han aclarado conceptos: y todo ello como en voz baja y con más afán de oír que de ser escuchado.» Apparently, however, the most provocative

---

[79] Jorge Semprún, *Autobiografía de Federico Sánchez*, p. 54.
[80] *Historia del PCE*, p. 248.
[81] José Luis Cano, Letter of 23 January 1978.
[82] «Breve NODO del Congreso», *Correo Literario*, 3, No. 51 (1 July 1952), p. 10.
[83] *Antología del II Congreso de Poesía* (Salamanca: Diputación Provincial, 1953).
[84] Ricardo Molina, «Ita et nunc», *Cántico*, 2, No. 3 (August-September 1953).
[85] Alfonso Canales, «El III Congreso de Poesía», *Caracola*, No. 23 (September 1954).

discussion centered upon «social» poetry.[86] Celaya maintained that poetry could change beliefs and better the world. His opposite, Rafael Romero Moliner, held that poetry arose from what is most distinct and personal and that it was directed to similar tastes in readers. In *Poesía de España,* Angel Crespo described the effect this stance had on Celaya's poetry: «El nuevo cambio radical, aunque presuponible de nuestro poeta, se produce en 1954. Sus agresivas declaraciones en el III Congreso de Poesía en Santiago anticipan al Celaya sin polvo o paja existencialista o lecetista que habla en *Cantos iberos...*»[87] Thus, even before all the poems of *Cantos iberos* appeared, Celaya disturbed the equanimity of his peers in poetry with the Marxist challenge.[88]

Cantos iberos arises from Celaya's concern to develop SocReal theory. He explores basic questions, such as what role the poet ought to play and who his probable readers are, and expands appropriate themes — instrumental language, commitment, the uses of violence, and the problem of Spain.

Celaya's most concise definition of the relation between life and literature is «La poesía es un arma cargada de futuro», a lyrical interpretation of his ideological shift from capitalist to Marxist, now set to music.[89] Motivated by socialist morality, Celaya writes to «create consciousness». Furthermore, he is a «verse engineer», who writes poetry to «build» the hope of others. To stress his eschewal of frivolity, Celaya draws from the lexicons of industry and martial affairs. But recognizing the incipient triteness of the Marxist challenge too often repeated, he clothes it with a seductive oxymoron:

> Me siento un ingeniero del verso y un obrero
> que trabaja con otros a España en sus aceros.
>
> Tal es mi poesía: poesía-herramienta
> a la vez que latido de lo unánime y ciego.
> Tal es, arma cargada de futuro expansivo
> con que te apunto al pecho. (PC, 631)

While the pretense of SocReal writers is that they are engaged in a down-to-earth activity on a par with that of manual laborers, the coming-into-

---

[86] FANNY RUBIO, «Teoría y polémica en la poesía española de posguerra», *Cuadernos Hispanoamericanos,* No. 361-362 (July-August 1980), pp. 203-04.

[87] [ANGEL CRESPO], «Gabriel Celaya», *Poesía de España,* p. 4.

[88] Prior publication of poems from *Cantos iberos:* «La poesía es un arma cargada de futuro», *Verbo,* No. 28 (December 1953); «A Sancho Panza», *Caracola,* No. 24 (October 1954); nine poems in *Verbo,* No. 29 (December 1954). The first edition of *Cantos iberos* was published by *Verbo* in 1955.

[89] HR, 47: «Paco Ibáñez ha cantado este poema y lo ha hecho muy popular. Si alguien tiene la paciencia de compulsar su letra con mi texto, verá que Paco ha suprimido algunos versos y que ha repetido otros, libremente, a modo de estribillo. Tales modificaciones fueron hechas, desde luego, con mi conformidad, porque a la canción hay que darle lo suyo.»

being of Celaya's emergency poetry owes something to an agency known among pretty bourgeois writers as inspiration:[90]

> Con la velocidad del instinto,
> con el rayo del prodigio,
> como mágica evidencia, lo real se nos convierte
> en lo idéntico a sí mismo. (PC, 631)

It is important to remember that Celaya's description is metaphorical. The homology between poet and engineer lies in the shared motive to work for the good of society. In fact, Celaya demystifies the image of the poet as esthete in order to dignify valuable, though usually belittled callings. This indirect route for propaganda still exhorts a classless society as its goal or, as the poem has it, «*futuro expansivo*».

Celaya speaks on the same issues in «Vivir para ver», the concluding poem of the work. Since the conventions of SocReal poetry are overly familiar to readers, Celaya is compelled to embellish them or risk offending the *cognoscenti*. He writes an enticing evocation of the poetry —romantic, surrealist, pure— that he ethically rejects. Analyzed according to his addressees, this poem consists of four sections, one directed to vanguard poets, another to pure poets, the third to both groups together, and last to the *pueblo*. The sections are preceded by an introductory stanza and followed by a general challenge. Like Lenin, Celaya believes that the enlistment of liberal intellectuals is an indispensable condition for the victory of socialism. «'The bourgeois intellectuals', said Lenin, 'cannot be expelled and destroyed, but must be won over, remoulded, assimilated and re-educated.'»[91] Celaya criticizes the vanguard poets for eluding the implications of their rebelliousness; they dissipated their efforts in playfulness, while ignoring the calls of the real revolution. He condemns the pure poets, creators of songs unblemished by rhetoric or emotion, for having washed their hands before evidence of mankind's suffering. He accuses both groups of excessive individualism. Behind these charges is Celaya's belief that such poets merely repeated anachronistic, nineteenth-century protests of mediocrity to a philistine bourgeois audience incapable of changing (Inq, 225-26). Celaya believes that, if more conscious of history, these poets would speak for the ascendent class, shape its awareness, and thereby create for themselves a new public. This of course is Celaya's purpose in writing *Cantos iberos,* as he makes clear in the section of «Vivir para ver» addressed to the masses. Repeatedly telling them they

---

[90] GABRIEL CELAYA, «Doce años después», *Acento Cultural,* January 1959, p. 18: «No pretendo negar con esto lo que más o menos vagamente llamamos inspiración. Pero sí quiero recordar que la inspiración no es un privilegio de los poetas. Se da en otros muchos órdenes de trabajo.»
[91] FEDYUKIN, *The Great October Revolution and the Intelligentsia,* p. 9.

are not alone, Celaya praises the solidarity of «many faces and one faith». Then he invites them to listen to verses intended to achieve action:

> Escuchad, camaradas, mis poemas iberos
> de hombre que, recorrido por vuestras mudas vidas,
> quisiera con sus versos lograr, no la belleza,
> sino la acción que pueden y deben los poetas
> promover con sus versos de conmovida urgencia. (PC, 636-37)

A poem as aggressive as this cannot end with an invitation, thus Celaya adds a challenge, reminding his listeners that neutrality is counterrevolution:

> levantaos, sed hombres que aceptan sus deberes,
> escuchad lo que el pueblo con alarma os exige,
> pensad que ser neutrales es pronunciarse en contra. (PC, 637)

Of two poems on the theme of language, Celaya dedicates one to the Arcipreste de Hita, Juan Ruiz. In epistolary style, Celaya celebrates his reverence for Castilian language and literature. Proclaiming the Medieval cleric-poet a literary ancestor, he exults in their shared admiration of life's simple pleasures: comradeship, food, and sex. Celaya praises their belief in the heterogeneity of life, which makes the Arcipreste a forerunner of the dialectical materialists:

> Con lo malo y lo bueno, con barro y dignidad,
> con materia sagrada y un impalpable imán,
> Juan Ruiz, tú bien entiendes lo que llamo unidad. (PC, 615)

To protest over-refined language, Celaya praises the materiality of Spanish words in «Hablando en castellano», title and anaphoric beginning of all fourteen stanzas. He finds new esthetic effect in the sensuous physicality of sounds: Words and referents merge. Celaya admires the robust sounds of «squared-off» syllables, the «angry» accents that make words solidly real: «decir tinaja, ceniza, carro, pozo, junto, llanto, / es decir algo tremendo, ya sin adornos, logrado» (PC, 617). Humble, honest words like these, representing functional utensils and adornments, help him tell the truth about a new way of life based on simple virtues. Spanish offers him the perfect medium for his purpose:

> Hablando en castellano,
> los nombres donde duele, bien clavados,
> más encarnan que aluden en abstracto.
> Hay algo en las palabras, no mentante, captado,
> que quisiera, por poeta, rezar en buen castellano. (PC, 617)

«Con los labios de la herida» (PC, 621) focuses on the moment when the speaker renounces his pampered ego forever in a symbolic healing that unites self with consciousness. The sacrifice of the ego to the collectivity, which obsessed the Protagonista in *Lo demás es silencio,* finds its solution in the concept of a consciousness, superior to both its personal and collective aspects, which synthesizes the paradox of «I-Other». Ego and community are no longer antagonists, the speaker is no longer estranged from himself or his fellows; he is an integral part of a social order based on equality. In this state of superconsciousness, the ego remains itself yet yields to otherness, rather than being reduced it grows.[92] This resolution, which eliminates ambivalence, frees love to become an unrestrained force for hope, for the betterment of mankind.

Lenin's aggressive policy that violence is not incompatible with love of mankind and may be necessary to secure the Revolution does not express a high regard for the ethics of means over ends. The naturally peaceable Celaya rationalizes violence by transmogrifying terrorists into devotionaries of an esoteric cult: «Tan sólo la certeza de estar cumpliendo un rito / convierte en inocentes a los adelantados» (PC, 612). Then he issues a call for direct action and armed struggle:[93]

> Matar, si no comprendes
> que en el muerto te matas a ti mismo, es engaño.
> Mas no obstante, debemos
> luchar, matar acaso,
> conservándonos puros, sabiendo lo que hacemos. (PC, 612)

Having established his ideological credentials in these poems, Celaya falls to the task of creating popular poetry. His goal of moral renewal adds dignity to the endeavor, his compassion for the *pueblo,* the simple life, revolutionary purpose, and action on behalf of a good cause bring honor to his role as agitprop cadre. Stylistically, he seeks to mimic Medieval bards, to channel sentiment and history into the dramatic flow of ballad fragments. Esthetically, he wishes to improve upon motifs that are familiar topics, introduced by poets in the 1930s. Still he begins, as did De Nora a decade earlier, by pleading with Spain to modernize her image in «Dime que sí» (PC, 599). Despite a reasonable request and passionate commitment, he receives no answer in this poem. Thus he feels he has grounds for creating his own version of Spanish history. He might have used the Marxist method unimaginatively, pointing out how bad everything is now and how much better it would be after a revolution. Al-

---

[92] GABRIEL CELAYA, «Doce años después», *Acento Cultural,* p. 20: «Hay un estado de conciencia que no es ni personal ni colectivo, en el que ciertas aparentes antinomias se funden. El yo arde, y uno es doblemente quien es, entregándose. Se da a los otros, renunciando a muchas cosas que creía personalmente importantes, y al darse no se reduce, crece, perdiéndose.»
[93] Note to this poem in HR, 38: «Aunque la Censura no lo advirtiera, creo que la apelación a la acción directa y a la lucha armada es evidente en este poema. Estábamos en 1954, piénsese.»

though Celaya does not avoid this entirely, he deftly shapes the argument in «Defendamos nuestra vida». Instead of offering a thesis and antithesis, he proclaims repeatedly the synthesis of «Todo es verdad. Todo es mentira» (PC, 629). He alleges that extant histories of Spain are fictitious, hiding the oppression of class relationships:

> ¡Disfraces de fantasía para unos pocos que imperan
> y aburridos uniformes para los hombres sin más!
> Una danza macabra y un perpetuo carnaval. (PC, 629)

Building his case concerning the problem of Spain, Celaya concludes the poem with a list of facts omitted from Francoist history books, yet remains on the safe side of the line between literature and sociology. For, while neotraditionalists like Calvo Serer affirm that there is no problem of Spain, Falangists like Laín Entralgo believe that there is; however, Marxists like Celaya not only believe there is a problem, they know the correct solution as well.[94]

Starting his new history, Celaya shapes the new man. Like a god with a talent for potting, he takes a handful of clay and shapes a vessel uniting mankind, where everyone works for the benefit of all. Man and Spain are destined for a close relationship with this potter; following the crucifixion, he resurrects them, and they unite with him as one:

> España, tierra convulsa,
> corazón de greda y yeso
> ... ...
> mi España crucificada,
> luz hiriente, Cristo negro,
> más que en tu espíritu, vivo
> en tu carne y en tu pueblo,
> y en tu latido aún sin forma,
> ¡oh arcilla que palpo y beso! (PC, 604)

Searching for the essential Spain, Celaya retreats through the ages, rejecting such intrusive hegemonies as the Bourbons, Hapsburgs, Moors, Romans, and Greeks. Finally, he discovers the lode of true Spanishness in the hereditary substratum where the nation began: strange, terrible, ancient Iberia. Like De Nora and Otero, Celaya personifies Spain as a woman, «Fiera amante, madre amarga» (PC 601). Before such an imposing figure, he suffers mixed feelings, not knowing whether he adores or despises her. Still, he is certain that he exists in, for, and of Spain. Consubstantial, he cannot separate his own existence from hers, thus his anger toward her is redirected at himself as guilt:

---

[94] For a review of this polemic, see: ELÍAS DÍAZ, *Notas para una historia del pensamiento español actual 1939-1973* (Madrid: EDICUSA, 1974), pp. 69-79.

> Tú eres mi aire y mi tierra, tú, mi cuerpo y mi elemento,
> y al maldecirte, maldigo
> de mí mismo porque pienso que aún no cumplí lo que debo.
>
> (PC, 601)

As an act of penance he composes his Iberian songs, exalting the exploited class, the single class of the future. Finding a perfect correspondence between the national theme of Don Quijote and Sancho Panza and the Marxist theory of society, Celaya personifies the masses as «Sancho-bueno, Sancho-arcilla, Sancho-pueblo» (PC, 606). Then he glorifies them as truly Spanish, a class whose time has come, that understands freedom, social justice, and solidarity:

> Tu libertad es instinto. Tus verdades son sencillas:
> al pan, pan, y al vino, vino,
> y a cada cual lo debido:
> lo que le cumple por hombre con un único camino. (PC, 608)

Celaya now goes into action, creating a mind for the masses, haranguing them to join the struggle. Most of the agitprop poems are clearly stated calls, understood even by the uninitiated. Adept readers, however, appreciate the rich connotations of each simple word in, for instance, this stanza from «Todo está por inventar»:

> ¡Camaradas!
> nuestra lucha es eficaz.
> Vencedores o vencidos, salvamos la libertad,
> la dignidad de ser hombres,
> la alegría del mañana, la juventud natural. (PC, 623)

Celaya incorporates Carrillo's doctrine of peace. «La necesidad, la sencillez, la alegría» (PC, 609-10) is a song about fighting as a collective virtue when in the name of peace. «Manos a la obra» (PC, 610-11), a declaration of revolution, proposes to secure peace through celestial theft:

> La paz que todos queremos
> hay que robársela al cielo.
> ¡Camaradas, sed activos
> y haréis real la estructura que anticipan vuestros gritos!
>
> (PC, 611)

«España en pie», on the other hand, claims peace and freedom as natural rights not to be abrogated because of race, sex, or belief; it ends like a legal petition:

> Sólo quiero respirar
> y pido la libertad.
> La pido como mi pueblo

porque queremos la paz.
Soy español. Dicho está. (PC, 619)

A willing chronicler of the march to socialism, Celaya invents a slogan to outwit censors in «España en marcha»: «somos quienes somos» (PC, 605).[95] A strongly worded call to mass action, cleverly disguised as an invitation to stroll, slipped through the fish-net too:

¡A la calle!, que ya es hora
de pasearnos a cuerpo
y mostrar que, pues vivimos, anunciamos algo nuevo. (PC, 605)

Celaya varies the new slogan in «Todos a una», whose message is solidarity. Of course he cannot declare himself a member of the international Communist movement in direct terms, but nothing prevents him from doing the same indirectly: «digo quién soy, quiénes somos... Somos quien somos: varones / tan seguros de sí mismos que renuncian a su nombre... Somos millones, millones. / Somos la luz que se extiende. / ¡Miradnos! Somos el hombre» (PC, 620).

Through messages such as these, Celaya planned to create the consciousness of workers, educate them to socialism, and enlist them in the movement. At the time of writing *Cantos iberos,* Celaya faithfully followed SocReal theory. Of himself he wrote: «uno, muy ingenuamente, se imaginaba a ese pueblo esperando el santo advenimiento de sus poetas redentores. No había más que llamarle y respondería. Esto era tan seguro como la revolución inminente» (Inq, 224-25). Unlike surrealists or existentialists who either exalted or deploraron irrationality, Celaya as a Marxist considered it a product of consciousness that would vanish in the ideological metamorphosis from oppressed submission to liberated action. Celaya later took a more realistic view of how his agitprop poetry achieved its effect. Though he discovered that his readers were fewer than he hoped, they were among the potential leaders of Spain. To transform their views would be more effective, he felt, than to convert millions of workers, for the world is changed more permanently by the policies of leaders than by the inchoate actions of the masses.[96] Thus, the technique used in «Vivir para ver», for example, takes into account the actual readers of his elaborate and, at times, elegant propaganda. Multiple reeditions of the work suggest that the pool of readers may even include a few proletarians, life thus fulfilling literary convention.[97]

---

[95] HR, 36: «Más que cantar a España, lo que yo pretendía era cantar la resistencia. Apelar patrióticamente a España no era más que una trampa tendida a la censura para poder hablar de cosas que de otro modo no hubiera tolerado. Y esta vez conseguí engañar a la censura.»

[96] LUIS SÁNCHEZ BARDÓN, «Gabriel Celaya, un productor de base», *Informaciones de las Artes y las Letras,* 16 February 1978, p. 3.

[97] Referring to the success of the «El Bardo» collection, Amelia Romero and

1955-1956 were years of uncompromising changes for Celaya. After decades of psychological depression and professional dissatisfaction, he dedicated himself entirely to literature in Madrid (PC, 21). And, after intermittent involvement of literature with politics, culminating in *Cantos iberos,* Celaya joined enthusiastically with other writers, students, and political activists to create an authentic culture for the times, in accord with the PCE's policy of infiltration.[98] Therefore, Celaya's behavior in Santiago de Compostela may be construed as quasi-political and his collaborations in literary publications as inspired by political motives. For instance, he managed to publish an eleven-stanza fragment of «Las resistencias del diamante» (*Rocamador* No. 4, Fall 1955), a long poem narrating the escape of members of a PCE cell, based on an event in which Amparitxu Gastón was of exceptional importance (HR, 57). The entire poem was not published in Spain until 1977.[99] Earlier, *Las Españas,* published by Spanish exiles, sponsored Celaya, solicited a prologue from Max Aub, and issued «Las resistencias del diamante» in 1957; then, two «comrades», Marie Chevallier and François Martorell, translated and published it in Paris in 1960.[100] Furthermore, exacerbating statements such as «Poesía eres tú» in the *Antología consultada* and an open letter published in *Caracola* were Celaya's proof of party loyalty.[101]

Celaya's impact upon literary affairs was great. In response to the Marxist challenge, José García Nieto wrote «Carta a Gabriel Celaya», a pastiche, in which he emphasizes the ineffectiveness of poets, who lack a wide audience: «Nos decimos a solas, nos leemos a solas, / con un

---

José Batlló in Carlos Alvarez, *Estos que ahora son poemas... Epílogo de Amelia Romero y José Batlló* (Barcelona: El Bardo, 1969), p. 100, thanked Celaya «a cuya casi fabulosa capacidad de hacer una poesía comercial la colección debe como mínimo el cincuenta por ciento de su supervivencia».

[98] Celaya alluded to this without directly naming the PCE, because of censorship, in Eduardo García Rico, «Literatura y política (en torno al realismo español)», *Cuadernos para el Diálogo,* Supplement, No. 19 (1971), p. 23: «Debo añadir que en aquella época algunos creyeron que los grupos poéticos inconformistas, concentrados en las numerosas revistas que entonces se publicaban, constituían o podían constituir fermentos revolucionarios a explotar. Más tarde, y con razón, aquellos desviaron sus actividades hacia la Universidad.»

[99] Gabriel Celaya, *Parte de guerra,* pp. 11-63.

[100] *Ibid.,* p. 8.

[101] This excerpt from «Carta de Gabriel Celaya», *Caracola,* No. 29 (March 1955), is a good example of how Celaya lets his *partiinost* get the better of his well-intentioned *narodnost:* «Puesto que cantar es sentir como propio *lo otro,* el poeta más que nadie, vive, más allá de sí mismo, ese dolor, y en la medida en que lo vive, siente la necesidad de contribuir a curarlo. Y es por haber dicho esto por lo que algunos me llaman 'poeta social', y me acusan de propagandista (¿y por qué no decir misionero?) no es nunca 'publicista'. Y es evidente, también, que si quiere actuar sólo podrá hacerlo con medios poéticos, ya que de lo contrario, además de destruir su poesía, destruiría la eficacia misma de su instrumento. ¿Y en estas condiciones, qué puede hacer el poeta? Algo muy importante: cambiar la conciencia. Es decir, obligar a ver y a sentir lo que nuestra pereza de burgueses confortables quisiera ignorar.»

solo juguete veinte niños jugamos, / o veinte veces veinte, qué más da; no nos oyen.»[102] This drew in turn «A un poeta neutral», where Celaya marks the field, chooses his team, and stands ready to fight to the finish:[103]

> Basta ya de mentiras. Dividamos los campos.
> Yo no te quiero mal; soy sólo tu contrario,
> pecho a pecho distinto, diente a diente luciente.
> Te juzgo pernicioso. Lo digo. Juego limpio.
> ... ...
> Yo creo en ti; te estimo noblemente decente,
> mas te pido osadía, salud, fe, sí, más tripas. (HR, 93)

The restrictions of censorship forced Celaya to use clandestine contacts to publish abroad his works of political poetry. However, his bibliography still grew by leaps and bounds as he tirelessly wrote personal poetry, fiction, essays, and articles.[104] In 1956, Celaya's fame crossed the Atlantic to Mexico and the Pyrenees to France, where his poems appeared and articles were written about him.[105] After Celaya won the first Premio de la Crítica in 1956 for the non-political *De claro en claro,* news of him also traveled to Lisbon, Sao Paulo, Stockholm, Zurich, Prague, and Budapest (PC, 23-24). Back home, of course, Celaya was admired for his poetic originality. Leopoldo de Luis, after reading *Cantos iberos,* was intrigued by Celaya's notion of Iberia as a cultural cooking pot. In ciphered tribute, he called the second part of *Juego limpio* «La edad de los metales», whose final poem contains the obligatory substitution of *cuchillos* for *martillos*:[106]

> Olla redonda, patria, gran caldero
> para cocer el rojo caldo ibero
> que envenenan remotos cardenillos.
>
> Secreto corazón de plata madre.
> Guarda tu noche un can para que ladre
> a una luna de hoces y cuchillos.

This gesture suggests that *Cantos iberos* had more readers than the few reviews in periodical publications lead one to believe.[107] De Luis also

---

[102] José García Nieto, «Carta a Gabriel Celaya», *La red* (Madrid: Agora, 1955), p. 67; *Poesía española*, No. 46 (October 1955).

[103] An open letter to García Nieto, published in 1956, in which Celaya repeats his position at greater length appears in PV, 88-93.

[104] Gabriel Celaya, «Bibliografía», *Las cartas boca arriba*, pp. 119-27.

[105] Seirra, *Gabriel Celaya*, p. 39.

[106] Leopoldo de Luis, *Teatro Real. Juego limpio* (1957, 1961; Madrid: Espasa-Calpe, 1975), p. 149.

[107] PC lists two: p. 30, Trinidad Mercader, Review of *Cantos iberos, Al-Motamid*, No. 31 (April-June 1955; p. 32, Mariano Roldán, «Los *Cantos iberos* de Gabriel Celaya», *La Voz de España*, 14 September 1956. Another is: José Vicente

made amends for cautious colleagues, while bringing readers up-to-date about a time when *Cantos iberos* should have been mentioned and reviewed, but was not. The problem was not that Celaya's poetry was unpopular, but until certain people knew whether his first loyalty was to Spain or the PCE, Celaya's works were read avidly at home but publicized only abroad. In his review of *Pequeña Antología,* De Luis slips in an impression of *Cantos iberos*:[108] «En *Cantos iberos,* la poesía de Celaya se sustancia en temas de viva entraña española. Un españolismo libre de tópicos, aspero a veces, pero de admirable reciedumbre, bien representado aquí por los poemas 'Hablando en castellano' y 'A Sancho Panza'.»

Celaya's life became so intertwined with literature that the poet publicly acted out the role he programmed for the speaker in *Cantos iberos.* As a result of associating himself with the student protest movement, which from its first major activity in February 1956 grew yearly, Celaya had to pay substantial fines to the government in 1961 and 1966 for political aggressiveness.[109] The next year, along with other Spaniards —Carlos Barral, José María Castellet, Jaime Gil de Biedma, and José Angel Valente— Celaya traveled to Havana to participate in a Congreso de la Cultura; he also was a judge for the Cuban Writers and Artists Union.[110] Thus, he was able to appreciate at first hand the progress achieved by the Revolution. Both Otero and Celaya, who promoted the superiority of the collective over the individual and the inevitability of socialism, saw the end of the Franco Regime, with the dictator's death in 1975, and the legalization of the PCE in 1977. Both reaped deserved honor in the cultural recuperation of the post-Franco era when all their titles appeared with a Spanish imprint, experiments in the anti-poetic sublime available at last to all Spaniards.

MATEO, Review of *Cantos iberos, Verbo,* No. 31 (Spring 1958). Also, compare: *Rocamador,* No. 10 (Spring 1957), p. 25: «De *Cantos iberos* se han ocupado cuatro revistas y pare usted de contar, y cuando más para dar una simple reseña de acuse de recibo, salvo excepciones que siempre existen.

Añadiremos que de este libro se han ocupado más en el extranjero que en España, lo que por sí solo ya dice bastante.»

[108] LEOPOLDO DE LUIS, Review of *Pequeña antología, Insula,* No. 126 (15 May 1957), p. 7.
[109] SEIRRA, *Gabriel Celaya,* pp. 40, 43.
[110] *Ibid.,* pp. 43-44.

5

POETRY OF SOCIAL PROTEST

The popularity of what was called social poetry during the 1950s and 1960s would be incomprehensible without taking into account socioeconomic progress ending Spain's autarky, indirectly creating a growing audience particularly in the university for poetry of protest. Between 1950 and 1975 the Spanish standard of living more than doubled while per capita income rose nearly four times.[1] This prosperity made university study more possible for those born after 1936 than for those born before. Once matriculated, however, students often became discontented with the antiquated university and obligatory membership in SEU, the Regime's student syndicate. They responded enthusiastically to mild university reforms under Ruiz-Giménez's policy carried out by Antonio Tovar, Chancellor of the University of Salamanca, Pedro Laín Entralgo, Chancellor of the University of Madrid, and Dionisio Ridruejo. Furthermore, official emphasis on book competitions, creation of new publications, and undertakings like poetry congresses, all part of the shift from *coexistencia* to *convivencia,* created an intellectual climate encouraging the expression of liberal ideals. Censorship hampered rather than impeded communication, causing anything published clandestinely to seem truthful, whether or not it was.[2] And in any case many intellectuals believed that to despair over censorship was to forget that free expression required exercise as well as an attitude; thus even the suppression of censorship could not promise a flourishing culture. Between 1951 and 1956 other influences enhancing the intellectual climate were increasing contacts between Spaniards on the one hand and Europeans and Americans on the other, the dialogue between Peninsular and exiled intellectuals, and, finally, the lapse of time since the end of the Civil War. This change of atmosphere fostered ideological sympathy for liberal, democratic, and even socialist ideas among Spaniards in general and especially among the younger generation.[3]

---

[1] «El nivel de vida se ha triplicado en los últimos quince años», *Ya,* 2 October 1977, p. 25.
[2] J. L. Aranguren as cited by ELÍAS DÍAZ, *Notas para una historia del pensamiento actual (1939-1973)* (Madrid: EDICUSA, 1974), p. 106.
[3] *Ibid.,* p. 118.

After a decade of severe repression these changes, which inspired unrealistic hope for improvement, touched off student strikes and demonstrations whose frequency and intensity increased. At first, students tried to introduce change through supplemental instruction within the auspices of the SEU. The first Congreso Nacional de Estudiantes Españoles, for example, approved «aulas de cultura», offering current perspectives on the major arts and sciences.[4] This resulted in a series of informal addresses by Gerardo Diego, Vicente Aleixandre, Dámaso Alonso, Gabriel Celaya, José García Nieto, José Hierro, Rafael Morales, Leopoldo Panero, Dionisio Ridruejo, and Luis Felipe Vivanco.[5]

In university lecture halls a widening breach separated the faculty, judging issues in terms of the 1930s, from the student body, which grew up during years of peace and consequently wanted explanations of the Spanish situation not emotional appeals to the past.[6] Members of the Generation of 56 —José-Carlos Mainer's term— used nominally Falangist periodicals sponsored by the SEU and others, underwritten by provincial and municipal governments, as testing-grounds for their ideas. They also welcomed Argentine editions of works out-of-print or otherwise unavailable in Spain. The dissemination of these inexpensive series had a direct bearing on both student discontent and the vogue for social poetry; indeed, the stimulus of these works helped intellectual life recover some of its prewar vigor.[7] Taking advantage of the more favorable climate, young writers such as Alfonso Sastre made a determined effort to bring the

---

[4] «Conclusiones del I Congreso Nacional de Estudiantes Españoles», *Alcalá*, No. 31 (25 April 1953).

[5] «Las leyes y la poesía», *Alcalá*, No. 50 (10 February 1954): «El SEU de Derecho, alentado por el Departamento de Actividades Culturales, inicia ahora con 'Aula de Literatura' aliada a la ya existente en Filosofía, unos encuentros de la Poesía con la Universidad...»

[6] RODRIGO FERNÁNDEZ CARVAJAL, «Reflexiones sobre la formación política», *Alcalá*, No. 55 (25 April 1954): «... hoy día es muy grande entre nosotros lo que suele llamarse 'distancia social', esto es, se diferencian sobremanera las mentalidades del cuerpo docente y del cuerpo discente. La experiencia política del primero, y consecuentemente su sistema de ideas y entusiasmos, fluye de nuestra trágica y gloriosa historia entre los años 1931 y 1939; historia en la cual todos, más o menos activamente, intervinieron. El cuerpo discente, por el contrario, ha crecido en años de paz. Lo que para los maestros es recuerdo personal, para los alumnos es referencia libresca, sustancialmente semejante a la que podría tener de las guerras carlistas un joven de 1900. La referencia histórica como justificante de un estado de cosas actual es necesaria y lícita, pero no suficiente... Tales personas exigen, de modo más o menos consciente y riguroso, una justificación de orden actual.»

[7] EDUARDO G. RICO, «Literatura y política (en torno al realismo español)», *Cuadernos para el diálogo*, No. 19 (1971), p. 43. Concerning social literature, compare CASTELLET's view quoted in «Mesa redonda. La literatura social», *Camp de L'Arpa*, No. 1 (May 1972), p. 14: «La literatura social es un movimiento concreto y determinado que surge de una generación, la nuestra, y que tiene su origen extraliterario en el fracasado congreso de escritores del año 1956; movimiento también relacionado con la politización de la Universidad a partir de febrero del 56; en este momento comienza la literatura social...»

social question to wider attention. As early as 1950, Sastre and José María de Quinto called for an alternative to traditional bourgeois theater, a repertory examining diverse social and political tendencies through works by internationally respected playwrights —John Steinbeck, Arthur Miller, Jean-Paul Sartre, and others—, reasoning that only a substantial change of offerings could attract new audiences.[8] Sastre viewed his *teatro de agitación social* as related to tendencies like «*realismo socialista*» in the USSR, «*social-realismo*» in Mexico, and the European tendencies of «*neorealismo*» and literature called «*existencialista*».[9] At the same time, he supported the purpose of Socialist Realist art —its capacity to revolutionize and purify its public— because the writer, «[s]in llegar, en la mayoría de las ocasiones al enrolamiento en unas formas políticas o religiosas determinadas, intenta provocar estados de ánimo y de conciencia prepolíticos, que muchas veces apuntan a una acción política purificadora».[10] Writers and artists, he believed, should work toward a better world, integrating the realms of morality and art.

Young people, whose attitude differed significantly from that of the government according to a survey made when Spain entered the United Nations in 1955, turned from the Regime and Falangism toward liberalism and socialism.[11] Critical, intellectually curious, they exceeded allowable limits of liberalization when their discussions led to petitions, demonstrations, and even street-fighting in the name of founding independent student associations. The resultant university crisis in 1956 was viewed with such alarm by the Regime that it resorted to open confrontation, suspending certain minimal rights of the Fuero de los Españoles in effect since 1945. What ensued for student leaders —Ramón Tamames, Enrique Múgica, and others— were detentions and searches without due process.[12] Ridruejo, considered a major figure in the reform that led to the crisis, was detained as well. The Education Minister, Ruiz-Giménez, was dismissed immediately and the Chancellor of the University of Madrid, Laín Entralgo, shortly thereafter.

While few doubted the sincerity of Ruiz-Giménez in promoting *convivencia*, the motives of the Regime were suspect because increased freedom apparently was allowed primarily in order to smooth diplomatic relations with the United States and the United Nations. Though the Regime appropriated the rhetoric of liberalism, Franco responded with customary rigor when his authority was challenged in 1956. Intellectuals such as José Luis Aranguren, hopeful for democracy, found the stifling

---

[8] [Teatro de Agitación Social], *Verbo*, No. 21 (February 1951), pp. 46-47.
[9] ALFONSO SASTRE, *Drama y sociedad* (Madrid: Taurus, 1956), pp. 69, 71.
[10] ALFONSO SASTRE, «Arte como construcción», *Acento Cultural*, No. 2 (December 1958), p. 66.
[11] DÍAZ, *Notas para una historia*, p. 123.
[12] *Ibid.*, pp. 124-25.

of student activism evidence that the Regime's liberalism was based on an internal contradiction: it permitted freedom of thought, but not the translation of thought into action.[13]

The Regime and individuals under its umbrella of power adopted liberal rhetoric for various reasons. The Regime's primary motive was to veneer its fundamentally authoritarian nature with some democratic practices. The issue was more complex for those with economic ties to the Dictatorship, either through civil service employment or the receipt of honors or awards.[14] On the one hand, such individuals spoke favorably of liberal principles —social and political tolerance, enlightenment and rationalism, and democracy with guaranteed human rights and rule by law. Their self-serving behavior, on the other hand, tacitly supported what was a police state using armed intervention to subdue its citizens.

The Dictatorship nonetheless permitted authentic dissent by what has been called an «amoebic opposition», representing the political spectrum from Christian democrats to members of the PCE.[15] Promoting differing goals, most aimed toward a peaceful political transition allowing, among other things, independent workers' unions, open political associations, amnesty for political prisoners, democratic socio-economic measures, separation of Church and State, and freedom of expression. For lack of institutionalized roles, since overt political activities were not allowed by the Regime, the opposition showed its discontent by the unusual means of literary works —more poetry than fiction, more essays than theater—, research reports, and opinion polls.[16] By gathering no mass following, intellectualized politicism was tolerated.

Abroad, the opposition had more latitude for action. One highly developed ideological strategy against the Regime was the translation, publi-

---

[13] [Equipo Reseña], *La cultura española durante el franquismo* (Bilbao: Mensajero, 1977), p. 152.

[14] ANTONIO LÓPEZ PINA, EDUARDO L. ARANGUREN, *La cultura política de la España de Franco* (Madrid: Taurus, 1976), pp. 145: «[Hay que] hacer mención del hecho, de que un sector significativo de la Falange y de la clase alta han desplegado considerables esfuerzos para que los valores liberales sirvieran de ornato externo a su política de apoyo a la luz del día del franquismo y de la *'situación'*; han intentado apropiarse de los mismos con *fines estéticos,* estrictamente económicos o de promoción personal.»

[15] JOSÉ AMODIA, *Franco's Political Legacy: From Dictatorship to Façade Democracy* (London: Allen Lane, 1977), pp. 217-20.

[16] In relation to essays, see THOMAS MERMALL, *The Rhetoric of Humanism* (New York: Bilingual Press, 1976), pp. 4-5: «In the late 1950s, with the gradual relaxation of censorship, there emerged among some writers a relatively critical attitude... the liberals (most of them Orteguians and Christian Democrats) came under the gradual indirect challenge of socialist and Marxist thinkers. But the undeclared polemic did not center around concrete socio-political problems, a type of encounter the regime would not permit. It became, rather, a conflict of total views of the nature of man, society, and culture. In other words, the post-Civil War essay become for the most part the expression of a conflict of humanisms...»

cation, and promotion of Spanish novelists in France, Italy, and socialist nations.[17] Another strategy was to gain attention through periodical publications. A special issue of *Esprit* entitled «Demain L'Espagne» and commemorating the twentieth anniversary of the Civil War, included an «Anthologie de l'espérance» with poems by Machado, Hernández, Alberti, Garciasol, Celaya, Crémer, De Nora, Otero, and Hierro; as well as an article by José María Castellet concerning the writer's condition in Spain, where a «*farwest*» mentality emboldened some writers to act as watchdogs over others; an unsigned article by a writer fearing reprisal, who observed that censorship was practically non-existent for poetry although it curbed discussion in general publications and dampened readers' enthusiasm for prose works; and a study of recent literature, calling attention to the adverse conditions in which it was written.[18] Efforts of lesser magnitude during the 1950s —poems and essays contributed to European and Latin American publications— wakened foreign interest in Spanish literature.

In this milieu, most poets publishing poems progressive enough to be considered protest adapted techniques from Socialist Realism but rejected its political philosophy because they favored a non-apocalytpic, pluralistic change in the Regime. They belonged near the center of a spectrum on which farthest to the left were Marxists and their sympathizers, while on the right were those who used social themes without referring to specific political principle or urgent need for social concern. With varying degrees of enthusiasm, such ideologically diverse poets were associated in the public mind with poetry of protest during the 1950s and 1960s.

POETRY IS COMMUNICATION

Vicente Aleixandre, recognizing the direction of postwar poetry, coined a dictum —«Poesía: comunicación»— as title for his aphorisms published in *Espadaña,* and left the systematic development of this principle to a disciple, Carlos Bousoño.[19] Of the many names suggested for the new tendency, that most widely used was «*poesía social*». One of the first poets using the term publicly for his own poetry was, surprisingly, Ramón de Garciasol, whose poems, book reviews, and essays appeared regularly in

---

[17] ALFONSO SASTRE, *La revolución y la crítica de la cultura* (Barcelona: Grijalbo, 1970), p. 148, refers especially to the project realized by Castellet, Barral, and Juan Goytisolo, whom he identified as «el más dogmático comisario exterior».

[18] «Demain L'Espagne», *Esprit,* No. 242 (September 1956): «Anthologie de l'espérance»; «Notes sur la condition d'écrivain en Espagne», «Le rideau du silence», and «Nouvelle littérature espagnole».

[19] VICENTE ALEIXANDRE, «Poesía: Comunicación (Nuevos puntos)», *Espadaña,* No. 48 (December 1950); CARLOS BOUSOÑO, *Teoría de la expresión poética* (Madrid: Gredos, 1952).

such publications sponsored by the Regime as *Escorial*. He held that, just as all deeds were social, being acts by men in society, all poetry including his own was social because it existed in a particular setting at a particular moment of history.[20]

This belief that poetry was a vital part of reality distinguished from other human activities only by its method of expression was shared also by several of the poets in the *Antología consultada*. Eugenio de Nora, for instance, trying to end dispute over the term social poetry, repeated the argument that all poetry was social, written by people and directed to people; he believed, moreover, if a poet was great it was because he drew support from an entire people and directed his poetry to all mankind.[21] Victoriano Crémer cited Aleixandre's dictum, adding that it was up to the poet to discover his addressee.[22] José Hierro asserted that the sign of the age was collective and social; therefore, the poet, shaping his time and being shaped by it, had to narrate the wrongs threatening mankind.[23] Due to these and similar observations, the anthology was recognized as an authoritative source for the precepts of social poetry.

Ricardo Molina expanded debate beyond immediate reference to the *Antología consultada*. In *Cántico* he raised questions about social poetry, apparently to curb blatant propagandizing by such poets as Celaya without naming names.[24] He cautioned that *poésie engagée* was a double-edged sword, which gave the poet a new field to explore, but could trap him into sectarian propagandizing.[25] Although he admitted poetry conveyed

---

[20] Ramón de Garciasol, «Poética», *Correo Literario*, 1, No. 13 (1 December 1950), p. 3: «El poeta amanece en el hombre ya hecho, y el hombre se da en sociedad y se hace en soledad. En este sentido, todos los hechos son sociales, la poesía entre ellos. La poesía de siempre, a pesar de la terminología preceptiva, es poesía social, circunstancia vital, intransferible, irrenunciable en tanto en cuanto deba seguir siendo.
Digo poesía social, refiriéndome a la que brota del hecho trascendental de vivir, y la vida no se da en fantasmas, sino en hombres; no en el vacío, sino en un tiempo y una sociedad concretos.»
Garciasol was anticipated by Pedro Salinas in an article published in *Revista de las Indias*, No. 76 (April 1945), collected in *La responsabilidad del escritor* (Barcelona: Seix Barral, 1961), p. 206: «Anda sonando por ahí ese bordón de que el arte debe ser social. Si se dice sinceramente, es forma de perisología. Todo arte —desde Mallarmé a la copla popular— es social, busca *socios*, es decir, participantes, amigos. Las más de las veces se enuncia esa muletilla con intención solapada, apuntando a que el arte debe ser dictado por tal o cual necesidad política del momento.»

[21] Francisco Ribes, *Antología consultada de la poesía joven española* (Santander: Hermanos Bedia, 1952), p. 151.

[22] *Ibid.*, p. 65.

[23] *Ibid.*, 107.

[24] In a survey focusing on the social role of poets since prehistoric times, he named Pablo Neruda as the representative figure of the modern age, see: Ricardo Molina, *Función social de la poesía* (Madrid: Guadarrama, 1971).

[25] Ricardo Molina, «La poesía comprometida», *Cántico*, 2, No. 3 (August-September 1954).

ideas, he himself rejected subservience to doctrines. As for techniques, Molina criticized what to him appeared to be rhetorical, rather than genuine anguish, a pose intended to vouch for the speakers' authenticity, but which endlessly repeated became monotonous and hypocritical.[26] If social poetry were to be authentic, he thought it would have to approach social problems with epic objectivity in the manner of a Whitman or a Verhaeren, who were neither revolutionary nor conservative, but rather generously open to the present.[27] Concerning the communion between writers and the people, Molina remarked that the masses —whether Roman plebeians, Medieval serfs, Renaissance peddlers, or workers and peasants of later centuries— neither liked nor understood their contemporary artists: Art was by the bourgeoisie for the bourgeoisie.[28]

Social poetry earned scholarly interest at the inauguration of the academic year in 1955, when Vicente Aleixandre, addressing the Instituto de España, and Emilio Alarcos Llorach, speaking before the University of Oviedo, analyzed the ascendant social poetry.

Aleixandre adopted a conciliatory tone in his lecture, later published as «Algunos caracteres de la nueva poesía española».[29] He synthesized the poetics, noting typical attitudes, prevalent themes, frequently employed techniques, and supported his generalizations with illustrative poems by ten poets.[30] Unlike contentious critics making general charges, Aleixandre named practitioners of the new poetry.[31] For him, the speaker's attitude had to impart authenticity, though this alone was not sufficient to assure a good poem. He found that the speaker usually rejected an estheticist vision of life and showed a temporal awareness that led to one of two tones: anguish or optimism. Claiming that social themes were as legitimate as traditional ones, Aleixandre identified life in its historical dimension, situated in a «here» and «now», as the primary theme and as subordinate ones he listed patriotism, the common man, injustice, com-

---

[26] RICARDO MOLINA, «Autenticidad y humanidad», *Cántico*, 2, No. 6 (February-March 1955).

[27] RICARDO MOLINA, «La poesía social como épica contemporánea», *Cántico*, 2, No. 6 (February-March 1955).

[28] RICARDO MOLINA, «Sobre la comunión entre escritor y pueblo», *Cántico*, 2, No. 8, (June-July 1955).

[29] VICENTE ALEIXANDRE, *Obras completas*, 2 (Madrid: Aguilar, 1977), pp. 489-515.

[30] Aleixandre quotes the following: A selection from *La casa encencida*, by LUIS ROSALES, «Para un esteta» by JOSÉ HIERRO, «Voz de lo negro» by BLAS DE OTERO, «La tarde de la ascensión del Señor» by CARLOS BOUSOÑO, «Una tarde cualquiera» by HIERRO, «La mañana» by JOSÉ MARÍA VALVERDE, «Los traperos» by RAFAEL MORALES, «A Andrés Basterra» by GABRIEL CELAYA, «Recordaré primero», by EUGENIO DE NORA, and «La madre» by DÁMASO ALONSO.

[31] Other poets he mentions are: Victoriano Crémer, Leopoldo de Luis, Angela Figuera, Angel Crespo, Alfonso Costafreda, Aparicio (Antonio?, Francisco?), José Luis Cano, Dionisio Ridruejo, José Suárez Carreño, José García Nieto, Ramón de Garciasol, Concha Zardoya, Jaime Ferrán, and José Angel Valente.

munication, and solidarity among men. He also called the use of narrative techniques, everyday language, references to ordinary objects and the world of the habitual essential to an art addressing the «majority». In short, Aleixandre dignified social poetry, pointing out common areas with poetry written by Rosales, Bousoño, and García Nieto.

Aleixandre gave a comprehensive view of the tendency while Alarcos Llorach's «La poesía de Blas de Otero», later expanded into a book, deepened appreciation for poetry written by its principle figure. Otero, a known Marxist, seldom appeared in literary publications. A stylistic analysis of his poetry by a respected academic therefore was a mark of recognition and acknowledgement of his significance to postwar poetry. That Alarcos Llorach delivered his lecture before an audience including the Governor of the province, the Chancellor of the university, the Mayor of the city, and the Archbishop indicated a major step toward the cultural openness envisioned by Ruiz-Giménez.[32]

Both Aleixandre and Alarcos Llorach claimed importance for social poetry, showing that its faults according to traditional criteria were actually the virtues of a new style. As Aleixandre pointed out, this esthetic was as justifiable as that of the pure poetry it criticized.

At the same time, Rafael Millán issued an anthology, *Veinte poetas españoles,* in which he considered poems by Crémer, Otero, and Celaya to be social poetry.[33] He placed the work of other poets in various categories: Eugenio de Nora's in Neoromanticism, Salvador Pérez Valiente's in *Tremendismo,* Ramón de Garciasol's in Metaphysical poetry, José Hierro's in its own category, already the object of imitation by others, Angela Figuera's also in a category by itself, written by the only woman included in the anthology, and that of Rafael Morales and Leopoldo de Luis in religious social poetry. The presence of social poetry in Millán's anthology was confirmed when ten of the twenty poets were included in *Poesía social,* a work edited by an eleventh, De Luis.[34]

By the late 1950s, the predominance of social poetry was an accepted, though not always celebrated fact in discussions about trends in poetry. Carlos Bousoño, concerned about the disappearance of «artistic individualism», said Spanish poetry entered a new period around 1947 when solidarity with mankind eclipsed the lyric tradition dating from the Romantics.[35] Irrationalism, cultivated by poets for over a century, was

---

[32] FANNY RUBIO, *Las revistas poéticas españolas 1939-1975* (Madrid: Turner, 1976), p. 294.

[33] RAFAEL MILLÁN, *Veinte poetas españoles* (Madrid: Agora, 1955), pp. 9-13.

[34] Those included in both anthologies are Celaya, Crémer, Crespo, Figuera, Garciasol, Hierro, Morales, De Nora, Otero, and Pérez Valiente.

[35] CARLOS BOUSOÑO, «La poesía de Dámaso Alonso», *Papeles de Son Armadans,* 11, Nos. 32-33 (1958), pp. 299-300; «Ante una promoción nueva de poetas», *Agora,* Nos. 27-28 (January-February 1959), p. 4; «Aclaración», *Agora,* Nos. 35-36 (Sep-

overtaken by objectivity, in the process yielding many mediocre poems. However, Bousoño recognized that political factors prolonged this artistic direction: «Si se pone de moda una poesía de sentido antigubernamental, por ejemplo, tal poesía acaso dure lo que dure el gobierno contra el que se levanta».[36] He noted that techniques extensively used between 1947 and 1957 to convey anguish, such as irony, the run-on line, and the judicious use of word play, had all but disappeared before emphasis on religious commitment, social commitment, at times explicitly political, and the affirmation of life's virtues; however, the dialectical origin of social poetry, he asserted, was a state of anguish resolved with commitment.

Aquilino Duque, without analyzing social poetry, judged it in terms of poetic truth and found it both ineffective and transitory: ineffective because the social poet wrote for himself and those like him, not the masses, transitory because it would lose its validity when living conditions of the oppressed improved.[37] Only beauty of expression assured the survival of poetry, he affirmed, citing as good social poetry that of Quevedo, Blas de Otero, and Miguel Hernández.

Polemical statements about social poetry were evidence of political discrepancies in the view of *Rocamador,* which compared the panorama to a republic of left-wing radicals and right-wing conservatives — extremist groups that seemed «*partidos poéticos*».[38] The publication urged that extrapoetic factors be set aside since no poem ought to be published solely for its political content. Furthermore, it deplored the fact that naming favorite poets was interpreted in terms of political leanings: Celaya, Otero, Neruda, and Vallejo placed one on the left; Diego, Valverde, Aleixandre, Garciasol, Anglada, and García Nieto placed one on the right.

Following recognition of the social esthetic came its vogue. The poetry that De Nora, Otero and Celaya published between 1945 and 1955 set the standard, but imitators used social themes and forms independently of the *raison d'être* of Socialist Realism: proselytization of PCE doctrines. For instance, in poems of homage to Celaya and Otero respectively, Leopoldo de Luis and Angela Figuera avoided Marxist watchwords.[39] Like

---

tember-October 1959), pp. 35-36; «Poesía contemporánea y poesía postcontemporánea», *Papeles de Son Armadans,* No. 34 (August 1964), pp. 121-84.

[36] CARLOS BOUSOÑO, «Aclaración», p. 36.

[37] AQUILINO DUQUE, «Poesía social», *Poesía Española,* No. 72 (July 1958), pp. 1, 20-24.

[38] The following articles in *Rocamador* are summarized: «Eclecticismo», No. 2 (Spring 1955), pp. 1-2; «Poesía y política», No. 15 (Spring 1959); «Inautenticidad», No. 23 (Summer 1961); «A propósito de prosaísmo», No. 26 (Summer 1962).

[39] See: LEOPOLDO DE LUIS, «A Luis, el carpintero de al lado de mi casa» and «Mina oscura», *Poesía (1946-1968)* (Barcelona: Plaza y Janés, 1968), pp. 129-30, 180; ANGELA FIGUERA AYMERICH, «Epílogo a Blas de Otero» and «Hombre naciente», *Antología total* (Madrid: CVS Ediciones, 1975), pp. 62-63, 99-100.

most of the poets who were associated with the fashion at its height —José Hierro, Ramón de Garciasol, Rafael Morales— they lived in Madrid, were active in literary affairs, and their poems, book reviews, and opinions appeared in numerous publications. For the most part they wrote conservative variations of the poetry of De Nora, Otero, and Celaya, benefiting from the crest of social poetry's popularity. Exception to this pattern was a group of poets in Barcelona centered around Carlos Barral that revived Socialist Realism by using new themes and satiric techniques.

I. *Angela Figuera Aymerich*

Angela Figuera, born the same year as Cernuda and Alberti, should have been a member of the Generation of 1927, but since she first published in 1948, was regarded as the senior member of the Generation of 1936. Perhaps the most profound influence on Figuera was Neruda, whom she imitated by creating a striking persona to convey her ethical ideals: solidarity, justice, and peace.[40] The persona was original, a feminine voice in a literary world with few published poetesses, and socially critical, addressing issues from the perspective of humanist commitment. Additionally, she shaped topics such as war and peace, social injustice, and traditional themes like love from a feminist position.

For Figuera, the Civil War was a turning point; she lost her teaching post in 1936 because she supported the Republicans. Afterwards, the reign of hatred and injustice, and disregard for freedom made her determined to express solidarity in her poetry: «Vivir viéndolo todo y sufríendolo todo *con todos*...».[41] Even employment in the Biblioteca Nacional, which might have fostered a prudent silence, failed to quiet her criticism of the Spanish predicament.[42] A measure of her achievement is the admiration of León Felipe, who retracted his statement that the «españoles de éxodo y del viento» had taken Spain's poetry when he discovered that it still remained in the voices of Alonso, Otero, Celaya, Crémer, De Nora, De Luis, and Figuera.[43]

In her first work of social poetry, *Vencida por el ángel,* Figuera explored motives for social commitment. Two poems trace an ethical transformation from self-absorption to social concern. In «Egoísmo» seven

---

[40] CHARLES DAVID LEY in *Spanish Poetry since 1939* (Washington D.C.: Catholic University of America, 1962), p. 110, that «at a public reading in 1953 of her latest poems— under the auspices of the government-subsidized review *Poesía española*— declared herself a disciple of Neruda's (and a friend to Gabriel Celaya and Blas de Otero)».

[41] LEOPOLDO DE LUIS, *Poesía social* (Madrid: Alfaguara, 1965), pp. 65-66.

[42] ANTONIO NÚÑEZ, «Encuentro con Angela Figuera», *Insula,* No. 327, p. 4.

[43] ANGELA FIGUERA AYMERICH, *Antología total (1948-1969)* (Madrid: CVS Ediciones, 1975), pp. 129-30. Further references to this edition appear in the text preceded by AT.

central stanzas describing life and death as chaos are self-accusations of a former pure poet: «Contra el sucio oleaje de las cosas / yo apretaba la puerta» (AT, 43-44). The title poem, «Vencida por el ángel» (AT, 44), relates the inner struggle of the speaker, who barred the outside world only to become engaged in a metaphysical duel with an angel that leaves her anguished, humiliated, and grieving for the world. These poems prepare for the speaker's acceptance of solidarity.

El grito inútil examines solidarity from a feminist viewpoint. The speaker of «¿Qué vale una mujer? ¿Para qué sirvo?» (AT, 51-52), alternates rhetorical questions with longings for the beauty of the past. The remaining poems are based on standard topics, some of which are: an ironic celebration of the postwar period, a plea for solidarity, poverty represented as putrefaction; a plea for peace —«Serán las madres que digan: 'Basta'»— a celebration of deplorably exploited manual labor; an observation that protesting hunger in poems does not put bread on the table, and, finally, a catalogue of callings that excludes poets: «No sé si tengo sitio. / Los poetas sobramos» (AT, 52-59). The collection ends with an intertextual tribute to Otero:

> Así te encuentran todos un poco taciturno.
> Y los lectores dicen «¡oh!, ¡oh!» sobre tus versos.
> Y hasta te recriminan las personas decentes
> por pretender un día que las niñas bajaran
> ese blanco percal de sus cortas braguitas
> (braguitas, ¿es posible?),
> para rogar a Dios con inocencia. (AT, 63)

Belleza cruel, written between 1953 and 1957, was unpublishable in Spain until the 1970s; meanwhile, it received an award and publication in Mexico in 1958.[44] Its nineteen poems are divided among three sections, each with at least one poem presenting Figuera's ideological position. In reading order, the first section, subtitled «Belleza cruel» as is the first poem, presents her views on humanism and poetry; the second, «Caso acusativo», contains testimonial poems; and the last, «Hombre naciente», also name of the final poem, includes a harangue to youth and declarations concerning the proper path to the future. Figuera regarded the *«poemas rabiosos»* of this work as the most exact representation of her feelings about the postwar period; as late as 1974 she refused to adopt the more personal introspective style that replaced social poetry during the 1960s.[45]

In the title poem the speaker, desiring a carefree life, feels guilty when reminded of people's fear, hunger, and concealed rage, for pursuing esthetic

---

[44] ANGELA FIGUERA AYMERICH, *Belleza cruel* (Barcelona: Lumen, 1978). Page numbers to this edition are indicated in text preceded by BC only if references do not appear in AT.
[45] ANTONIO NÚÑEZ, «Encuentro con Angela Figuera», p. 4.

ideals, for seeking beauty everywhere. The implication is that in a normal state of affairs, where hard work earns adequate wages and neighbors treat each other charitably, the poet may pursue beauty, while under Spain's abnormal conditions poets pursuing beauty must be criticized. «El cielo», contrasts the speaker's «*Colegas queridísimos*», who have an unimpeded view of heaven, with herself, seeing only sullen clouds hanging above the bended backs and sweat-blinded eyes of miners and prisoners. An accusation of complicity between the Regime and guilty poets, alluded to by previous mention of «*tirano*» and «*fiscales*», concludes the poem:

> No puede verse el cielo desde el fondo del cáncer,
> desde el fondo más hondo del infierno más negro,
> desde el fondo de todos los que están en el fondo,
> los que son tierra sucia que pisáis sin mirarla
> cuando váis extasiados
> por las líricas nubes. (BC, 20)

According to Figuera, the ideal poet is a humble figure like the saint in «San Poeta Labrador» (AT, 93-94), who worked tirelessly in the furrowed fields, a poet-saint cultivating his land as he did his poetry:

> Iba un puñado de belleza
> por cada puñado de grano.
> Y un puñadito de verdad.
> (Esto sin que lo viera el amo.) (AT, 93)

Part of his duty was labor, the other prayer. Always hoping for a miracle —angels tending his fields, abundant crops to harvest—, he nevertheless plowed fields to bring about the slow miracle of progress through effort. The poet's sympathy is topic of «Si no has muerto un instante» (AT, 89), a propositional statement based on an epigraph from Nazim Hikmet. The speaker turns Hikmet's observation that he suffers personally whenever injustice prevails into a general imperative — he who does not suffer for others deserves death: «Al hoyo, y acabado.» The final poem «Hombre naciente» (AT, 99-100), echoes Otero's phrase, «Pido la paz y la palabra». Under a white flag, the speaker pleads for a land without weapons and ruins, then begs mankind to begin a life based on hope.

Figuera's poetry unlike that of Socialist Realists never condones violence, nor does it often refer to political commitment. Two exceptions are «Niño con rosas» (BC, 15-16) and «La rosa incómoda» (BC, 21-22), which when innocently read appear whimsical, but remembering that the rose is symbol of the Partido Socialista Obrero Español, may be read as signs of commitment.

Figuera believed that the proper sociopolitical solution was good will toward others accompanied by methodical labor, topic of the harangue, «Veinte años» (AT, 97-99). Composed on the occasion of her son's twentieth birthday, the poem is addressed to those on the threshold of manhood. The speaker refuses to discuss the ignominy, destruction, death, hatred, and vengeance of «*aquello*» in order to tell «*esto*», instructions to build a peaceful Spain upon the ruins. To express her uncompromising aversion to war, Figuera speaks as Eve in «Guerra» (BC, 30-32). Mother of Cain and Abel, she saw mortality in their flesh and crime in their eyes when they were born, as if prescient of tragedy. Unable to temper Cain's ire with Abel's docility and Abel's innocence with Cain's reverence, she rues having created war.

Solidarity with the unfortunate was a central tenet in Figuera's outlook. She developed this theme in «Sólo ante el hombre» by contrasting her reverence toward God and nature with her egalitarian regard for mankind — «Sólo ante el hombre me comprendo y mido / mi altura por su altura y reconozco / su sangre por mis venas y le entrego / mi vaso de esperanza, y le bendigo, / y junto a él me pongo y le acompaño» (AT, 88-89). Addressing one «*hermano*» after another, the speaker of «Canción del pan robado» uses bread as a symbol for wages. This permits a number of allusions —«¿Es el camino / tan largo de la espiga hasta mis labios?»; «El pan que salga de los hornos, / pan bien cocido y bien ganado, / será el pan nuestro cada día, / ni discutido ni menguado» (BC, 60-61)— suggesting economic exploitation by thieves portrayed as a hyena, a kite, and a vulture. Having vowed solidarity with the unfortunate, Figuera gave testimony of their desperately unfair lives in the poems of «Caso acusativo». The speaker of «Balance» (BC, 33-35) employs satiric epithets in addressing the bourgeoisie, insisting that they calculate the balance they owe for benefits received. Her tone softens when addressing the «*pueblo*», eternal creditor in Spain's economy, and ends with a plea to God: «Y hágase al fin tu voluntad / así en España / como en el cielo.» Figuera's most unusual poem of testimony is «Carta abierta» (AT, 90), addressed to «Jesús de Nazaret», signed by a poor carpenter barely able to feed his children, who invites Christ to return to earth to work miracles again. The theme of «La justicia de los ángeles» (BC, 40-47) is optimistic; angels correct earthly injustice in four individual cases of impoverishment.

The underlying optimism of Figuera's poetry gave rise to appeals for divine justice in poems such as these. Unlike the optimistic Socialist Realists, who assumed ultimate victory for the oppressed through their own actions, Figuera promoted the view that, human effort failing, divine agency would right wrongs.

II. *José Hierro*

Owing even less to Socialist Realism than Figuera, José Hierro developed a style depending upon testimonial techniques, yet which also conveyed profound awareness, avoiding explicit challenges. Like Figuera, he found his life changed by the Civil War; soon after Franco's victory, he was arrested, sentenced, and jailed until 1944 for involvement in the Resistance.[46] Following his release, Hierro wrote poetry, eventually attracting a large number of loyal readers. Said to be the poet obtaining the most votes for the *Antología consultada,* he soon was called one of Spain's foremost living poets.[47] Official honors came in the wake of recognition: During the late 1950s, Hierro assumed an editorship for *La Estafeta Literaria,* a Regime-funded publication directed by Rafael Morales, and later was responsible for the Ateneo de Madrid, sponsored by the Regime.

After appearing in the *Antología consultada,* Hierro was classified in the minds of many as a social poet. Phrases cited earlier from the essay accompanying his poems, «Algo sobre poesía, poética y poetas», were quoted as evidence.[48] Perhaps most responsible for earning him a place among social poets was the statement that he detested the idea of escape to an ivory tower because the poet must bear the weight of his age, his poetry the trace of historical events. Nevertheless, these few assertions seem to have been quoted out of context; Hierro's views on poetry differed significantly from those of the Socialist Realists. In contrast to Celaya, for whom poetry was a weapon, for Hierro it was a gift; the poet, a visionary, elaborated inspiration logically by identifying a rhythm, then a meter —in effect, the poem's music— and, finally, selected words to fit the lines.

Hierro first discussed his poetic theory as «practical poetry».[49] He pointed out that pure poetry risked coldness and pedantry, but its gravest risk, the one responsible for its demise in his view, was that words were its final goal not a means to a higher goal. In the 1950s he thought that the opposite extreme had been reached: Problems and messages took precedence over the poetic word. Furthermore, Hierro asserted that the audience for pure poetry, *la inmensa minoría,* was exactly the same as *la inmensa mayoría,* though their names differed. Ever since Medieval times, he added, small groups of poetry readers were the contemporary audience for whatever poetry was written. And, since those unaccustomed to poetry seldom read it, the genre was by definition for a select audience. Hierro cautioned poets against believing that uninformed illiterates incapable of analyzing the beauty of a poem were an appropriate audience.

Hierro expanded this two-category system to one having four in the prologue of *Poesías completas,* where he divided poets according to the

---

[46] AURORA DE ALBORNOZ, «Aproximaciones a la obra poética de José Hierro», *Cuadernos Hispanoamericanos,* No. 341 (November 1978), p. 274.
[47] CHARLES DAVID LEY, *Spanish Poetry since 1939,* pp. 115, 118.
[48] FRANCISCO RIBES, *Antología consultada,* pp. 99-107.
[49] JOSÉ HIERRO, «Poesía pura, poesía práctica», *Insula,* No. 132 (November 1958), pp. 1, 4.

goal of their poetry: The *estetas* contemplated beauty, the *testimoniales* bore witness, the *políticos* not only bore witness, they offered political solutions, and the *religiosos* addressed God.[50] One advantage of this classification was that it permitted Hierro to separate himself from committed poets, whether religious or political, without having to join the *estetas*. Hierro defined testimonial poetry as that in which the poet spoke as a witness for the «defense» or the «prosecution», without being drawn toward political or religious commitment. He thought testimonial poetry necessary in times such as the postwar period, but still believed poetic precision the most important poetic quality. Hierro separated his own poems between *reportajes* and *alucinaciones*. The former offered a direct, narrative treatment of a theme, telling something about objective reality. The latter were contemplative, irrational imaginings, making use of such techniques as temporal juxtaposition, fusion of times and places, doubling of the speaker, personification of the inanimate, and such symbols as *mar, azul, alas, vuelo*.[51] He offered no solutions to social problems to avoid falling into propaganda, striving for objectivity rather than passion.

When Hierro commented on social poetry for De Luis in 1965, he indicated that, if during the 1950s all poetry was supposed to be social, a decade later none was, regardless of the fact that both positions were probably exaggerated.[52] In his own case, he found that certain social themes emerged naturally rather than by plan, although he suspected most of his poems were too personal in tone to be considered social. Hierro claimed neither to follow fashions, such as social poetry, nor reject them; rather, he followed his intuition, allowing poems to «teach him about himself».

Hierro's works bearing traces of social poetry are *Tierra sin nosotros* and *Quinta del 42,* written when he was developing techniques used in testimonial poems. In the first of these works, strategically placed poems set a tone of resistance affecting interpretation of the work as a whole. The motive for resistance arises in the contrast between a prior time of joyful promise, a lost paradise, and the sorrowful, painful present. In «Entonces» the speaker thinks of the time before *aquello,* unwilling to accept that it was irrevocably past:

> Cuando se hallaba el mundo a punto
> de que el prodigio sucediese.
> Cuando tenía cada instante
> un ritmo nuevo y diferente,
> cada estación sus ubres llenas,
> rebosantes de blanca leche... (CSDM, 24)

---

[50] JOSÉ HIERRO, *Cuanto sé de mí* (Barcelona: Seix Barral, 1974), pp. 11-18. Further references to this edition appear in the text preceded by CSDM.
[51] ALBORNOZ, «Aproximación a la obra poética de José Hierro», p. 28.
[52] LEOPOLDO DE LUIS, *Poesía social*, pp. 217-20.

This poem and «Generación», introducing a section called «Nosotros», contain no explicit references to the Civil War, yet to read them outside such a context diminishes the effect of social criticism. The «*prodigio*» just cited and the «*viento glorioso*» of «Generación» are vehicles for the speaker's ideals, promises of the future, which when destroyed taught the lesson of human limits. «Generación», while dealing with existentialist themes, draws a more pessimistic conclusion. De Nora, for example, argued that the lesson of human mortality, *destino,* must be taught by the poet, Hierro regarded *destino* as the seal of tragedy, for man not only must disappear, but his effort to survive death through his work is also doomed:

> Así pasamos, como un soplo
> de brisa azul sobre la piedra.
> Sin dejar rastro, como el oro
> de las hojas, cuando coronan
> la frente grave del otoño...
>
> Porque no queda ni una sola
> rosa plantada por nosotros. (CSDM, 43)

Though despairing the futility of human effort, the speaker writes poems as a rebellious act against time and oblivion. In the final poem, he confesses awareness of the transitory nature of existence and the inevitability of death, his protest unresolved in a fragment grammatically lacking a principal clause: «Pero morirme sin rebelarme, / someterme sin resistencia» (CSDM, 84).

In this collection there are two testimonial poems anticipating «Reportaje» that deal directly with Hierro's memories of prison. «Canción de cuna para dormir a un preso» (CSDM, 44-46) is a rhythmic lullaby capturing a delicate moment when the speaker tries to soothe anxiety pretending that his listener is a child and that what happened did not; darkness and sleep provide a temporary escape from the present. The speaker's perspective in the other poem, «A un lugar donde viví mucho tiempo», looks back to the time of imprisonment. Most of the poem is addressed to the prison building itself; the speaker recalls forced exercise in the patio, monotonous views of gray skies, companions who died, and the indifference of the institution toward the men it housed. This apparent resignation, nonetheless, is betrayed by passion in the final lines: «Días de ayer, ¡Dios os / perdone lo que habéis hecho de nosotros!» (CSDM, 59).

Among the poems of *Quinta del 42* «Para un esteta» is especially important as a declaration of Hierro's beliefs. The speaker contrasts the attitude of an esthete to his own. For the esthete, words are like beautiful flowers, for the speaker they lack «aroma». The former holds beauty as the highest value, the speaker values most life (and death). The esthete's refusal to acknowledge life's transitory nature and the impermanence of his works earn a reminder that man's duty is to live and die. This existentialist tone affects «Encadenados», to cite just one example in which the human tragedy is that men survive, abandoned by God:

> Se murió la esperanza
> y siguieron viviendo.
> Sólo los perros mueren
> al morirse su dueño. (CSDM, 235)

«Reportaje» claims to be an objective report of reality, though an attentive reading shows that the «report» is filtered through sentiments. The speaker contrasts the temporality of life with the timelessness of imprisonment, where hours, seasons, and years blend into each other: Measured time is meaningless for the incarcerated. This lack of change creates in prisoners a thirst for mutability that some satisfy with stoic resignation, others with protest: «Porque sin una evidencia / de tiempo, yo no estoy vivo» (CSDM, 243).

Hierro's preoccupation with experience modified by states of consciousness discernible in this poem, one of his most objective, is a direct consequence of his belief that the poet «escribe para entenderse a sí mismo».[53] His belief in poetry as a means of self-knowledge and his ideological independence were alien to the tenets of Socialist Realism, by which the poet exposed reality ideologically, offering not only testimony concerning wrongs but encouragement to bring about sociopolitical solutions. Hierro's outlook resembled that of Claudio Rodríguez, José Angel Valente, and Jaime Gil de Biedma; who together set attitudes and modes of later poetry.[54]

III. *A Christian Response*

In face of the politicized atheism of Socialist Realist poetry, religiously committed poets promoted a traditional humanist vision of man and society in which mankind played a central role without any apocalyptic upheaval called for or expected. The Christian God of love and the Christian code of morality informed the ethos of their social poems; social injustice and misfortune called for divine redress. Poets looked compassionately toward society's victims, as did the Socialist Realists, but their motives were different and directed toward other goals. Both groups protested, but only the Socialist Realists called for political revolution. Setting aside Marxist commitment as the major characteristic of

---

[53] *Ibid.*, p. 220.
[54] José Olivio Jiménez, *Diez años de poesía española (1960-1970)* (Madrid: Insula, 1972), p. 18.

social poetry, numerous poets saw themselves engaged in authentic protest. As the roster of social poets lengthened during the 1950s, the explanation may be that suggested by J. M. Cohen: Poets who avoided commitment to a particular political view expressed sentiments «as acceptable to a root-and-branch Falangist as to a secret socialist or anarchist».[55] That is, Marxist sympathizers were not the only readers adept at supplying missing details to protest in cipher. Non-Marxists were adept readers in their own way, finding protest in a defiant stance, a rebellious pose, or an emphatic rhetoricism. Always present, then, was the possibility that readers would interpret protest to their own liking, discounting radical stands conflicting with their personal views, or conversely, taking all stands as reflecting their own awareness. Nevertheless, poets cognizant of factional differences made clear distinctions among themselves.

Protesting the excesses of «*prosaísmo utilitarista*», Rafael Morales claimed beauty an essential value of poetry, a means by which the poet could relate to others.[56] At the same time he expressed a particular understanding of beauty in such works as *Poemas del toro* and *El corazón y la tierra*. That is, he wished to redefine beauty, long thought to result from pure sensuality or esthetic play, by humanizing it through the expression of intellectual and affective truths. Beauty, for Morales, did not reside in the theme of a poem but rather in its expression. Because he believed it possible to poeticize what was usually considered ugly, insignificant, or beneath the attention of poets, he used such unexpected topics as lepers, idiots, ragmen, and garbage pails.

In accord with Christian neohumanism, he viewed these humble subjects as aspects of life in a universe of love. His characteristic outlook showed pity toward the less fortunate; but his pity was not always free from patronization, as these lines addressed to a leper suggest:

> ¡Ay, mírala, qué bella es la muchacha,
> qué delicada y pura junto al aire!
> Pero no la desees: olvida, olvida.
> No sirves ya, leproso, para amante. (PC, 122)

Other poems from *Los desterrados,* dedicated to those «banished» from normal society —marginal figures like the loveless, the forgotten, the elderly, the blind— are lyrical evocations, not the social indictments typical of Socialist Realist poems. Morales called himself a Romantic inspired by sorrow for others, one who wrote, according to his statement in the *Antología consultada,* «para la mayoría».[57] Though this comment would

---

[55] J. M. COHEN, «Since the Civil War. New Currents in Spanish Poetry», *Encounter,* 12, No. 2 (February 1959), p. 47.

[56] RAFAEL MORALES, *Poesías completas (1940-1967)* (Madrid: Giner, 1967), pp. 7-21. References to this edition appear in the text preceded by PC.

[57] FRANCISCO RIBES, *Antología consultada,* pp. 126-27.

suggest that he sought Otero's audience, his sentimentalized manner, not unattractive when judged by criteria other than Socialist Realist, undermined his social concern. This is obvious in «Los traperos» (PC, 159-60), where interest focuses on the ragmen's sacks. Morales used adjectives of disassociation —*silenciosos, solitario, frío*— and disparagement —*sucios, mutilados, muertos*— to paint a somber image of scavenged rubbish. At the same time, he used pathetic description to engage the readers' sympathy: The sacks are «*dolorosos*», a pair of shoes «*de un muchacho muerto*», a doll «*sin brazos y sin ojos*», and a fan «*tímido*». In the concluding stanza the ragmen, bowed under the weight of their sacks, simply disappear into the night, without reference to them as historical beings, victims of an unfair society. Though Morales stated that he wrote for the majority, he added that he knew neither why he wrote poetry nor what he sought in doing so, an attitude at odds with that of the Socialist Realists, highly conscious of their motives for writing.[58] Finally, Morales called attention to his distance from Celaya and Otero in this reflective aphorism: «¿Poesía realista? Jamás. ¿Poesía de la realidad? Siempre».[59]

In contrast to Morales, Gloria Fuertes did not hesitate to associate her name with that of Celaya, whom she mentioned in «Inesperada visita» and «Esta noche comprendo», although elsewhere she acknowledged differences among social poets.[60] In her own poetry Fuertes sought «*comunión-comunicación*» with readers to move and surprise them. Therefore she relied upon a direct, conversational style in poems addressed to humanity. Moreover, referring to the debate over pure and impure poetry, she preferred «useful» language over the «useless» perfection sought by poets writing only for themselves. These poets are the addressees of «No perdamos el tiempo», in which the speaker exhorts listeners to notice widespread poverty and forget such topics as the infinite sea, the rosy dawn, and the perfumed rose. Instead she urges:

> Debemos de inquietarnos por curar las simientes,
> por vendar corazones y escribir el poema
> que a todos nos contagie.
> Y crear esa frase que abrace todo el mundo,
> los poetas debiéramos arrancar las espadas,
> inventar más colores y escribir padrenuestros. (OI, 45)

---

[58] *Ibid.*, p. 125.
[59] RAFAEL MORALES, «Poética», *Agora*, Nos. 51-52 (January-February 1961), p. 24.
[60] GLORIA FUERTES, «Inesperada visita» and «Esta noche comprendo», *Obras incompletas* (Madrid: Cátedra, 1977), pp. 51-52, 175. Subsequent references to this edition appear in the text after the abbreviation OI.
  Referring to the first years of the postwar period she wrote: «Por aquel entonces, sin ponernos de acuerdo, Blas de Otero, Celaya, Hierro, Alcántara —y tantos nombres que añadirán a esta relación los estudiosos—, escribíamos poemas declarando incluso nuestra filiación, dirección y profesión para llamar la atención a los transeúntes que luego iban o no pasar por nuestras páginas» (OI, 24).

The mention of *padrenuestros* suggests that prayer was among Fuertes' remedies for social injustice, a view consistent with her vision of an omnipresent God sufficiently approachable to receive familiar address. In «Un hombre pregunta» (OI, 43-45), «Oración» (OI, 47-48), «A lo mejor un día...» (OI, 53), and «Poema» (OI, 55), Fuertes portrayed a benevolent deity, responsive to genuine love and need, and therefore found among impoverished slum-dwellers and mankind's servants —whether doctors, poets, or well-intentioned bankers—, but not among the insincere, ungenerous, or unfeeling, whatever their pretensions. Fuertes sought a mystical attitude toward the poetic process whatever her milieu: «Yo me hundo en lo espiritual / haciendo un poema en el arrabal» (OI, 55).

To create the speaker of *Poemas del suburbio* (1954) and *Aconsejo beber hilo* (1954), Fuertes, daughter of working-class parents, drew details from personal experience beginning with her name cited in the first line of «Nota biográfica» (OI, 41). As an anti-aristocratic gesture the speaker of «El vendedor de papeles o el poeta sin suerte» (OI, 52) offers verses gratis when fees are not forthcoming. This mild irreverence toward a pursuit usually regarded more seriously reappears as self-mockery in «Voy haciendo versos por la calle» (OI, 89). Avoiding the Marxist bluster of an Alberti or an Otero, the speaker of this poem is annoyed by distractions —the streetcar she rides is noisy, her absorption in the poem's creation risks interruption. This down-to-earth speaker provides glimpses of the life of the poor— despair at not having money to purchase shoes and clothing in «No tengo nunca nada» (OI, 99) and the daily inconveniences of overcrowding, underpaid wages, excessive working hours, and inadequate food in «Estamos bien» (OI, 101). To achieve immediacy, Fuertes created other personae to deliver first-person accounts of poverty, eliminating an intermediary speaker between readers and protagonists. Among these diverse victims of poverty are a seventy-year-old man about to die in «La ida del hombre» (OI, 64), a reformed prostitute in «La arrepentida» (OI, 64-65), a destitute young woman in «La pobre» (OI, 105-06), and various homeless beggars in «El mendigo de los ojos» (OI, 63), «Pobre de nacimiento» (OI, 65-66), and «Melancolía del mendigo» (OI, 83). Fuertes demonstrated in these poems that she preferred a testimonial manner to that of the propagandist; only a few of her poems express direct protest.

Like other social poets, Fuertes emphasized her solidarity with the poor, sometimes speaking directly to them, other times expressing their perceptions before other listeners, presumably those able to take corrective measures. In an example of the first approach, «Carta», the speaker acknowledges letters, noting the trade or workplace of senders. Through repetitive phrases and rudimentary syntax, she affirms her awareness of their individual misfortunes, her sympathy for their plight, but admits her inability to make drastic changes: «Yo no puedo de lo que me decís haceros nada. / ... / pobres de mil oficios no estáis solos / aquí un poeta os canta, / luego vendrán más» (OI, 113-14). This sense of powerlessness is apparent too in Fuertes' poems directed to the customary poetry-reading public. Three in particular convey this effect despite their sensivity to socio-economic issues. The speaker of «Mal sueño» catalogues groups —the suspicious, the warlike, the pedants, the envious, in short, those who oppress others— that she would «eliminate» gladly, yet the poem ends indecisively: «yo / que detesto la pena de muerte, / no sé lo que haría» (OI, 51). «Las flacas mujeres» may be taken as a death warrant for those who plan wars, if the last lines are read as mock humility:

> Y yo pido perdón al Gran Quien Sea,
> por desearles una buena caja,
> con cuatro cirios de los más curiosos. (OI, 67)

Similarly, «Aviso», which protests the sort of bureaucrat found in the stock market and government ministries who lowers wages, ends with an order that is tantamount to a death warrant: «Enterrad a ese hombre cuanto antes» (OI, 97).

These poems, whose context is liberal commitment to gradual change, differ from those written by Otero and Celaya because in Fuertes' the threats are rhetorical while in Otero's and Celaya's they echo actual political policies. For the same reason, the message of «Yo arreglaría el mundo», which is not unlike «La poesía es un arma cargada de futuro», is less convincing than that of Celaya's. Despite words like, *balas, hangares* and *aviones* mentioned in earlier lines, these lines are inoffensive:

> Vive empeñado el fiel corazón mío
> en que yo sea como un loco soldado
> y plise a los que odian con el pie de mis cantos. (OI, 59)

Fuertes was not calling for a new social order but merely an improvement in society as it was. In this regard, her poems in the testimonial mode nudge the reader's conscience rather than «transform» it; they remind readers of the need for concern without demanding Marxist commitment. While Fuertes accepted association with Celaya, her poems suggest that political differences existed between them.

Ramón de Garciasol published several collections beginning in the 1950s that he considered to be social poetry. Like Morales and Fuertes, he counted himself among those «rehumanizing» a poetic tradition dehumanized by estetes; he «rooted» himself in the humane current based on knowledge and freedom, restraint, and seriousness.[61] Because of these qualities, Garciasol pointed out that his poetry was «discrepant and non-

---

[61] RAMÓN DE GARCIASOL, *Antología provisional* (Madrid: Aguilar, 1967), p. 24. Further references to this edition are preceded in the text by AP.

conformist», for which some labeled it metaphysical, others social (AP, 22). Although Garciasol did not deny the label of social, his poetry, like that of Morales, lacked a left-wing political outlook. Among remarks he submitted to De Luis for *Poesía social,* for instance, was a definition of the social poet based on Christian morality: «El poeta social —tanto más cuanto más altura poética logre—, denuncia la existencia de un cáncer moral cuya medicina es *ama al prójimo como a ti mismo*».[62] Furthermore, since he ignored the ideological outlook of others, he regarded as fellow social poets Crémer, Figuera, Otero, Celaya, De Nora, and Hierro, as well as the less frequently named Leopoldo de Luis, Gloria Fuertes, Salvador Pérez Valiente, and Martín Descalzo.[63]

A vehement rhetorical manner rather than left-wing political ideas defined Garciasol's nonconformity. What he protested sometimes derived from the human condition with its temporal limits, other times was ambiguously indicated, trivial, or incomprehensible. For instance, in «Hombre» the speaker opens with imperatives: «¡Espera, tiempo! ¡Espera, carne! ¡Vida, espera!» (AP, 40). The body of the poem explores time as motive for man's fear of death, of being subject to natural law. The conclusion is an optimistic view of time assuring the possibility of growth and change, and the curing of unwelcome aspects of reality. The speaker concludes with imperatives glorifying time: «¡Tiempo, vamos! ¡Florece, carne! ¡Vida, sigue!» (AP, 41). Garciasol utilized emphatic rhetoric to a similar purpose in «Arenga a las rosas y a los hombres». By juxtaposing *rosas* and *hombres* four times in the last half of the poem, he joined two central ideas; first, that roses should grow over the weapons of war, transforming the warlike and, second, that men should awaken to the good and the beautiful, turning their backs on fear. Serious protest seems to ring through the following lines:

> ... ...
> vamos a proclamar la resistencia
> de amor contra la guerra.
> Están sembrando el aire de temores
> para amargarnos la alegría,
> para que nos matemos tú y yo, hermano... (AP, 62)

However, the context of this call for resistance is unclear. The identity of *we* and *they,* crucial to engaging readers' sympathy, is vague. If the poem's range of reference is Spain, the protest is anachronistic, an echo from the 1930s. If, on the other hand, the protest refers to the world, most readers will applaud, few favor war. The *vosotros* address in «Vencido» permits the speaker to distinguish himself from his addressees:

---

[62] LEOPOLDO DE LUIS, *Poesía social,* p. 124.
[63] RAMÓN DE GARCIASOL, «Notas sobre la nueva poesía española (1939-1958)», *Acento Cultural,* No. 2 (December 1958), p. 19.

> Vosotros sois el día: sois. Marchaos.
>
> Olvidadme y seguid. Cantad de nuevo.
> En alto la canción y las banderas.
> Olvidaos de haberme conocido. (AP, 52)

The differences between this poem published in 1952 and De Nora's «Lamento» written more than a decade earlier are significant. The context of De Nora's poem was, according to the appended note, protest of the dehumanized contemporary world.[64] Its cry for freedom and allegations of censorship, however, alerted readers to a more immediate context: Franco's Spain. De Nora's poem was obviously nonconformist. This is not so with Garciasol's poem. A sensitized line, which might indicate authentic protest, such as «La noche es buena / para ocultar la sangre entre las sombras» is not followed by a vow to act but by the speaker's refusal of social engagement: «Quiero quedarme solo, cara a cara / con Dios, con mi dolor, conmigo a solas» (AP, 52). In the absence of textual clues to meaning, sometimes extra-poetic information is instructive. Since the lines cited above were written by a politically conservative poet, «la canción y las banderas» of the opposition might be those of recalled Civil-War communists and anarchists rather than of contemporary postwar Falangists.

On the poets discussed in this section, Leopoldo de Luis wrote least about his own poetry and most about that of others. To his credit are numerous articles and book reviews, more than a dozen collections of his own poems, and several anthologies, among them, *Poesía social*, from which he excluded himself though he wrote two works based entirely on social themes.

Teatro real envisions Spain as a somber theater in which actors repeat their roles, each deaf to the words of the others.[65] Those like the speaker, who sense the truth of this farce, understand its futility and parody. Among scenes played is one of a shipwreck. «Naufragio en tierra» (P, 121-23) contrasts the stage setting —actors, backdrop sea, mock ship— with an allegorical ship of state on a sea of hunger and terror, whose captain and sailors tell each other that the ship, on an unknown course, is not sinking. In «Patria oscura», referring to the working class «a la que falta luz, como alegría / y pan» (P, 138), the speaker states that he feels as one with them, even to sharing their captive voice. As a poet he offers words as remedy:

> Esta pobre palabra, como a tientas,
> es una mano hacia la luz; ceniza

---

[64] See Chapter 3, p. 60.
[65] LEOPOLDO DE LUIS, *Poesía (1946-1968)* (Barcelona: Plaza y Janés, 1968). References to this edition appear in the text preceded by P.

> quiere apartar hacia la lumbre; humana
> esperanza de amor la justifica. (P, 139)

Speaking for a utilitarian poetic, De Luis compared writing poetry to carpentry. In «A Luis, el capintero de al lado de mi casa», reminiscent of Celaya's «A Andrés Basterra», the speaker says he creates products as necessary as his neighbor's. Both serve the needs of men, but the poet's effort has the more noble goal: «De las palabras crece un manifiesto / de sangre y de verdad. Una esperanza / luminosa y común» (P, 130). The message De Luis reiterated was that of light, symbol with which end two of the poems just mentioned. In one, above the gesturing actors on the shadowy stage «Sólo la luz, la luz sigue alumbrando» (P, 117) and, in the other, within sight of the doomed sailors «El falso faro / de un reflector está haciendo señales» (P, 123). While some of these details suggest a parallel between De Luis and Celaya, De Luis used the term *luz* symbolically while Celaya made his message as explicit as conditions permitted.

The introductory poem of *Juego limpio*, «Con los míos estoy», has the identity marks of a self-effacing rather than militant speaker, one who idealistically dreams of making the world an imitation of heaven:

> No me resigno a que las cosas vayan
> por la Tierra peor que por el Cielo.
> Para cumplir con mi verdad escribo.
> (Perdón si soy molesto.) (P, 144)

This parenthetical apology contrasts with the bravado of the Marxist challenge. De Luis believed in social commitment, though not in the Marxist version. His messages were more inclusive, more general:

> Nosotros extraemos en el bosque
> del tiempo estas verdades, estas pocas
> palabras, ramas con que se mantiene
> tras la ceniza aún la lumbre roja:
> *libertad, esperanza, amor, mañana,*
> *hijo, alegría, corazón, no importa.* (P. 159)

He spoke for a better future, but did not advance violent solutions; he employed many of the key words, but in his catalogue they lack the political focus a poet like Otero would have achieved. Such a focus would be contrary to his open-minded liberal outlook, ready to take into consideration views other than his own, avoiding a dogmatic stand on any issue, whether in poetry or criticism.

This same open-mindedness is apparent in the anthology *Poesía social* —testimonial to the dominance of poetry of protest in the postwar period— including representative poets, their commentaries, and poems. In the introduction, De Luis sought to identify social poetry's inherent characteristics through the ages, regardless of distinctive features occurring at particular moments. He rejected the view that social poetry was a school or a movement, comparable to pure poetry, modernism or surrealism «con sus postulados, sus manifiestos, sus pontífices y sus ortodoxias».[66] Instead, he defined *poesía social* as a genre contrasting with *poesía política, poesía civil, poesía satírica, poesía popular,* and others. De Luis named its generic characteristics: realism, historicity, narration, and protest without a specific objective or solution. To social poets, he attributed commitment to truth above any one ideology. While valuing social poetry by Miguel Hernández and Rafael Alberti, De Luis also discussed social poetry from the Middle Ages to the postwar era. Attending to tone rather than ideological bias, De Luis identified Garciasol as author of the first postwar social poem and Camilo José Cela as another initiator of the tendency.[67] While these assertions were possible within a liberal outlook avoiding specific political issues, they seem erroneous from the Marxist view that poetry, or any other realm, is inevitably political. The assertions, in short, indicate the ideological separation between the first social poets and those who followed.

Eugenio de Nora challenged De Luis' definition of social poetry, accusing the latter of making a false distinction between *poesía social* and *poesía política,* which he himself considered inseparable. For De Nora, true social poetry, being political, raised consciousness by unchaining the processes by which men bettered themselves.[68] Moreover, he held that all moral stands carried political implications, acknowledged or not. For De Luis, a moral stand was not a political one; but his belief that the poet's commitment to truth «al margen de todo dogma y consigna» constituted a non-political stand disregarded historical and biographical information. As a result, De Luis differentiated his own social poetry from the «social» poetry of De Nora, Otero, and Celaya, which was political in his view. Thus the proliferation of social poetry occurred as poverty and injustice became socially acceptable topics among poets across the political spec-

---

[66] LEOPOLDO DE LUIS, «La poesía social, otra vez», *Insula,* No. 247 (June 1967), p. 4.

[67] LEOPOLDO DE LUIS, *Poesía social,* p. 49: «... en la posguerra, en 1942, escribió el poema 'Quejas a Rubén Darío', anticipo, en cierto modo, de la tónica de su libro *Defensa del hombre.* En ese poema se rechaza la poesía narcisista y de valores puramente sensuales para pedir una poética que asuma la misión de remover las conciencias y que combata por que no se tome al hombre a esclavitud ni a juego.»

And pp. 52-53: «... es autor de un poema aparecido en la revista *Garcilaso* (núm. 25), en el año 1945, con un tono infrecuente entonces. Se titula 'La risa de Dios' y disonaba, como digo, en el concierto de la poesía de la época, con su agria invectiva contra los hombres de Estado, culpables del dolor de los pueblos. Es un poema de tono apocalíptico, que predice la ira divina y se expresa con elementos del superrealismo.»

[68] *Ibid.,* p. 251.

trum, who cultivated social themes as the latest style. As a style however, social poetry was subject to the whims of popularity. Among the statements in *Poesía social* were comments by Crémer, Hierro, and Valente that by the mid-1960s social poetry's popularity was declining. The 1965 anthology itself, a codification of a genre with two decades of selected poems, was a «monument» to the no longer ascendant poetic tendency described by Francisco Ribes in 1952.[69]

IV. *Fellow Travelers*

On the twentieth anniversary of Antonio Machado's death, 22 February 1959, Spanish intellectuals from the interior joined others from abroad in Collioure, France, to remember the elder poet with a show of solidarity as a public, and publicized, affront to the Franco Regime. The event was sponsored by the PCE; among militants and sympathizers attending were Jorge Semprún, Tuñón de Lara, Max Aub, León Felipe, and according to rumors, Santiago Carrillo.[70] Enthusiastically promoted by Spaniards in exile, the tribute attracted fewer from the Peninsula than expected. Nevertheless, crossing the border were Menéndez Pidal; physicians Marañón, Lafora, and Hernando; university professors Laín Entralgo, Garrigues, Andrés, Gallego Díaz, Montero Díaz, Lapesa, and Marías; novelists Cela, Goytisolo, Fernández Santos, Sánchez Ferlosio, and Aldecoa; film directors Bardem and Berlanga; painters Millares, Guinovart, and Zamorano; dramatists Sastre and Buero Vallejo; and poets Aleixandre, Alonso, Bleiberg, Celaya, Otero, and De Nora. This homage and other activities, such as manifestos on behalf of free expression, amnesty for the exiled, and an end to repression, were signs of growing responsibility assumed by intellectuals of the opposition in cultural and political affairs.

Of the younger intellectuals at Collioure, perhaps the most like-minded group centered around Carlos Barral and included, among others, José María Castellet, José Agustín Goytisolo, Jaime Gil de Biedma, and Angel González. Barral called this group perhaps the first during the postwar period not bound by the loyalties of Madrid's literary world that facilitated appearance in anthologies and publications.[71] However, they were regarded as outsiders when they wished to be taken into account seriously; therefore to gain attention they undertook a two-part publishing endeavor consisting of a poetry collection and an anthology. The collection's political intent was to offer inexpensive, widely distributed editions of poetry,

---

[69] JULIA UCEDA, «La traición de los poetas sociales», *Insula*, No. 242 (January 1967), pp. 1, 12.
[70] Names are reported by: DARÍO PUCCINI, *Romancero de la resistencia española (1936-1965)* (México: Biblioteca Era, 1967), p. 51, n. 74; CARLOS BARRAL, *Los años sin excusa* (Barcelona: Barral, 1978), pp. 181-82.

breaking the confinement of customary publication channels. The «Colección Colliure», taking the Spanish spelling of Machado's burial place, was directed by Castellet, edited by Jaime Salinas, and published by Barral. Scheduled during the initial phase were reprinted works by Celaya, De Nora, and Otero and new ones by Goytisolo, Gil de Biedma, Barral, López Pacheco, Caballero Bonald, Valente, González, Crespo, and Fuertes. All but volumes by Otero and De Nora had appeared when the collection was discontinued in 1965.[72]

Springing from the same motives as the «Colección Colliure», *Veinte años de poesía española (1939-1959)* was the group's reinterpretation of Spanish poetry in light of the European tradition.[73] These poets believed the evolution toward realism was not acknowledged sufficiently in Madrid's poetry circles, led by members of the Generations of 1927 and 1936.[74] The existence of realism in recent European poetry, of course, meant that Spanish realism coincided with an international tendency. Thus the poetry of Alberti, Celaya, and Otero and their followers such as José Agustín Goytisolo and Angel González, was not marginal, as those in Madrid thought, but rather in the European literary forefront.

Indebted to Socialist Realism, the thesis Castellet developed in the anthology's introduction postulated that the rise of realism was more than the diffusion of a literary style, it was part of a long process whereby bourgeois poets criticized their own class, which ignored them, before a collective addressee, the masses, with whom the poets shared an interest in social renewal. Previously, poets felt only disdain toward the bourgeoisie. But when the independence and superiority they esteemed proved illusory, they turned from the evasion of symbolism to the *engagement* of realism. For mature poets the decision presented a contradiction, never entirely resolved, between a dependence upon symbolist techniques to express an attitude of realism. In Spain this process of social and artistic evolution occurred against the backdrop of twentieth-century social malaise, reaching a crisis in the Civil War. Castellet named 1930 as when the symbolist tradition lost momentum; poets thereafter attempted to repro-

---

[71] *Ibid.*, p. 189.
[72] FANNY RUBIO, *Las revistas poéticas españolas (1939-1975)*, p. 210, n. 46.
[73] JOSÉ MARÍA CASTELLET, *Veinte años de poesía española (1939-1959)* (Barcelona: Seix Barral, 1960).
[74] JOSÉ MARÍA CASTELLET, *Un cuarto de siglo de poesía española (1939-1964)* (Barcelona: Seix Barral, 1965), pp. 12-13. Those of the Generation of 1927 probably were Aleixandre, Diego, and Alonso, but precisely who were the Generation of 1936 is not entirely clear. LEOPOLDO DE LUIS, *La poesía aprendida* (Madrid: Bello, 1975), p. 177, observes: «... este tema de la generación del 36 es controvertible, y habría que matizarlo mucho, pues, según creo, la del 36 es una generación escindida que tras la guerra civil, no pudo ya reagruparse homogéneamente. Muerte, cárcel y exilio lo impidieron. No cuenta sino con individualidades y con grupos de signo distintos.»

duce a reality of massive social change through direct, colloquial language. Because seemingly irreversible changes toward a single-class society accompanied poetic realism, Castellet believed that the very concept of poetry would change forever, symbolism would disappear along with the bourgeoisie.

The body of the anthology established a chronological sequence of poems in support of the thesis of increasing realism. Though the variation of topic and style in poems is wider than Castellet's dogmatic stand would suggest, the anthology redefined the canon of poets giving prominence to Socialist Realists and those they influenced. Taking into account both editions of the anthology, poets most frequently cited from the Generation of 1927 were Alberti, Guillén, Aleixandre, and Cernuda; from that of 1936, Otero, Celaya, and Hierro; and from the younger generation, Goytisolo, Valente, and Gil de Biedma. Overall, the three most cited poets were Otero, Alberti, and Celaya in that order. Those most active between 1959 and 1964, judging from the number of poems added to the second edition, were Alberti, Valente, Guillén, Otero, Celaya, Fuertes, and Gil de Biedma.

In representative reviews, critics regardless of ideological preference agreed that Castellet's argument lacked objectivity. Carlos Vélez, who said he was in the same «ideological camp» as Castellet, nevertheless criticized the latter's method of selecting poems according to a prior thesis when poems should be assembled first then interpreted.[75] Furthermore, he thought Castellet erred by imputing early importance to poems by Hernández, Felipe, and Alberti when, due to various kinds of interference, they became known only later. Similarly, he thought it was inaccurate to stress Machado's prophetic speech about realism because it was not generally available until the 1957 edition of *Los complementarios* appeared. Finally, he criticized the prominence of Catalan poets to the exclusion of others whose poetry was more realistic.[76] Manuel Mantero judged the anthology devisive for aggravating ideological differences among poets when, he believed, questions of politics, history, and economics should be studied in their own realms, not in poetry.[77] After noting the parallel of

---

[75] CARLOS VÉLEZ, Review of *Veinte años de poesía española*, *Acento Cultural*, Nos. 9-10 (July-October 1950), pp. 47-49.

[76] He named the following as examples, *Ibid.*: «Andúgar, Alcántara, Bengoechea, Joaquín Fernández, Sahagún, Cabañero, P. Tomé, Martín Descalzo, Pérez Valiente, Hidalgo, Alcaide, etc.»

[77] MANUEL MANTERO, Review of *Veinte años de poesía española*, *Agora*, Nos. 46-48 (August-October 1960), pp. 44-47. Mantero conveys his own position in the following lines from «Es una confesión», *Poesía (1958-1971)* (Barcelona: Plaza y Janés, 1972), pp. 43-44:

Hierro, Leopoldo, Otero,
Celaya, Crémer, hinco

Castellet's thesis with Celaya's view of poetry as a weapon and Otero's as a path to peace and freedom, he asserted that Juan Ramón Jiménez was highly esteemed among many young poets, contrary to Castellet's denial. Recognizing both the benefits and the defects Castellet's commitment had for the anthology, J. L. García Molina commended the editor for raising the issue of poetry's relation to social conditions, but rejected as too simplistic the notion that contemporary poetry progressed from the pole of symbolism to that of realism, an abstract formulation of a problem based on historical facts.[78] Finally, in a carefully argued refutation of Castellet's thesis, E. Inman Fox held that there existed no real break with the symbolist tradition; except for certain works like *Cantos iberos* and *Pido la paz y la palabra,* which he called artistically reactionary in their didacticism, poetry still blurred the real world with that of the imagination to achieve a spiritual effect.[79]

José Agustín Goytisolo, Jaime Gil de Biedma, and Angel González, among the younger poets in Castellet's anthology, were perhaps those who most self-consciously cultivated a SocReal perspective. They examined reality to transform it, reviving topics of solidarity, pleas, and prophesies, but avoided ingenuous didacticism applying critical irony to the norms by which the bourgeoisie and the Regime, to mutual advantage, perpetuated injustice. The emphasis on SocRealism in their poetry of the late 1950s and early 1960s drew attention away from other characteristics, perhaps more significant, acquired during their formation «en el tardío simbolismo, con trastiendas psicologistas y utillaje de tradición barroca».[80]

Once writing in the SocReal tradition, however, Goytisolo, Gil de Biedma, and González developed familiar topics from an appropriate moral position. This, rather than a novel message, is the primary feature of Goytisolo's «Los celestiales», a chronicle of postwar poetry from the moment when poets (in the favor of the Regime) announced it was time to forget civil strife and compose melodious verses until the present moment, when other poets —singing, satirizing, loving mankind— lose them-

> mi lanza en vuestra sombra
> ....
> con vosotros estamos
> en deuda. Pero digo
> que mi generación
> tiene un signo distinto.

---

[78] J. L. GARCÍA MOLINA, Review of *Veinte años de poesía española,* La Caña Gris, No. 3 (Winter 1960-61), pp. 6-9.

[79] E. INMAN FOX, «Poesía 'social' y la tradición simbolista», *Actas del Tercer Congreso Internacional de Hispanistas* (México: El Colegio de México, 1970), pp. 355-63.

[80] CARLOS BARRAL, *Los años sin excusa,* p. 190.

selves amid crowded streets as they «lanzan gritos, pidiendo paz, pidiendo patria, / pidiendo aire verdadero».[81] In this reworking of a familiar topic, with sonorous hendecasyllables and alexandrines, the speaker reveals his bias against evasive poets through epithets such as «*celestiales*» and «*gente de orden*» and ironic description of their refined but vacuous behavior. His sympathy for the «*poetas locos*», on the other hand, indicates whom he truly admires.

The most expressive poet of the group on the topic of taking a stand was Gil de Biedma, whose collection *Compañeros de viaje* captured the revised SocReal esthetic.[82] This is explicitly realized in «En el nombre de hoy» (LPV, 75-76), where the speaker identifies himself as a writer of social poetry. Imitating documentary diction, he gives the date and time, 3:00 p.m., 26 April 1959, and names his fellow travelers: Barral, González, Goytisolo, Celaya, Otero, and others. Gil de Biedma also commented on significant political events and figures. In a tribute to the courage of striking miners, «Asturias, 1962» (LPV, 110), the speaker compares different sorts of silence, some like that following the Civil War are destructive for they muffle communication, others like that during the strike are charged with anticipation of change. A similar note of looking to a brighter future ends the poem «Un día de difuntos», where the speaker recounts his visit with a group of intellectuals to socialist leader Pablo Iglesias' grave, celebrating solidarity:

... pienso que en todos la imagen de aquel día,
   la visión de aquel sol
   y de aquella cabeza de español yacente
   vivirán como un símbolo, como una invocación
   apasionada hacia el futuro, en los momentos malos. (LPV, 113)

Gil de Biedma adopts a feminine persona, parenthetically identified as the exiled Republican María Zambrano, in «Piazza del Popolo» (LPV, 68-70). Hearing a solidarity song in Rome, the speaker vividly recalls an earlier moment elsewhere when now deceased companions rose in unison to sing the same song.

Clearly following Otero in taking a position, Angel González pledged commitment in a carefully rhymed sonnet, «Donde pongo».[83] Like Otero's poem «En la inmensa mayoría» this one uses religious metaphors to indicate unquestioned commitment. With customary code words —*esperanza*,

---

[81] José Agustín Goytisolo, *Salmos al viento* (Barcelona: Lumen, 1980), pp. 27-29. References to this edition appear in the text with the abbreviation PV.

[82] Reprinted in: Jaime Gil de Biedma, *Las personas del verbo* (Barcelona: Seix Barral, 1978). References to this edition appear textually with the initials LPV.

[83] Angel González, *Palabra sobre palabra* (Barcelona: Seix Barral, 1968), p. 132. Additional references to this edition are in the text preceded by PSP.

primavera, fe—, with antonyms —*siempre* and *nunca* or *jamás*—, González affirmed his belief in Marxism:

> Al siempre va. Mantengo mi postura.
> Si sale nunca, la esperanza es muerte.
>
> Si sale amor, la primavera avanza.
> Pero nunca o amor, mi fe segura:
> jamás o llanto, pero mi fe fuerte.

A difficult topic to disguise sufficiently from censors, and therefore one seldom very explicit in poetry of protest, is that of the tyrant. Nevertheless, these poets explored the theme, making heavy use of ironic statment as a primary critical technique. The speaker of González's «Elegido por aclamación» tells of an individual who first declared himself «Jefe», then challenged any who objected to so indicate, but «[i]nmóvil mayoría de cadáveres / le dio el mando total del cementerio».[84] The speaker also knowingly suggests that the Civil War was the result of a misunderstanding, the people said «*urnas*», the leader heard «*armas*». Finally, he quotes the leader's empty statement about the perfection of democracy and his unfulfilled assertion that the popular will shall prevail. The cumulative effect of such language of innuendo points to the sham and violence of the Regime. Gil de Biedma gave the same topic an allegorical rendering in «El arquitrabe».[85] The architrave, base of the entablature capping pilasters, is a suggestive analogy for a tyrant, whose Regime, upheld by the pillars of society, must be reinforced by the «scaffolding» of traditionalist ideas. Behind this comparison, the speaker mocks those who presume themselves intimates of the leader, oppressively serious individuals who censure any evidence of happiness: «Uno sale a la calle / y besa a una muchacha o compra un libro, / se pasea, feliz. Y le fulminan: / *¿Pero cómo se atreve?* / ¡El arquitrabe...!» (LPV, 49).

Commonly, early poems of protest were in praise of the proletariat and condemned class enemies only in general terms. Poems by this group, however, refer infrequently to the proletariat, and single out recognizable bourgeois types for satiric treatment. By ridiculing contradictions of behavior and prudent conformity to financially beneficial customs, these poems supported the revolution, undermining the superstructure. Angel González, indicating Marxist bias in «Todos ustedes parecen felices...» (PSP, 27-28), contrasted the appearance of his bourgeois addressees with the true nature of their behavior. The speaker affirms that their smiling words of love conceal feelings of disgust for the masses, their love for a few conceals hatred of the many. González isolated the «perfect» bureau-

---

[84] JOSÉ MARÍA CASTELLET, *Un cuarto de siglo de poesía española*, p. 479.
[85] For an explication of this poem, see: SHIRLEY MANGINI GONZÁLEZ, *Jaime Gil de Biedma* (Madrid: Júcar, 1977), pp. 37-40.

crat in «Nota necrológica» (PSP, 171-74). A threadbare petty bourgeois, whose moral conscience was guided by faith in paternalistic government —«*o se piensa o se cumple*»—, he never reflected upon his complicity with the Regime, aspiring only to long life and pensioned retirement, future denied him by fatal asthma.

Goytisolo satirized the censor in «Vida del justo» (PV, 49-51), by contrasting the two sides of his nature. On the one hand, the censor carried pious books in public, upheld established values in the «Centro de Información», and confessed regularly, but on the other, he visited prostitutes and leered at his secretary. Another type of powerful figure in the Regime was the financial magnate, topic of «Apología del libre» (PV, 31-32). Adding one hyperbole to another, the speaker in effect condemns his addressee for his exploitation of others, for ignoring laments and curses of victims, for exulting in his triumph over them. Hypocrisy and opportunism are mixed in the protagonist of «El señalado» — «está y no está con todos» (PV, 40). Changeable in his outlook, among some he praises democracy and freedom, among others he calls for Unity, Family, and Order. Concludes the speaker: «El señalado sabe que el futuro es su imperio.»

According to Goytisolo, bourgeois procedures for dealing with filial disobedience, sexual attraction, and death guarantee social stability; honesty, authentic feeling, genuine love for others, however, lose to hypocritical conformity. Temporarily forgetful of his careful upbringing, the «prodigal son» strayed to a netherworld of cabarets and bohemian companions, causing malicious gossip. But the speaker reassures that reality will return him to his proper position: «será un varón conservador / gloria y ejemplo del redil / un recto, un probo ciudadano / un elefante de piedad» (PV, 45). «Idilio y marcha nupcial» relates the courtship and marriage between a couple with «noble thoughts», who love each other with «canonical seriousness», and who, at the sound of the Grand March, know they will love each other forever. The irony of the poem is indicated by the pretentious preparations for the ceremony and by the speaker's pronouncement that «[a]hora queda muy lejos todo aquello / del arrebato pasional oh fruto / nefasto de poetas licenciosos...» (PV, 35). «Las visitas» (PV, 33-34) presents a proper funeral. The elaborate ritual is in keeping with its cost, the attending physician gives his voice a «serious» tone, relatives and servants weep softly, and the visitors, knowing they are «heralds of the ephemeral», maintain a «studied» silence.

Finally, neither Gil de Biedma nor González believed that Spain should remain under the spell of the past. In «Apología y petición» (LPV, 80-81), the speaker analyzes the contention that Spain is cursed with immemorial poverty and bad government and concludes that, while this belief encourages fatalist acceptance, an economic explanation of the problem would reveal that corrupt entrepreneurs and bribed officials were those who sequestered Spain. González used allegory in «Entreacto» (PSP, 122-24) to equate the Franco dictatorship (signaled indirectly) with a play based on treason, whose last act was about to begin. The speaker notes indications of the inevitable end in torturous dialogues about a time gone by, delivered by garishly made-up actors, whose faces are etched by desperation, cowardice, and terror.

This group, then, added momentum to the waning SocReal tendency in Spanish poetry by integrating it within the similar European tendency; looking beyond national borders, they enhanced their own prestige and that of the poetry of protest.

By 1965 when *Poesía social* and *Un cuarto de siglo de poesía española* appeared, the twenty-year vogue for poetry of protest lessened. That is not to say that all poets turned from social themes; González published *Tratado de urbanismo* in 1967 and Goytisolo, *Algo sucede* in 1968. Younger poets added titles to the tendency also: Manuel Vázquez Montalbán, *Movimientos sin éxito* (1969) and *Una educación sentimental* (1970); J. P. González Martín, *Nuevos heraldos negros o manual del hambriento* (1969); Carlos Alvarez, *Estos que ahora son poemas...* (1969) and *Como la espuma lucha con la roca* (1976). Moreover, some critics still defended poetry directed to the masses. Carlos Vélez, for example, affirmed that social poetry, like all poetry, came about as a result of a certain dissatisfaction in the poet, who turned to creation in the name of commitment to self, a group, or mankind.[86] Social poetry differed from other genres only in that its origin and destination was man, its purpose freedom, and its privileged forms revolutionary or religious. Furthermore, believing that all people were entitled to read poetry, yet realizing that in Spain only the «clan of 600» actually did, Vélez thought that poetry whose characteristics were simplicity, clarity, brevity, and musicality and therefore appropriate for the mass media, ought to be advertised like any product. In short, he proposed heightening the realism of poetry by seeking the lowest common denominator of a style.

Socialist Realism, however, was no longer the ruling poetic concept. The new opposition, displacing that of pure and committed poetry, was between poetry of «communication» and that of «knowledge» or «discovery». Barral's early critique of poetry as communication pointed out theoretical inaccuracies and undesirable practical consequences of this poetic concept.[87] Toward the end of the 1950s, critic after critic noted

---

[86] CARLOS VÉLEZ, «Notas sobre la poesía social», *Acento Cultural*, No. 1 (November 1958), pp. 13-14; «Resumen y esperanza», *Acento Cultural*, Nos. 9-10 (July-October 1960), pp. 28-29; «Forma y expresión para una poesía popular», *Acento Cultural*, Nos. 9-10 (July-October 1960), pp. 29-37.

[87] CARLOS BARRAL, «Poesía no es comunicación», *Laye*, No. 23 (April-June 1953), pp. 23-26.

failings in the theory, building the case against poetry as an instrument. José Angel Valente oriented poetry according to the rising concept because he believed the presence of ideology in poetry the greatest barrier to true realism; ideology's ready supply of topics and messages prevented the rediscovery of reality, the task of the poet.[88] César Armando Gómez criticized Socialist Realism as a threat to artistic freedom, its dogmatism the contrary of creation.[89] Enrique Badosa argued that while widespread concern for social issues would naturally be reflected in literature, the use of literature for propaganda purposes was an artistic debasement.[90] Luis López Anglada noted that what interested poetry readers was to identify with the spiritually superior artist through the interpretive testimony of his work: if the religious poet brought about conversions, or the political poet, revolutions, these were consequences independent of poetry.[91]

The shift of interest from sociopolitical efficacy as measure of poetic excellence to profundity of expression was generally recognized by the mid-1960s. Increasingly, poets sought to express the mystical, personal symbols and heterodox values of subjective reality rather than concern for the welfare of neglected social groups according to orthodox (Marxist, Christian) symbols and values; they were striving for carefully wrought poems rather than prosified, conversational language.

---

[88] JOSÉ ANGEL VALENTE, *Las palabras del tribu* (Madrid: Siglo XXI, 1971), pp. 30-31.
[89] CÉSAR ARMANDO GÓMEZ, «Del arte como libertad», *Acento Cultural*, No. 3 (January 1959), pp. 5-7.
[90] ENRIQUE BADOSA, *La libertad del escritor* (Barcelona: Plaza y Janés, 1968), pp. 27-28, 47.
[91] LUIS LÓPEZ ANGLADA, «La poesía como testimonio y como expresión», *Acento Cultural*, No. 6 (January-February 1960), pp. 25-27.

CONCLUSION

This study was undertaken to discover and document the characteristics of nonconformist poetry through a reconstruction of the poetry of protest as a systemic tendency developing where literary and extra-literary —political, ambient— concerns affected each other. Previous studies, using other methodologies, acknowledged the relationship of this literary tendency to its cultural milieu without exploring what that relationship implied. Here, therefore, close attention was paid to implications for textual interpretation, with supporting data offered whenever possible.

The developing tendency's context came to light, through careful reading of some fifty postwar literary periodicals. These contained information about leading figures, their political and poetic credos, polemics in which they engaged, and critical judgments of their works at the time of publication, as well as background information on the effects of censorship, the postwar interest in existentialism and Marxism, and the honoring of exiled and deceased writers of the political opposition. In a comparison of this historical data with conclusions of critics, writing at a distance of one to three decades, a frequently missed dimension was disclosed: the range of meanings adduced from the same work by readers following different ideologies and methodologies.

The poetry of protest shared several characteristics common to other literary tendencies in form, though not, obviously, in exact content. Looking to the literary tradition, the poetry of protest adapted certain meters, verse forms, and themes, while deliberately excluding others; showing preference for free verse, epic narrative, and social themes. Similarly, it rendered homage to certain poets, ignoring others; esteeming above all, Antonio Machado. The poetry of protest, as shown, most often appeared in customary channels: literary periodicals, anthologies, small-press books. Furthermore, it was read according to specific conventions, those deriving from Socialist Realism, which limited possible meanings to an accepted, though not always observed, range. While sharing normal characteristics with other tendencies, the poetry of protest differed in one most important respect: it ran the risk of surveillance by governmental authorities and members of the clergy. The risk seldom became reality, however. Censorship of it, in fact, was selectively enforced and, generally, with decreasing rigor. Despite cases of political censorship, those of Blas de Otero and Gabriel Celaya, for example, it is worth remembering that a great quantity of this poetry was printed. Rather, documentation suggests that we distinguish between censorship of what was printed in Spain and the censoring opinion of traditional-minded critics who did not favor published poetry they considered Marxist.

Balancing close readings of the poetry of protest against data collected from literary publications, I uncovered a pattern of development which may be divided into two phases; the first lasting until 1950, the second, until the mid-1960s.

During the first phase, the poetry of protest derived from the prewar concept that regarded literature as related to sociopolitical reality. In other words, the sociopolitical context of the poem, the «here and now», entered into interpretation. The formation of the tendency, nevertheless, was gradual rather than sudden. At first discussed under various names —neoromanticism, *rehumanización, tremendismo*—, the poetry of protest established conventions, the most salient of which was the belief that poetry exercised power over objective reality. Poets whom most regarded as mentors were, foremost, Antonio Machado, then Miguel Hernández, Pablo Neruda, Rafael Alberti, and César Vallejo. Dámaso Alonso's *Hijos de la ira,* often cited as relevant to this poetry, was related obliquely, more on comments taken out of context than upon the work's actual characteristics. In fact, critics consistently agreed upon the importance of 1944 as the date when the tendency was initiated only after 1960. Poets important to this phase were Victoriano Crémer and Eugenio de Nora. The former's early poetry satirized neoclassicism and *garcilasismo,* his later testimonial poetry was social criticism. Crémer's principal role in the tendency's development, however, was his editorial supervision of *Espadaña.* De Nora, foremost poet writing quasi-political poetry of resistance, extended his influence through poems and articles, primarily in *Espadaña.* More than any other in the 1940s, he put into practice the theory of Socialist Realism, converting a Marxist outlook, hostile to the Franco Regime, into a poetic norm. Other lesser known poets opposing the Regime used allegory, elegy, and document to veil criticism under the clothing of metaphors comprehended by adept readers.

In the second phase of this tendency, the issue of commitment came to the fore. The early united opposition to the Dictatorship polarized into antagonistic positions by 1950: one Marxist, committed to social revolution; the other traditional liberal, committed to gradual transition to political freedom. Marxists, who took the initiative, accused peers of moral evasion, thus polarizing the literary world. The first public airing of the topic occurred in issues of *Espadaña,* where De Nora challenged Crémer and others to adopt a Marxist outlook. The controversy then encompassed the *Antología consultada,* which, if rejected by authoritarian supporters of the Regime, was debated at length by traditional liberals, who admired the poetry, but objected to the Socialist Realist credo which lay behind it. Shortly thereafter, Celaya and others defended Socialist Realist poetics in the third annual poetry congress, where few poets were sympathetic to what I call the Marxist challenge. Undaunted, Celaya and Otero, occasionally joined by others, wrote poetry on behalf of the proletarian movement, which proselytized doctrines of the PCE. Notably, they traced the typical metamorphosis of an alienated bourgeois who becomes a committed Communist; notoriously they wrote what is more properly «agitation propaganda». This poetry awakened reaction from traditional liberals. Some poets —Angela Figuera Aymerich, José Hierro, Gloria Fuertes, Leopoldo de Luis, Garciasol, and Rafael Morales— adapted the themes of Socialist Realism to their own more conservative outlooks. Finally, the poetry of protest, like any other tendency, neither disappeared quickly nor maintained its influence indefinitely; rather, it fell from favor under criticism by new arbiters of style, the poets of the younger generation.

LIST OF WORKS CITED

POETS:

ALBERTI, RAFAEL: *Poemas del destierro y de la espera*. Madrid: Espasa-Calpe, 1976.
— *Poesía (1924-1967)*. Madrid: Aguilar, 1972.
— *El poeta en la calle*. Paris: Librairie du Globe, 1966.
ALONSO, DÁMASO: *Hijos de la ira. Diario íntimo*. Elías L. Rivers, ed. Barcelona: Labor, 1970.
ALVAREZ, CARLOS: *Estos que ahora son poemas... Epílogo de Amelia Romero y José Batlló*. Barcelona: El Bardo, 1969.
ANA, MARCOS: *Las soledades del muro*. Madrid: Akal, 1977.
AZCOAGA, ENRIQUE: *El canto cotidiano*. Madrid: Editorial Hispánica, 1943.
BLEIBERG, GERMÁN: *Selección de poemas 1936-1973*. London: Grant and Cutler, 1975.
CELAYA, GABRIEL: *Las cartas boca arriba*. Madrid: Turner, 1974.
— *Cantos iberos*. Madrid: Turner, 1976.
— *El hilo rojo*. Madrid: Visor, 1977.
— *Itinerario poético*. Madrid: Cátedra, 1977.
— *Lo demás es silencio*. Madrid: Turner, 1976.
— *Parte de guerra*. Barcelona: Laia, 1977.
— *Poesías completas*. Madrid: Aguilar, 1967.
CRÉMER, VICTORIANO: *Caminos de mi sangre*. Madrid: Adonais, 1947.
— *Las horas perdidas*. Valladolid: Halcón, 1949.
— *Nuevos cantos de vida y esperanza*. Barcelona: Instituto de Estudios Hispánicos, 1952.
— *Poesía total (1944-1966)*. Barcelona: Plaza y Janés, 1970.
— *Tacto sonoro*. León: Espadaña, 1944.
FIGUERA AYMERICH, ANGELA: *Antología total*. Madrid: CVS Ediciones, 1975.
— *Belleza cruel*. Barcelona: Lumen, 1978.
FUERTES, GLORIA: *Obras incompletas*. Madrid: Cátedra, 1977.
GALLEGO, JOSÉ LUIS: *Prometeo XX*. Barcelona: El Bardo, 1970.
GARCÍA NIETO, JOSÉ: *La red*. Madrid: Agora, 1955.
GIL, ILDEFONSO-MANUEL: *Poemas de dolor antiguo*. Madrid: Editorial Hispánica, 1945.
— *Homenaje a Goya (poemas)*. Zaragoza: Ediciones del Pórtico, 1946.
GIL DE BIEDMA, JAIME: *Las personas del verbo*. Barcelona: Seix Barral, 1978.
GONZÁLEZ, ANGEL: *Palabra sobre palabra*. Barcelona: Seix Barral, 1968.
GOYTISOLO, JOSÉ AGUSTÍN: *Salmos al viento*. Barcelona: Lumen, 1980.
HIDALGO, JOSÉ LUIS: *Obra poética completa*. María de Gracia Ifach, ed. Santander: Institución Cultural de Cantabria, 1976.
HIERRO, JOSÉ: *Cuanto sé de mí*. Barcelona: Seix Barral, 1974.
LUIS, LEOPOLDO DE: *Poesía (1946-1968)*. Barcelona: Plaza y Janés, 1968.
— *Teatro real. Juego limpio*. Madrid: Espasa-Calpe, 1975.

MILLARES SALL, AGUSTÍN: *El grito en el cielo*. Las Palmas de Gran Canaria: Cuadernos de Poesía y Crítica, 1946.
MILLARES SALL, JOSÉ MARÍA: *El canto a la tierra*. Las Palmas de Gran Canaria: Cuadernos de Poesía y Crítica, 1946.
MORALES, RAFAEL: *Poesías completas (1940-1967)*. Madrid: Giner, 1967.
NORA, EUGENIO DE: *Amor prometido*. Valladolid: Halcón, 1946.
— *Cantos al destino (1941-1945)*. Madrid: Editorial Hispánica, 1945.
— *Contemplación del tiempo*. Madrid: Adonais, 1948.
— *España, pasión de vida (1945-1950)*. Barcelona: Instituto de Estudios Hispánicos, 1954.
— *Poesía (1939-1964)*. León: Diputación Provincial, 1975.
[NORA, EUGENIO DE]: *Pueblo cautivo*. Fanny Rubio, ed. 1946; rpt. Pamplona: Peralta, 1978.
— *Siempre*. Madrid: Insula, 1953.
OTERO, BLAS DE: *Ancia*. Madrid: Visor, 1975.
— *Angel fieramente humano. Redoble de conciencia*. Buenos Aires: Losada, 1977.
— *Con la inmensa mayoría (Pido la paz y la palabra. En castellano)*. Buenos Aires: Losada, 1972.
— *Esto no es un libro*. Río Piedras: Editorial Universitaria-Puerto Rico, 1963.
— *País*. José Luis Cano, ed. Barcelona: Plaza y Janés, 1971.
— *Que trata de España*. Madrid: Visor, 1977.
ZARDOYA, CONCHA: *Corral de vivos y muertos*. Buenos Aires: Losada, 1965.

ANTHOLOGIES:

Antología cercada. Las Palmas de Gran Canaria: El Arca, 1947.
Antología del II Congreso de Poesía. Salamanca: Diputación Provincial, 1953.
Antología parcial de la poesía española (1936-1946). León: Espadaña, 1946-1949.
CANO, JOSÉ LUIS: *El tema de España en la poesía contemporánea*. Madrid: Revista de Occidente, 1964.
CASTELLET, JOSÉ MARÍA: *Veinte años de poesía española 1939-1959*. Barcelona: Seix Barral, 1960.
— *Un cuarto de siglo de poesía española (1939-1964)*. Barcelona: Seix Barral, 1965.
GONZÁLEZ MARTÍN, J. P.: *Poesía hispánica 1939-1969 (Estudio y antología)*. Barcelona: El Bardo, 1970.
LUIS, LEOPOLDO DE: *Poesía española contemporánea. Antología (1939-1964). Poesía social*. Madrid: Alfaguara, 1965.
MANTERO, MANUEL: *Poesía española contemporánea: Estudio y antología (1939-1965)*. Barcelona: Plaza y Janés, 1966.
MILLÁN, RAFAEL: *Veinte poetas españoles*. Madrid: Agora, 1955.
MORENO, ALFONSO: *Poesía española actual*. Madrid: Editora Nacional, 1946.
PUCCINI, DARÍO: *Romancero de la resistencia española*. México: Biblioteca Era, 1967.
RIBES, FRANCISCO, ed.: *Antología consultada de la joven poesía española*. Santander: Hermanos Bedia, 1952.

CRITICISM: BOOKS

ALARCOS LLORACH, EMILIO: *La poesía de Blas de Otero*. Salamanca: Anaya, 1966.
ALONSO, DÁMASO: *Poetas españoles contemporáneos*. Madrid: Gredos, 1952.
BADOSA, ENRIQUE: *La libertad del escritor*. Barcelona: Plaza y Janés, 1968.
BLANCO AGUINAGA, CARLOS; JULIO RODRÍGUEZ PUÉRTOLAS, IRIS M. ZAVALA: *Historia social de la literatura española. (En lengua castellana.)* Vol. 3. Madrid: Castalia, 1979.

LIST OF WORKS CITED

BOUSOÑO, CARLOS: *Teoría de la expresión poética*. Madrid: Gredos, 1952.
CANO, JOSÉ LUIS: *La poesía de la generación del 27*. Madrid: Guadarrama, 1973.
CANO BALLESTA, JUAN: *La poesía de Miguel Hernández*. Madrid: Gredos, 1962.
— *La poesía española entre pureza y revolución (1930-1936)*. Madrid: Gredos, 1972.
CELAYA, GABRIEL: *Inquisición de la poesía*. Madrid: Turner, 1972.
— *Poesía y verdad (Papeles para un proceso)*. Pontevedra: Ediciones Litoral, 1959.
— *Poesía y verdad*. Barcelona: Planeta, 1979.
CIPLIJAUSKAITÉ, BIRUTÉ. *El poeta y la poesía: del romanticismo a la poesía social*. Madrid: Insula, 1966.
COHEN, JOHN MICHAEL: *Poetry of this Age*. London: Hutchinson's and Co., 1960.
CONCHA, VÍCTOR G. DE LA: *La poesía española de posguerra. Teoría e historia de sus movimientos*. Madrid: Prensa Española, 1973.
DAYDÍ-TOLSON, SANTIAGO, ed.: *Vicente Aleixandre. A Critical Appraisal*. Ypsilanti, Michigan: Bilingual Press, 1981.
«Demain L'Espagne». [Issue dedicated to Spain.] *Esprit*, No. 242 (September 1956).
EAGLETON, TERRY: *Marxism and Literary Criticism*. London: Methuen, 1976.
Espadaña. Revista de poesía y crítica. [Includes introductory study.] Rpt., León: Espadaña, 1978.
FERRÁN, JAIME; DANIEL P. TESTA, eds.: *Spanish Writers of 1936. Crisis and Committment in the Poetry of the Thirties and Forties*. London: Tamesis, 1973.
GALÁN, JOAQUÍN: *Blas de Otero, palabras para un pueblo*. Barcelona: Ambito Literario, 1978.
GERULAITIS, RENATE, ed.: *Oakland Symposium on Socialist Realism in Literature*. Rochester, Michigan: Oakland University, 1975.
GONZÁLEZ, SHIRLEY MANGINI: *Jaime Gil de Biedma*. Madrid: Júcar, 1977.
GRANDE, FÉLIX: *Apuntes sobre poesía española de posguerra*. Madrid: Taurus, 1970.
HAUSER, ARNOLD: *Teorías del arte. Tendencia y métodos de la crítica moderna*. Madrid: Guadarrama, 1975.
HIRIART, ROSARIO: *Un poeta en el tiempo: Ildefonso-Manuel Gil*. Zaragoza: Diputación Provincial, 1981.
«Image of Spain». [Issued dedicated to Spain.] *The Texas Quarterly*, 4, No. 1 (1961).
JAMES, C. VAUGHAN: *Soviet Socialist Realism. Origins and Theory*. London: Macmillan Press Ltd., 1973.
JIMÉNEZ, JOSÉ OLIVIO: *Diez años de poesía española 1960-1970*. Madrid: Insula, 1972.
— *Cinco poetas del tiempo*. Madrid: Insula, 1964.
LAMANA, MANUEL: *Literatura de posguerra*. Buenos Aires: Nova, 1961.
LECHNER, JAN: *El compromiso en la poesía española del siglo XX. Parte segunda, de 1939 a 1974*. Leiden: Universitaire pers Leiden, 1975.
LEY, CHARLES DAVID: *Spanish Poetry Since 1939*. Washington, D.C.: Catholic University of America, 1962.
LUIS, LEOPOLDO DE: *Antonio Machado*. Madrid: SGEL, 1975.
MAINER, JOSÉ-CARLOS: *Literatura y pequeña burguesía*. Madrid: EDICUSA, 1972.
MOLINA, RICARDO: *Función social de la poesía*. Madrid: Guadarrama, 1971.
MORATIEL, SERGIO: *La poesía en acción de Victoriano Crémer*. León: Imprenta Diocesana, 1973.
RAFFUCCI DE LOCKWOOD, ALICIA M.: *Cuatro poetas de la «Generación del 36»*. Universidad de Puerto Rico: Colección UPREX, 1974.
RUBIO, FANNY: *Las revistas poéticas españolas (1939-1975)*. Madrid: Turner, 1976.
SALINAS, PEDRO: *La responsabilidad del escritor*. Barcelona: Seix Barral, 1961.

SASTRE, ALFONSO: *Drama y sociedad*. Madrid: Taurus, 1956.
— *La revolución y la crítica de la cultura*. Barcelona: Grijalbo, 1970.
SEIRRA, PIERRE-OLIVIER: *Gabriel Celaya*. Paris: Seghers, 1970.
SERRANO PLAJA, ARTURO: *Antonio Machado*. Buenos Aires: Schapire, 1944.
SESÉ, BERNARD: *Antonio Machado (1875-1939)*. Madrid: Gredos, 1980.
TERTZ, ABRAM [ANDREI SINYAVSKY]. *On Socialist Realism*. Czeslaw Milosz, ed. New York: Pantheon, 1960.
TUÑÓN DE LARA, MANUEL: *Antonio Machado, poeta del pueblo*. Barcelona: Laia, 1975.
VALENTE, JOSÉ ANGEL: *Las palabras del tribu*. Madrid: Siglo XXI, 1971.
VIVANCO, LUIS FELIPE: *Introducción a la poesía española contemporánea*. 2 vols. Madrid: Guadarrama, 1974.
ZORITA, ANGEL: *Dámaso Alonso*. Madrid: EPESA, 1976.

CRITICISM: ARTICLES

ALBORNOZ, AURORA DE: «Aproximaciones a la obra poética de José Hierro». *Cuadernos Hispanoamericanos*, No. 341 (November 1978), pp. 273-90.
ALEIXANDRE, VICENTE: «Algunos caracteres de la nueva poesía española». *Obras completas*, vol. 2. Madrid: Aguilar, 1977, pp. 489-515.
BADOSA, ENRIQUE: «La conciencia de la muerte en la poesía de Miguel Hernández». *Laye*, No. 19 (May-June 1952), pp. 7-12.
«Balance poético, suma y sigue». *Verbo*, No. 15 (March-April 1949).
BARRAL, CARLOS: «Poesía no es comunicación». *Laye*, No. 23 (April-June 1953), pp. 23-26.
BARROW, GEOFFREY R.: «Some Otero Satires of Hypocrisy». *Neophilologus*, 64, No. 2 (April 1980), pp. 227-43.
BLANCO AGUINAGA, CARLOS: «El mundo entre ceja y ceja: releyendo a Blas de Otero». *Papeles de Son Armadans*, No. 254-255 (May-June 1977), pp. 147-96.
BOUSOÑO, CARLOS: «Poesía contemporánea y poesía postcontemporánea». *Papeles de Son Armadans*, No. 34 (August 1964), pp. 121-84.
CABA, PEDRO: «La decadencia de la poesía lírica». *La Estafeta Literaria*, No. 7 (1944), p. 5.
CANO, JOSÉ LUIS: «Recuerdo y homenaje a Juan Guerrero». *Insula*, No. 113 (15 May 1955), pp. 4-5.
— «Historia de una colección de poesía». *Cuadernos Hispanoamericanos*, No. 8 (1949), pp. 345-52.
— «Historia y sentido de una colección de poesía: Adonais». *El libro español*. Revista del Instituto Nacional del Libro Español, 2, No. 17 (1959), pp. 274-76.
— «Romanticismo y antirromanticismo en nuestra poesía actual». *Correo Literario*, 1, No. 11 (1 November 1950), p. 9.
CASAMAYOR, ENRIQUE: «Tremendismo poético». *Cuadernos Hispanoamericanos*, No. 9 (May-June 1949), pp. 745-53.
CELAYA, GABRIEL: «Carta de Gabriel Celaya». *Caracola*, No. 29 (March 1955).
— «Doce años después». *Acento cultural*, January 1959, pp. 17-20.
— «Veinte años de poesía». *Egan*, No. 2 (April-June 1948), pp. 27-31.
COHEN, J. M.: «Since the Civil War. New Currents in Spanish Poetry». *Encounter*, 12, No. 2 (February 1959), pp. 44-53.
CONCHA, VÍCTOR G. DE LA: «*Espadaña* (1944-1951) (Biografía de una revista de poesía y crítica)». *Cuadernos Hispanoamericanos*, No. 236 (August 1969), pp. 304-63.
CRÉMER, VICTORIANO: «Esquema para un cuadro sinóptico sobre poesía y trabajo». *Poesía Española*, No. 8 (August 1952), pp. 1-7.

LIST OF WORKS CITED

— «Para una biografía de *Espadaña*». *Peña Labra,* No. 14 (Winter 1974-1975), pp. 2-6.
DEBICKI, ANDREW P.: «Satire and Dramatic Monologue in Several Poems of Dámaso Alonso». *Books Abroad,* 48, No. 2 (Spring 1974), pp. 276-85.
DÍAZ MÁRQUEZ, LUIS: «La temática de la poesía de Damaso Alonso». *Cuadernos Hispanoamericanos,* No. 209 (May 1967), pp. 231-65.
DUQUE, AQUILINO: «Poesía social». *Poesía Española,* No. 72 (July 1958), pp. 1, 20-24.
FERNÁNDEZ CARVAJAL, RODRIGO: «Notas a la poesía joven». *Cisneros,* No. 11 (1946), pp. 96-103.
FOX, E. INMAN: «Poesía 'social' y la tradición simbolista». *Actas del Tercer Congreso Internacional de Hispanistas.* México: El Colegio de México, 1970, pp. 355-63.
FRUTOS, EUGENIO: «Los poetas dicen». *Verbo,* May-June 1947.
— «La poesía actual y el romanticismo», *Correo Literario,* 1, No. 6 (15 August 1950), pp. 1, 4.
GALAN, F. W.: «Literary Change and Systemic Change: The Prague School of Literary History, 1928-48». *PMLA,* 94, No. 2 (March 1979), pp. 275-85.
GAOS, VICENTE: «De Luis Rosales a José García Nieto. Diez años de poesía: 1935-1945». *La Estafeta Literaria,* No. 25 (1945), p. 5.
GARCÉS, JESÚS JUAN: «Algunas notas urgentes sobre la poesía contemporánea». *La Estafeta Literaria,* No. 8 (1944), p. 5.
GARCÍA RICO, EDUARDO, ed.: «Literatura y política (en torno al realismo español)». *Cuadernos para el Diálogo,* Supplement No. 19 (1971).
GARCIASOL, RAMÓN DE: «Notas sobre la nueva poesía española (1939-1958)». *Acento Cultural,* No. 2 (December 1958), pp. 17-20, ii-iv.
GULLÓN, RICARDO: «La joven poesía española (en torno a una Antología)». *Insula,* No. 81 (15 September 1952), pp. 1, 5.
HIERRO, JOSÉ: «Poesía pura, poesía práctica». *Insula,* No. 132 (November 1958), pp. 1, 4.
Interview with Juan Guerrero. *La Estafeta Literaria,* No. 3 (15 April 1944), p. 9.
JAUSS, HANS ROBERT: «Literary History as a Challenge to Literary Theory». *New Directions in Literary History.* Ralph Cohen, ed. Baltimore: Johns Hopkins, 1974, pp. 11-41.
LAMA, ANTONIO G. DE: «Si Garcilaso volviera». *Cisneros,* No. 6 (1943), pp. 122-24.
— «Poesía y verdad. La poesía actual». *Espadaña,* No. 9 (1944).
— «Poesía y verdad. Antologías». *Espadaña,* No. 27 (1947).
LECHNER, JAN: «Preliminares para un estudio de las poéticas de posguerra». *Entre la cruz y la espada: en torno a la España de la posguerra. Homenaje a Eugenio G. de Nora.* Madrid: Gredos, 1984, pp. 205-09.
LEY, CHARLES DAVID: «Some Spanish Poets of Today». *Bulletin of Hispanic Studies,* 22, No. 86 (April 1945), pp. 69-76.
— «Influencia de Pablo Neruda y de otros poetas hispanoamericanos en la moderna poesía de España». *Actas del Tercer Congreso Internacional de Hispanistas.* Carlos H. Magis, ed. México: El Colegio de México, 1970, pp. 543-52.
LÓPEZ DE ABIADA, JOSÉ: «Observaciones en torno a la poesía de posguerra». *Insula,* No. 407 (October 1980), pp. 3-4.
LÓPEZ SANTOS, L.: «Fichas provisionales. Como la Poesía del último siglo». *Espadaña,* No. 2 (1944).
«Mesa redonda. La literatura social». *Camp de L'Arpa,* No. 1 (May 1972), pp. 14-18.
MIRÓ, EMILIO: «España, tierra y palabra, en la poesía de Blas de Otero». *Cuadernos Hispanoamericanos,* No. 356 (February 1980), pp. 274-97.
NERUDA, PABLO: «Sobre una poesía sin pureza». *Caballo Verde para la Poesía,*

No. 1 (October 1935; rpt. Nendeln-Liechtenstein: Verlag Detlev Auvermann KG, 1974).
[Nora, Eugenio de]. Juan Martínez, pseud.: «Poesía y verdad. Carta abierta a Victoriano Crémer». *Espadaña*, No. 46 (n. d.).
«Orientaciones de nuestra poesía». *Verbo*, No. 14 (January-February 1949).
Ridruejo, Dionisio: «El poeta rescatado». *Escorial*, 1, No. 1 (November 1940), pp. 93-100.
Rubio, Fanny: «Teoría y polémica en la poesía española de posguerra». *Cuadernos Hispanoamericanos*, No. 361-362 (July-August 1980), pp. 199-214.
Siebenmann, Gustav: «Los cambios estéticos en los últimos 40 años de poesía en España». *Boletín de la Asociación de Profesores de Español*, No. 7 (October 1972), pp. 83-92.
Silver, Philip: «Tradition as Originality in *Hijos de la ira*». *Bulletin of Hispanic Studies*, 67 (April 1970), pp. 124-30.
— «On Entering Creation: A Second Look at *Hijos de la ira*». *Books Abroad*, 48, No. 2 (Spring 1974), pp. 286-96.
Smith, Barbara Hernnstein: «Poetry as Fiction». *New Directions in Literary History*. Ralph Cohen, ed. Baltimore: Johns Hopkins, 1974, pp. 165-87.
Torreolla, Rafael S.: «La literatura de mañana». *La Estafeta Literaria*, No. 12 (1944), p. 29.
Valbuena Prat, Angel: «El momento actual de la poesía española». *La Estafeta Literaria*, No. 15 (1944), p. 15.
Valente, José Angel: «Poesía para el pueblo». *Cuadernos Hispanoamericanos*, No. 18 (November-December 1950), pp. 471-72.
Valverde, José María: «Notas de entrada a la poesía de César Vallejo». *Cuadernos Hispanoamericanos*, No. 7 (January-February 1949), pp. 57-84.
Vilanova, Antonio: «Poesía española y poesía europea». *Entregas de Poesía*, No. 1 (January 1944).

Sociopolitical Background: Books

Abellán, Manuel L.: *Censura y creación literaria en España (1939-1976)*. Barcelona: Ediciones Península, 1980.
Amodia, José: *Franco's Political Legacy: From Dictatorship to Façade Democracy*. London: Allen Lane, 1977.
Barral, Carlos: *Los años sin excusa*. Barcelona: Barral, 1978.
Crémer, Victoriano: *El libro de San Marcos*. León: Nebrija, 1980.
La cultura española durante el franquismo. [Equipo Reseña, eds.] Bilbao: Mensajero, 1977.
Díaz, Elías: *Notas para una historia del pensamiento español actual (1939-1973)*. Madrid: EDICUSA, 1974.
Espina, Antonio: *El cuarto poder: cien años de periodismo español*. Madrid: Aguilar, 1960.
Fernández Areal, Manuel: *La libertad de prensa en España*. Madrid: EDICUSA, 1971.
Heilbroner, Robert L.: *Marxism: For and Against*. New York: W. W. Norton and Co., 1980.
Historia del Partido Comunista de España. Varsovia, Poland: Ediciones «Polonia», 1960.
Jackson, Gabriel: *The Spanish Republic and the Civil War 1931-1936*. Princeton: Princeton University Press, 1965.
López Pina, Antonio; Eduardo L. Aranguren: *La cultura política de la España de Franco*. Madrid: Taurus, 1976.

LIST OF WORKS CITED

MACHADO, ANTONIO: *Los complementarios y otras prosas póstumas.* Guillermo de Torre, ed. Buenos Aires: Losada, 1957.
MERMALL, THOMAS: *The Rhetoric of Humanism.* New York: Bilingual Press, 1976.
PRADOS Y LÓPEZ, MANUEL: *Etica y estética del periodismo español.* Madrid: Espasa-Calpe, 1943.
RUIZ-GIMÉNEZ, JOAQUÍN: *Diez discursos.* Madrid: Educación Nacional, 1954.
SEMPRÚN, JORGE: *Autobiografía de Federico Sánchez.* Barcelona: Planeta, 1977.
VILAR, SERGIO: *Manifiesto sobre arte y libertad. Encuesta entre los intelectuales y artistas españoles.* Barcelona: Fontanella, 1964.

SOCIOPOLITICAL BACKGROUND: ARTICLES

ALONSO BLANCO, CARMEN: «Los mitos del siglo». *La Hora,* No. Extraordinario (24 June 1950).
ARANGUREN, JOSÉ LUIS L.: «La condición de la vida intelectual en la España de hoy». *La Torre,* 1, No. 4 (October-December 1953), pp. 83-97.
— «La evolución espiritual de los intelectuales españoles en la emigración». *Cuadernos Hispanoamericanos,* No. 38 (1953), pp. 123-57.
BELLOW, SAUL: «Spanish Letter». *Partisan Review,* 15, No. 2 (February 1948), pp. 217-30.
BLANCO, JUAN EUGENIO: «Más sobre los intelectuales», *Laye,* No. 4 (June 1950), p. 11.
FERNÁNDEZ CARVAJAL, RODRIGO: «Reflexiones sobre la formación política». *Alcalá,* No. 55 (25 April 1954).
— «Contramovimiento». *Alcalá,* No. 1 (25 June 1953).
PILAPIL, VICENTE R.: «Opus Dei in Spain». *The World Today,* May 1971, pp. 211-21.
RUBIO, JOSÉ LUIS: «Razones frente al socialismo». *La Hora,* 2, No. 21 (25 March 1949), p. 5.
RUIZ, J.: «Intelectuales enrolados». *Laye,* No. 1 (March 1950), p. 7.
RUIZ-GIMÉNEZ, JOAQUÍN: «Entre el dolor y la esperanza». *Alcalá,* No. 23-24 (10 January 1953).
— «La democratización de la cultura». *Cuadernos para el Diálogo,* No. 20 (May 1965), pp. 5-7.
TORRE, GUILLERMO DE: «Hacia una reconquista de la libertad». *La Torre,* No. 3 (July-September 1953), pp. 107-26.

PUBLICATIONS CONSULTED

Acanto. Madrid: 1946-1948.
Acento Cultural. Madrid: 1958-1960.
Alamo. Salamanca: 1964-1968.
Alba. Vigo: 1948-1956.
Alcalá. Madrid: 1952-1953.
Aldonza. Alcalá de Henares: 1964-1967.
Amanecer. La Coruña: 1958.
Ambito. Gerona: 1951, 1956-1958.
Ansí. Zaragoza: 1952-1953.
Arquero de Poesía. Madrid, Barcelona: 1953-1959.
Aturuxo. El Ferrol: 1952-1961.
Camp de L'Arpa. Barcelona: 1972-1974.
La Caña Gris. Valencia: 1960-1961.
Cántico. Córdoba: 1947-1955.
Caracola. Málaga: 1952-1958.

Cisneros. Madrid: 1943-1945.
Claraboya. León: 1963-1968.
Corcel. Valencia: 1942-1945.
Correo Literario. Madrid: 1950-1952.
Cuadernos de Agora. Madrid: 1956-1964.
Cuadernos para el Diálogo. Madrid: 1963-1969.
Dabo. Palma de Mallorca: 1951-1954.
Demócrito. Madrid: 1946-1947.
Deucalión. Ciudad Real: 1951-1953.
Egan. San Sebastián: 1948-1963.
Entregas de Poesía. Barcelona: 1944-1947.
Escorial. Madrid: 1940-1943.
Espadaña. León: 1944-1950.
El Español. Madrid: 1942-1943.
La Estafeta Literaria. Madrid: 1944-1957.
Fantasía. Madrid: 1945-1946.
Fénix. Madrid: 1943-1944.
Finisterre. Madrid: 1946, 1948.
Gánigo. Santa Cruz de Tenerife: 1953-1957.
Garcilaso. Madrid: 1943-1944.
Grímpola. Madrid: 1957-1967.
La Hora. Madrid: 1947-1956.
Horizonte. Barcelona: 1968-1969.
Indice. Madrid: 1951-1970.
Insula. Madrid: 1946-1980.
Laye. Barcelona: 1950-1953.
Lazarillo. Salamanca: 1943-1944.
Mediterráneo. Valencia: 1943-1945.
El Molino de Papel. Cuenca: 1955-1957.
El Pájaro de Paja. Madrid: 1951.
Palabra Nueva. Valladolid: 1962-1965.
Papeles de Son Armadans. Madrid, Palma de Mallorca: 1956-1970.
Peña Labra. Santander: 1971-1975.
Poesía Española. Madrid: 1952-1970.
Rocamador. Palencia: 1955-1966.
Serra D'Or. Monserrat: 1959-1962.
Sigüenza. Alicante: 1952-1953.
Verbo. Alicante, Valencia: 1946-1958.
Vértice. Madrid: 1941-1945.
Vientos del Sur. Granada: 1943.

INDEX OF PROPER NAMES

Abellán, Manuel L., 1, 188.
Alarcos Llorach, Emilio, 37, 104, 117, 151, 152, 184.
Albareda, José María, 8.
Alberti, Rafael, 15, 23, 31, 32, 41, 43, 47, 51, 52, 55, 74, 80, 103, 108, 114, 116, 149, 164, 169, 171, 172, 180, 183.
Albi, José, 33.
Albornoz, Aurora de, 158, 159, 186.
Alcaide, Juan, 172.
Alcántara, Manuel, 163, 172.
Aleixandre, Vicente, 13, 29, 30, 31, 33, 34, 35, 36, 53, 73, 146, 149, 151-52, 153, 170, 171, 172, 184, 186.
Alonso, Dámaso, 13, 22, 31, 34, 35, 36-42, 53, 121, 146, 151, 154, 171, 183.
— *Hijos de la ira,* 29, 33, 34, 35, 36-42, 43, 170, 180, 183.
Alonso Blanco, Carmen, 19, 189.
Altolaguirre, Manuel, 31, 32.
Alvarez, Carlos, 5, 152, 177, 183.
Amodia, José, 148, 183.
Ana, Marcos, 119, 183.
Andúgar, Julián, 172.
Antología cercada, 73-81, 184.
Antología parcial, 31-32, 59, 67, 184.
Aparicio, Juan, 10, 11, 12.
Aragon, Louis, 24, 54, 74, 116.
Aranguren, Eduardo L., 148.
Aranguren, José Luis, 8, 25, 26, 145, 147, 188, 189.
Arias Salgado, Gabriel, 27.
Aub, Max, 73, 74, 142, 170.
Ayensa, Alfonso, 95.
Azcoaga, Enrique, 22, 32, 54, 183.

Badosa, Enrique, 23, 178, 184, 186.
Balbín Lucas, Rafael, 121.
Barral, Carlos, 99, 144, 149, 154, 170, 173, 174, 177, 186, 188.
Barrow, Geoffrey R., 114, 186.
Batlló, José, 142, 183.
Bellow, Saúl, 15, 189.
Bengoechea, Javier, 121, 172.
Blanco, Juan Eugenio, 18, 189.

Blanco Aguinaga, Carlos, 57, 67, 112, 184, 186.
Blasco, Ricardo Juan, 13.
Bleiberg, Germán, 12, 13, 14, 31, 67, 74, 81-82, 120, 170, 183.
Bousoño, Carlos, 31, 34, 36, 90, 120, 149, 151, 152-53, 185, 186.

Caba, Pedro, 34, 186.
Caballero Bonald, José María, 5, 121, 171.
Cabañero, Eladio, 172.
Calvo Serer, Rafael, 139.
Campbell, Roy, 134.
Canales, Alfonso, 134.
Canito, Enrique, 13.
Cano, José Luis, 13-14, 22, 26, 31, 33, 35-36, 40, 41-42, 80, 87, 90-91, 99, 122, 123-24, 134, 151, 184, 185, 186.
Cano Ballesta, Juan, 22, 23, 25, 54, 185.
Carriedo, Gabino-Alejandro, 79.
Carrillo, Santiago, 95, 170.
Casamayor, Enrique, 31, 186.
Castellet, José María, 21, 34-35, 41, 67, 144, 146, 149, 170, 171-73, 184.
— *Veinte años de poesía española,* 2, 21, 35, 42, 67, 171-73, 184.
Castillo Puche, José Luis, 41.
Castro Ovejero, José, 16, 86.
Cela, Camilo José, 10, 124, 169, 170.
Celaya, Gabriel, 3, 4, 5, 22, 24, 32, 33. 53, 60, 88, 89, 90, 96, 99, 108, 109, 116, 122, 124-44, 146, 149, 150, 151, 152, 153, 154, 163, 165, 166, 168, 170, 171, 172, 173, 174, 180, 181, 183, 185, 186.
— *Cantos iberos,* 4, 60, 128, 133, 135-44, 183.
— *Las cartas boca arriba,* 56, 124, 125, 127-28, 183.
— *Lo demás es silencio,* 127, 128-33, 138, 183.
Cernuda, Luis, 20, 30, 31, 32, 33, 46, 172.
Ciplijauskaité, Biruté, 13, 185.
Cirlot, Juan Eduardo, 22.
Cohen, John Michael, 52, 53, 111, 162, 185, 186.

Concha, Víctor G. de la, 12, 21, 29, 35, 42, 46, 82, 185, 186.
Conde, Carmen, 31, 88.
Costafreda, Alfonso, 67, 121, 151.
Couffon, Claude, 114.
Crémer, Victoriano, 10, 14, 23, 24, 25, 29, 31, 34, 35, 42-43, 59, 76, 82-86, 88, 90, 105, 120, 126, 149, 150, 151, 152, 154, 166, 170, 172, 180, 183, 186, 188.
— *Nuevos cantos de vida y esperanza*, 52, 82-85, 183.
— *Tacto sonoro*, 43-51, 183.
Crespo, Angel, 5, 125, 135, 151, 171.
Cuadra, Pablo Antonio, 13.

Dampierre, C. R., 37.
Darío, Rubén, 82, 101, 115, 169.
Daydí-Tolson, Santiago, 2, 36, 185.
Debicki, Andrew P., 38, 187.
Delclaux, Jaime, 121.
Delgado, Alvaro, 58.
Díaz, Elías, 8, 25, 26, 28, 139, 145, 147, 188.
Díaz Márquez, Luis, 40, 187.
Díaz-Plaja, Fernando, 11.
Diego, Gerardo, 31, 34, 135, 146, 153, 171.
Donahue, Moraima Semprún, 99.
Doreste, Ventura, 74-75, 77-78.
Duque, Aquilino, 153, 187.
Durán, Manuel, 22.
Durruti, Buenaventura, 45.

Eagleton, Terry, 54, 56, 185.
Echarri, Xavier de, 9.
Eluard, Paul, 75, 116.
Emmanuel, Pierre, 13, 75, 123.
Engels, F., 109.
Entrambasaguas, Joaquín de, 14, 32, 37, 90.
Espina, Concha, 34.
Espina García, Antonio, 10, 188.

Fedyukin, S., 98, 136.
Felipe, León, 31, 154, 170, 172.
Fernández, Joaquín, 172.
Fernández Areal, Manuel, 26, 188.
Fernández Carvajal, Rodrigo, 19, 30, 146, 187, 189.
Ferrán, Jaime, 101, 151, 185.
Figuera Aymerich, Angela, 5, 24, 86, 151, 152, 154-57, 166, 181, 183.
Foix, J. V., 54.
Fox, E. Inman, 173, 187.
Foxá, Agustín de, 10.
Franco, Francisco, 3, 6, 7, 8, 10, 15, 26, 50, 53, 55, 59, 76, 78, 88, 93, 144.

Frutos, Eugenio, 30, 187.
Fuertes, Gloria, 5, 163-65, 166, 171, 181, 183.
Fuster, Joan, 33.

Galan, F. W., 3, 187.
Galán, Joaquín, 114, 185.
Gallego, José Luis, 77, 183.
Gaos, Vicente, 12, 31, 80, 90, 187.
Garagorri, Pauline, 16.
Garcés, Jesús Juan, 34, 187.
García Gill, Gabriel, 37.
García Lorca, Federico, 13, 30, 31, 32, 33, 34, 43, 50, 52, 129.
García Molina, J. L., 173.
García Narezo, Gabriel, 74.
García Nieto, José, 12, 51, 80, 88, 91, 121, 142-43, 146, 151, 152, 153, 183.
García Rico, Eduardo, 142, 146, 187.
García Suárez, Pedro, 9.
Garciasol, Ramón de, 22, 87, 149-50, 151, 152, 153, 154, 165-67, 169, 181, 187.
Garfias, Pedro, 62.
Gastón, Amparo, 124, 142.
Gerulaitis, Renate, 55, 185.
Gil, Ildefonso-Manuel, 22, 81, 134, 183.
Gil de Biedma, Jaime, 5, 144, 161, 170, 171, 172, 173-77, 183.
Gómez, César Armando, 178.
Gómez Picazo, Elías, 8.
González, Angel, 5, 28, 170, 171, 173-177, 183.
González, Fernando, 32.
González, Shirley Mangini, 175, 185.
González Martín, J. P., 35, 177, 184.
González Nieto, Luis, 21.
Gorki, Maxim, 54, 56.
Goytisolo, José Agustín, 5, 23, 60, 170, 171, 172, 173-77, 183.
Grande, Félix, 25, 35, 185.
Guerrero, Juan, 14, 34, 187.
Guillén, Jorge, 31, 32, 172.
Guillén, Nicolás, 116.
Gullón, Ricardo, 90, 134, 187.

Hauser, Arnold, 5, 185.
Heidegger, Martin, 15, 16, 46, 52.
Heilbroner, Robert L., 72, 97, 188.
Hernández, Miguel, 7, 16, 22-23, 30, 31, 32, 41, 43, 52, 69, 75, 76, 81, 88, 114, 116, 149, 153, 169, 172, 180.
Hernández, Mario, 111.
Hidalgo, José Luis, 32, 73, 88, 172, 183.
Hierro, José, 5, 14, 23, 28, 32, 60, 80, 90, 121, 146, 149, 150, 151, 152, 154, 157-61, 163, 166, 170, 172, 181, 183, 187.

INDEX OF PROPER NAMES

Hikmet, Nazim, 116, 156.
Hiriart, Rosario, 81, 185.

Ibáñez, Paco, 135.
Ibáñez Martín, José, 8, 9.
Ibárruri, Dolores (La Pasionaria), 94, 95, 104, 107, 112-13.
Ifach, María de Gracia, 73.
Iglesias, Pablo, 174.

Jackson, Gabriel, 94, 188.
James, C. Vaughan, 54, 61, 96, 185.
Jauss, Hans Robert, 2, 187.
Jiménez, José Olivio, 21, 161, 185.
Jiménez, Juan Ramón, 20, 32, 34, 54, 173.
Johan, Angel, 80-81.

Khruschev, Nikita, 92.
King, Edmond L., 101.

Labordeta, Miguel, 124.
Lacalle, Angel, 21.
Laín Entralgo, Pedro, 7, 139, 147, 170.
Lama, Antonio G. de, 25, 29, 30, 31, 32, 33, 35, 37, 42, 43, 46, 52, 59, 62, 73, 86, 105, 126, 187.
Lamana, Manuel, 35, 57, 66, 185.
Lascaris-Comneno, C., 62.
Lechner, Jan, 1, 46, 79, 185, 187.
— *El compromiso en la poesía española*, 2, 12, 16, 22, 24, 31, 42, 45, 46, 51, 57, 66, 73, 79, 86, 105, 185.
Loceta, Juan de (See Gabriel Celaya).
Lenin, Vladimir Ilich, 56, 97, 136.
León, Sergio, 95.
Ley, Charles David, 23, 37, 40, 96, 134, 158, 185, 187.
— *Spanish Poetry since 1939*, 13, 32, 40, 57, 87, 154, 185.
Lezcano, Pedro, 77-79.
López de Abiada, José Manuel, 57, 58, 67, 187.
López Anglada, Luis, 86, 153, 178.
López-Bernasocci, José Manuel, 16.
López Gorgé, Jacinto, 91.
López Ibor, Juan, 8.
López Pacheco, Jesús, 171.
López Pina, Antonio, 148, 188.
López Santos, Luis, 34, 187.
Lorenzo, Pedro de, 121.
Luis, Leopoldo de, 2, 21, 32, 80, 88, 124, 143-44, 151, 152, 154, 159, 166, 167-170, 171, 181, 183, 184, 185.
Lumsden, Audrey, 38.

Machado, Antonio, 7, 20-21, 31, 32, 34, 37, 54, 114-15, 116, 123, 149, 170, 172, 179, 180, 183.
Mainer, José-Carlos, 7, 146, 185.
Malraux, André, 54.
Mantero, Manuel, 80, 172, 184.
Mao Zedong, 116.
Marías, Julián, 26, 170.
Martín Descalzo, J. L., 166, 172.
Marx, Karl, 103, 104, 113.
Mateo, José Vicente, 143.
Mayakovsky, Vladimir, 67, 116.
Mead, Robert G., 26.
Menéndez Pidal, Ramón, 134, 170.
Mercader, Trinidad, 143.
Mermall, Thomas, 148, 188.
Miller, James E., Jr., 100.
Millán, Rafael, 152, 184.
Millares Sall, Agustín, 74-76, 77, 184.
Millares Sall, José María, 74-76, 184.
Milosz, Czelaw, 96.
Miró, Emilio, 117, 187.
Molina, Ricardo, 37, 134, 150, 151, 185.
Montesinos, Rafael, 34.
Morales, Rafael, 23, 31, 90, 121, 146, 151, 152, 154, 158, 162-63, 165, 166, 180, 184.
Moratiel, Sergio, 43, 46, 47, 82, 86, 185.
Moreno, Alfonso, 32, 184.
Múgica, Enrique, 147.
Múgica, Rafael (See Gabriel Celaya).

Neruda, Pablo, 15, 24, 33, 40, 41, 54, 57, 60, 61, 62, 74, 76, 86, 99-100, 104, 114, 116, 127, 129, 150, 153, 154, 180, 187.
Nora, Eugenio de, 3, 10, 23, 24, 25, 28, 29, 31, 34, 35, 42, 57-72, 76, 77, 79, 80, 85, 86, 87, 88, 89, 90, 103, 108, 114, 124, 125, 138, 139, 150, 151, 152, 153, 154, 160, 166, 167, 169, 170, 171, 181, 184, 188.
— *Cantos al destino*, 57, 58, 59, 60-62, 184.
— *Contemplación del tiempo*, 57, 58, 59, 67, 184.
— *España, pasión de vida*, 3, 57, 58, 62, 67-72, 75, 184.
— *Pueblo cautivo*, 57-58, 62-68, 78, 184.
Núñez, Antonio, 116, 154, 155.

Ortega y Gasset, José, 7, 27.
Otero, Blas de, 3, 5, 13, 14, 22, 32, 38, 48, 53, 59, 76, 80, 86, 88, 89, 90, 98-124, 127, 134, 139, 144, 149, 151, 152, 153, 154, 155, 163, 164, 165, 166, 168, 170, 171, 172, 173, 174, 181, 184.

— *Ancia*, 100, 108-09, 111, 116, 121, 122, 184.
— *Angel fieramente humano*, 14, 32, 86, 100-04, 108, 115, 120, 184.
— *En castellano*, 109-16, 122, 124, 184.
— *Pido la paz y la palabra*, 109-16, 122, 124, 184.
— *Que trata de España*, 109, 116-20, 124.
— *Redoble de conciencia*, 100, 104-08, 120, 184.

Padilla, Heberto, 120.
Panero, Leopoldo, 21, 24, 25, 31, 37, 51, 88, 134, 146.
Pemán, José María, 10, 32, 43, 86.
Perdomo García, José, 15.
Pereda, Rosa María, 98.
Pérez Embid, Florencio, 13, 121.
Pérez Valiente, Salvador, 23, 32, 91, 152, 166, 172.
Pérez Villanueva, Joaquín, 134.
Pilapil, Vicente R., 8, 189.
Prados, Emilio, 31.
Prados y López, Manuel, 9, 189.
Preston, Paul, 95.
Puccini, Darío, 22, 53, 54, 170, 184.
Puig Palau, Alberto, 99.

Quinto, José María de, 147.

Raffucci de Lockwood, Alicia M., 84, 185.
Riba, Carles, 134.
Ribes, Francisco, 88, 90-91, 96, 170, 184.
— *Antología consultada*, 2, 58, 59, 67, 87-91, 122, 142, 150, 158, 162, 180, 184.
Ridruejo, Dionisio, 7, 10, 12, 20, 88, 145, 146, 147, 151, 188.
Rivers, Elias L., 38, 42.
Rodríguez, Claudio, 23, 161.
Rodríguez Puértolas, Julio, 57, 67, 184.
Rodríguez Spiteri, Carlos, 32.
Roldán, Mariano, 143.
Romero, Amelia, 141.
Romero Murubi, Joaquín, 32.
Romero Moliner, Rafael, 135.
Rosales, Luis, 12, 21, 25, 31, 34, 88, 151, 152.
Rubio, Fanny, 28, 58, 66, 135, 185, 188.
— *Las revistas poéticas*, 1, 7, 12, 13, 21, 22, 23, 86, 105, 129, 152, 171, 185.
Rubio, José Luis, 18, **189**.
Ruiz, J., 18, 189.
Ruiz, Rubén, 107.

Ruiz-Giménez, Joaquín, 25, 26, 27, 28, 134, 145, 147, 152, 189.
Rupert, Claude, 134.

Sáenz, Blas, 18.
Sahagún, Carlos, 172.
Salinas, Jaime, 171.
Salinas, Pedro, 31, 32, 34, 150, 185.
Sánchez Albornoz, Nicolás, 57.
Sánchez Bardón, Luis, 141.
Sartre, Jean-Paul, 16, 17, 147.
Sastre, Alfonso, 28, 146-47, 149, 170, 186.
Seirra, Pierre-Oliver, 124, 133, 143, 144, 186.
Semprún, Jorge, 95, 112, 124, 133, 134, 170, 189.
Serrano Plaja, Arturo, 20, 54, 84, 186.
Serrano Súñer, Ramón, 7.
Sesé, Bernard, 21, 186.
Siebenmann, Gustav, 35, 188.
Silver, Philip, 42, 188.
Sinyavsky, Andrei, 55, 96, 120, 130, 186.
Smith, Barbara Hernnstein, 4, 188.
Sobejano, Gonzalo, 36.
Soria, Carmelo, 57.
Sos, Eladio, 21.
Stalin, Josef, 54, 56.
Suárez Carreño, José, 124, 151.

Tamames, Ramón, 147.
Teira, Manuel, 73.
Tertz, Abram (See Sinyavsky, Andrei).
Testa, Daniel P., 101, 185.
Tomé, Padre, 172.
Torre, Guillermo de, 21, 26, 42, 54, 57, 66, 189.
Torrente Ballester, Gonzalo, 12, 13.
Torreolla, Rafael S., 34, 188.
Tovar, Antonio, 7, 13, 145.
Tuñón de Lara, Manuel, 21, 95, 114, 170, 186.

Uceda, Julia, 170.
Unamuno, Miguel de, 7, 16, 20, 30, 32, 37, 40, 47, 123.

Valbuena Prat, Angel, 12, 188.
Valbuena Briones, Angel, 101.
Valente, José Angel, 5, 23, 86, 134, 144, 151, 161, 170, 171, 172, 178, 186, **188.**
Valle, Adriano del, 32, 34.
Vallejo, César, 24-25, 86, 114, 116, 153, 180.

INDEX OF PROPER NAMES

Valverde, José María, 25, 31, 90, 151, 153, 188.
Vázquez Montalbán, Manuel, 177.
Vélez, Carlos, 122, 172, 177.
Vilanova, Antonio, 12, 188.
Vilar, Sergio, 123, 189.
Villalonga, Lorenzo, 10.
Vivanco, Luis Felipe, 10, 12, 20, 22, 25, 31, 146, 186.

Wilden, L. Dumont, 16.

Zambrano, María, 174.
Zardoya, Concha, 24, 32, 76, 151, 184.
Zavala, Iris M., 57, 67, 184.
Zhdanov, Andrey, 54, 56.
Zorita, Angel, 40, 186.
Zubiaurre, A. de, 31.
Zuñica, Joaquín, 88.